ALL THE NAMES OF THE LORD

Lists, Mysticism, and Magic

VALENTINA IZMIRLIEVA

THE UNIVERSITY OF CHICAGO PRESS
CHICAGO AND LONDON

VALENTINA IZMIRLIEVA is associate professor in the Slavic Department at Columbia University.

This book is a volume in the series Studies of the Harriman Institute, Columbia University.

The University of Chicago Press, Chicago 60637
The University of Chicago Press, Ltd., London
© 2008 by The University of Chicago
All rights reserved. Published 2008
Printed in the United States of America

17 16 15 14 13 12 11 10 09 08   1 2 3 4 5

ISBN-13: 978-0-226-38870-0 (cloth)
ISBN-10: 0-226-38870-0 (cloth)

Library of Congress Cataloging-in-Publication Data
Izmirlieva, Valentina.
    All the names of the Lord : lists, mysticism, and magic / Valentina Izmirlieva.
        p. cm.
    Includes bibliographical references and index.
    ISBN-13: 978-0-226-38870-0 (cloth : alk. paper)
    ISBN-10: 0-226-38870-0 (cloth : alk. paper)   1. God (Christianity)—Name.
I. Title.
    BT180.N2I96   2008
    231—dc22

                                                            2007044616

♾ The paper used in this publication meets the minimum requirements of the American National Standard for Information Sciences—Permanence of Paper for Printed Library Materials, ANSI Z39.48-1992.

FOR TOM

Silver and gold I have none,
but what I have I give you.
—Acts 3:6

All language . . . rests on a single name, never in itself proferable [*sic*]: the name of God. Contained in all propositions, it necessarily remains unsaid in each.
—Giorgio Agamben, "The Idea of the Name"

All has become names by the Middle Ages, and earlier.
—Joshua Trachtenberg, *Jewish Magic and Superstition*

Lists *mix* God and grocer; they are divinely grocerly and grocerly divine, in variable proportions.
—Francis Spufford, *The Chatto Book of Cabbages and Kings*

Anyone who tries to get to the bottom of everything is sliding down a dangerous slope.
—Flaubert, *Bouvrad and Pécuchet*

CONTENTS

ACKNOWLEDGMENTS

This book, like a baby monster, was in gestation for fifteen long years, during which it accumulated many debts. Some of the people who helped me nurse it to life are no longer here to accept my acknowledgments; others are probably so tired of the book that they would *not* want to hear any more about it. I should know better than to list all their names in a book that regards comprehensive lists as precariously ambitious. Conforming to the rules of the game, I will mention only some. All of them—the nameless with the named—have my deepest gratitude.

Several people were instrumental in the conception of this project: my first teacher of things medieval, Krassimir Stantchev (Rome), who introduced me to Dionysius the Areopagite; Klimentina Ivanova (Sofia), who taught me the joy of working with Slavonic manuscripts and much more; the late Klaus-Dieter Seemann (Berlin), who, by inviting me to participate in a conference on the "neglected" medieval genres, inadvertently pointed me in the direction of names and lists; and David Tracy (Chicago), who gave me not only the gift of his wisdom, but also the courage to pursue my studies far afield, into that inhospitable land which Theodore Adorno once called "the icy desert of abstraction."

Two teachers at the University of Chicago, Norman Ingham and Paul Friedrich, helped me mature as a scholar by encouraging me to follow two disparate paths of exploring naming and listmaking: medieval Slavic letters and tropology. Two other distinguished members of the University of Chicago community, Bernard McGinn and James Fernandez, though never my teachers directly, shaped much of my thinking on this project with their own inspired writing. Last in a series of binary lists, I should also acknowledge two seminars that enriched my understanding of religious practices and everyday worship, leaving an imprint on much of my later work. In 1998–99

I spent a year at the Martin Marty Institute for Advanced Study of Religion at The University of Chicago's Divinity School. It was truly a baptism by fire, and I will always be grateful to Frank Reynolds for never making me feel like an outsider, even though I was. In 2003 I had the pleasure of participating in the Summer Faculty Seminar at Worcester, Massachusetts, "Religious Hermeneutics and Secular Interpretation," organized by the Erasmus Institute and led by the incomparable Geoffrey Hartman. In both settings I found not only fantastic colleagues, but also friends for life. (While at Worcester, my husband and I learned of the impending arrival of our daughter, Hannah, which made the experience even more memorable.)

I gratefully acknowledge the institutional support of Columbia University at crucial moments of my work on the book: two summer Council Grants in the Humanities and Social Sciences, and a semester of research leave extended into a whole precious year by a Chamberlain Fellowship for service at the Core. A summer Harriman PepsiCo travel grant supported two weeks of work in Venice and Rome in 2002, without which the last chapter of the book would not have been written, and three generous publication grants from the Harriman Institute have been invaluable for the manuscript's final preparation.

This project could never have been completed without extensive work in manuscript depositories, archives, and libraries around the world. I am particularly grateful to Father Mateja Matejic and Dr. Predrag Matejic for granting me access to the rich microform collection of Slavonic manuscripts in the Hilandar Resource Center for Medieval Studies at The Ohio State University, along with financial support and practical advice. My gratitude extends also to curators, librarians, and staff members in the archival divisions of the Serbian National Library in Belgrade; the National Library SS Cyril and Methodius in Sofia, Bulgaria; The Library of Congress in Washington, D.C.; the Vatican Library; and the Pontifical Oriental Institute in Rome.

Ideas that eventually found their way into this book have been presented at various scholarly centers, most notably the Osteuropa-Institut at the Free University of Berlin, the Slavic Department and the Department of Religious Studies at Northwestern University, the Committee on Medieval and Renaissance Studies at Columbia University, the Seminar on Slavic History and Culture at Columbia University, and the Department of Cyrillo-Methodian Studies at Sofia University in Bulgaria. I am in debt to my receptive audiences in all these venues.

Earlier versions of several chapters in this book have appeared in other publications: chapter 6 as "The Aetiology of the Seventy-Two Diseases:

Investigating a Byzantino-Slavic False Prayer," in *Byzantinoslavica* (Prague) 59, no. 1 (1998): 181–95; chapter 7 as "From Babel to Christ and Beyond: The Number 72 in Christian Political Symbolism," in *Stara b"lgarska literatura* (Sofia) 35–36 (2007): 3–21; and chapter 8 as "The Peculiar Codex *Jerusalem 22:* Tracing the Slavic Kabbalah," in *Jews and Slavs: Slavic Manuscripts in the Holy Lands* (Jerusalem-Sofia: The Hebrew University of Jerusalem and The Cyrillo-Methodian Research Center, forthcoming). I thank the people involved in these publications.

My debt of gratitude extends to dear friends and colleagues who have offered me the benefit of their scholarly expertise, encouragement, and practical support: Michael Agnew, Susan Boynton, Victor Friedman, Boris Gasparov, Petko Ivanov, Kostas Kazazis, Julia Kristeva, Leo D. Lefebure, John McGuckin, Katia Mitova, and Norman Pereira. Among those who have read drafts of the entire manuscript, I am particularly grateful to Robert Belknap, Paul Kollman, Moshe Taube, Lawrence Frizzell, Nadieszda Kizenko, and the profoundly generous anonymous reviewer at the University of Chicago Press. All of them have offered invaluable corrections, additions, and comments that have helped make this book far better than I could have made it on my own. I owe special thanks to my student and friend Marijeta Bozovic, who has improved my manuscript with labor and love, gracing it with her impeccable sense of style.

This book about things magical and mystical has had its fair share of serendipity, never more conspicuous than in the final phase of its promotion (which is perhaps fitting, since it is also a book about the social promotion of texts). My entire experience with the University of Chicago Press and the Harriman Publication Series has been a blessing. The present version of the book has benefited much from the competent advice of Elizabeth Branch Dyson and Ron Meyer, and from the technical assistance of Mary Fahnestock-Thomas. To David Brent, who has championed this project through thick and thin all the way to production, I owe much more than I can possibly express.

Still, my greatest debt is to my family: my parents, Bojana Popova and Angel Popov; my brother, Alexander Popov; my parents-in-law, Betty and Jim Kitson; my daughter, Hannah, and—more than anyone else—my husband, Tom Kitson, who, with his Scottish love of understatement, would never "let me count the ways." Thank you!

INTRODUCTION

I do not aim foolishly to introduce new ideas. I want only to analyze and with some orderly detail to expand upon the truths so briefly set down by others.
—Dionysius the Areopagite, *The Divine Names*

As you set out for Ithaka,
hope the voyage is a long one,
full of adventure, full of discovery.
—C. Cavafy, *Ithaka*

"**B**lessed be the name of the Lord from this time on and forevermore. From the rising of the sun to its setting, the name of the Lord is to be praised," exults the Psalmist (Ps. 113:2–3); and Jesus echoes him in his simplest lesson of devotion, "Pray then in this way: Our Father in heaven, hallowed be your name" (Matt. 6:9).[1]

"The name of God" is such a commonplace of Christian language that we often ignore it. Lulled by familiar references to "the name" and "in the name" of the Lord, we rarely stop to consider how the word *name* works in relation to its lofty referent. What exactly is God's name? Is it hidden or revealed? Is it one or many? And if there are many, as the language of worship often suggests, can we know them all? By naming the creatures, Adam gained power over Creation. Could there be even greater power in knowing all the names of the Lord?

My subject in the following pages is a corner of the Christian experience where such questions have been made enormously significant both intellectually and existentially. My interest lies specifically in the practice of listing the names of God, a practice that often pluralizes the singular "name" of biblical language in extravagantly abundant litanies and inventories of gargantuan proportions. The practice is widespread, and its numerous purposes defy easy generalizations. Lists of divine names are used across written and oral discourses to glorify and to instruct, to protect and to subjugate, and are equally at home in all quarters of Christian culture: from theology to liturgy and magic, and from official ceremonial practices to the practices of everyday life.

To be sure, such extensive production of sacronymic catalogues is not unique to Christianity. Virtually all theistic religions share the Christian zeal for embracing the divine realm in a list, whether through the names of numerous gods and goddesses or through the numerous names of a single divinity. Archaeological discoveries in Mesopotamia even suggest that the listing of sacred names was perhaps the oldest practice of writing, since it governed the written production of the Sumero-Babylonian "list-science" (*Listenwissenschaft*).[2] For my purposes, however, I register these contexts only as a spectacular backdrop for a focused, in-depth inquiry.

Divine Names as Terms of Order

My study of Christian listmaking practices can be classified under the general rubric of rhetoric in the sense that it targets verbal performance and persuasion, the ability of words to produce social realities. Since I treat lists as rhetorical figures, or tropes, of serial arrangements, this project has particular affinities to the subfield of tropology—the discipline at the interface of poetics and rhetoric that Aristotle inaugurated to study verbal ingenuity and patterns of associative thought. The objectives of contemporary tropology branch along two analytical paths: formal and pragmatic. Formalists, primarily the linguists and the philosophers in the field, are interested in *what* a trope is, while pragmatists, best represented by cultural anthropologists (or the "an-trop-ologists," as James Fernandez prefers to call them), investigate *how* a trope operates in social space.[3] My bias lies with the second group. When I claim that I am concerned with the Christian practice of listing God's names, I mean not so much the way these lists are put together as the way they are put to use. What do lists do in Christian praxis? What is their locus in life, their internal justification, their enduring appeal for Christian communities? How does their performance change in shifting contexts? What do they accomplish for the people involved in their production and exchange? These and similar questions define the telos of this book.

Within the rhetorical discipline, my study is most at home in the niche carved by Kenneth Burke in his book *The Rhetoric of Religion: Studies in Logology.* Burke's introductory stipulations illuminate my own purpose well:

> [I]n this book we are to be concerned not directly with religion, but rather with the *terminology* of religion; not directly with man's relationship to God, but rather with his relationship to the *word* "God." Thus this book is about something so essentially rhetorical as religious nomenclature—hence the subtitle, "Studies in Logology," which is to say, "studies in words about words." . . . Since words-about-God would be as far-reaching as words can be, the "rhetoric of religion" furnishes a good instance of terministic enterprise in general.[4]

The key word in this passage is "nomenclature." Like Burke before me, I will be interested in religious rhetoric as a "terministic enterprise," in the potential of religious nomenclature not only to probe the limit *(terminus)* of language, but also to impose limits, boundaries, and restrictions on our picture of reality—in other words, to produce order.

With his typical aphoristic brilliance, Burke suggests that man is ruled by "a logic of entitlement,"[5] by the drive to sum up particulars under a single umbrella term toward ever higher levels of generalization. Searching for a title of titles, for an overarching "God-term," is the destiny of the symbolic animal, a part of the human condition. And because "God" is one of the better-known names for that terministic horizon, the search always has a religious aftertaste, even when its context is entirely secular. This, I suppose, makes religious nomenclature the most obvious territory for observing the "logic of entitlement" in action. Such, at least, has been the simple premise of my project.

Seeking to probe the terministic aspect of Christian rhetoric, I take as a case in point the most "far-reaching" of the "words-about-God"—the divine names—and propose to treat them as the ultimate Christian terms of order. Nomenclature does not by itself presuppose order, as classification does. Yet systematic knowledge tends to correlate the terms it uses with its own classifications—to correlate, as it were, its language and its vision of order—to the effect that its nomenclature becomes also a taxonomy.[6] And since Christianity offers a limiting case of such an enterprise, I claim that list-making, when used to organize the names of God, is a form of creating order. More specifically, I argue in the following chapters, from the point of view of particular texts in context, that a list of divine names, when articulated from a position of authority, seeks to impose a vision of order upon whole communities of Christians and shape their lives according to that vision.

Before engaging in the argument, however, let me first, by way of a general introduction, attempt a three-step explication of the highly condensed formula "imposition of a vision of order," taking the term *order* as my point of departure.

What Kind of Order?

Scholars have argued, in a number of theoretical idioms, that a representative aspect of religion is the human drive to make sense of everything, to indulge in a kind of "exegetical totalization"—in short, to propose universal order.[7] Abrahamic religions offer a perfect case in point, as one of their irreducible axioms is that human beings and matter both result from a single, creative consciousness, which itself transcends everything it generates. Such a hypothesis of origin presents the created world as a *cosmos* in the etymological sense of the term. Everything in this world is presumed to be radically contingent upon the free decision of the Creator. *Chance, accident, mistake* are but words to label the human inability to understand the logic of divine order. In the grand design of Providence, nothing lacks meaning or purpose: it is all part of a plan, part of a unified vision. Christianity, together with Judaism and Islam, thus offers a limiting case of a vision of order, with God the Creator as its single universal principle. (When Kenneth Burke claims that any "over-all term" is in essence a God-term, his implied notion of God is, of course, very Abrahamic if not entirely Christian.)[8]

Universal order may be appealing in itself, for it makes sense without a remainder, but it is not an easy concept to sell. The difficulty lies in the paradox implied in a vision of that scale: it is a vision of the *invisible*. Having to do more with imagination than with seeing, such a vision of order collapses, as it were, "the distinction between the physically visible and the visualized."[9] It is an imaginative conception of reality that defies the naked eye by presupposing a metaphysical omniscience, a triumph of unrestrained imagination over the senses, which are always limited.

William James has claimed that such "unseen order" is perhaps the most basic category of religious life: "Were one asked to characterize the life of religion in the broadest and most general terms possible, one might say that it consists of the belief that there is an *unseen order*, and that the supreme good lies in harmoniously adjusting ourselves thereto."[10] With this typically sweeping generalization, James suggests that what defines religious subjects as such is their acceptance of a vision of universal order as their own private reality (a "reality of the unseen"), a vision of order that informs both the epistemological context and the ethical horizon of their existence.[11] By translating thus the entire teleology of the religious experience in terms of "unseen order," James in effect contends that the success of any religious project hinges on the ability to make people believe in an order they cannot see.

I leave aside for now the important question of agency and emphasize only one aspect of this paradoxical demand that is particularly relevant to the current discussion. Since the unseen predictably resists visual representation, its most natural rhetorical venue is language—the medium of total imagination. Leading religious communities to believe in an unseen order, in other words, depends almost exclusively on *verbal* rhetoric: a "rhetoric of the invisible" that concerns itself with the visionary aspect of religious order (or its "theoretical" aspect, if you will, since the term *theory* comes from the Greek word for "spectacle," *thēoria*, and "to theorize," *theōrein*, means literally "to make visible").

If the rhetorical project of making people believe in what they cannot see is indeed fundamental to any religious enterprise as James suggests (and scholars of religion as different as Jonathan Z. Smith and Clifford Geertz appear to accept almost axiomatically), it is especially so for Christianity, where that concern has generated from the start a particularly strong sense of doctrinal urgency. Its most well-known biblical source is Jesus's reproach to Doubting Thomas: "Have you believed because you have seen me? Blessed are those who have not seen and yet have come to believe" (John 20:29).

The scene occurs at a pivotal moment in Christian history when Jesus appears to his collected disciples a second time after the Resurrection. The first time, he delegated the authority for spreading the divine Word to the apostles ("As the Father has sent me, so I send you" [John 20:21]); now he sanctifies the entire body of the Church as recipients of the Word. The Christianity of the future will be made of those who believe not because they have witnessed the deeds, but because they have *heard* the message. The Thomas episode thus represents a crucial transformation of the Christian community from a society of direct disciples, or *eyewitnesses*, to a universal community of a *verbal* tradition. The ear, rather than the eye, becomes the organ of faith from now on, as the focus of the Christian experience shifts from the revelatory event (the Incarnation) to the text that proclaims it (the New Testament).[12]

These changes have at least two major consequences for our subject: they push the unseen to the forefront of the Christian imagination, and they make its verbal representation—"the rhetoric of the invisible"—crucial for the social (re)production of the Christian identity.[13] I argue in the following chapters that lists of divine names play a strategic role in this new rhetoric as basic tools for making universal order *visible*—and thus operative—in the lives of Christian communities.

Lists as Figures of Display

Shifting the focus to the visual component of my initial formula, let me now ask the question How can a list make order visible? What internal characteristic of the list trope makes a catalogue of divine names an effective vehicle for putting the unseen Christian order on display?

To begin to answer this question, I must first go back to the concept of nomenclature and consider its principal affinity to classification and order. An order system, at its most basic, classifies objects in categories, while a nomenclature provides the terms—or "names"—for these classes. Nomenclatures allow us to articulate a classification, to translate it from the realm of abstractions into the realm of words. Nomenclatures, of course, do not presuppose order by themselves; we can have, as we usually do in real life, terminologies that are more or less unsystematic. Yet the ambition of any systematic knowledge is to correlate its vision and its language of order so that its nomenclature becomes also a taxonomy, and it is this internal tendency, this asymptotic movement of nomenclature toward systematicity that is important for us. Now I cannot think of a more direct, economical, and effective articulation of any nomenclature than a list, which makes the list, ideally at least, the optimal articulation of a taxonomy as well. When we present the terms of order in a list, we represent the entire order system to which they belong, putting that system on display, so to speak, for everyone to see. That is what I mean when I claim that some lists make order visible.

Years ago I was told of a little boy who could not bear to have his toys put away. Each time his mother put them in a toy box, the boy would take them out and line them up across his room. "I need to see them," he argued in his defense. "That is how I know that I have them." I kept coming back to this example when I started thinking theoretically about lists. My hunch was that a mere *list* of the toys would have the same effect, for I imagined a verbal list to be a substitution for a lineup, its symbolic representation. It took another child to show me that in action.

Four years ago, when I was already deeply involved in this project, friends from Sweden came to visit with their two-year-old daughter, Dara. The first thing Dara did each morning of their stay was to list, in a solemn ritual of roll-call, all the children from her daycare center in Stockholm. It was a touching sight to see this little girl, still sleepy in her bed, reciting with special care the names of her friends, pointing with each name to a particular place in a circle that remained invisible to the rest of us. The order of the names was always the same, probably the one her Swedish teacher used at home. And when her own name came up, Dara would point to herself and bow with a little smile, glad to be included in the circle, to be part of the order as she knew it. The listing ritual was clearly an exercise of verbal magic: of conjuring up the presence of her friends in their actual absence; of making them visibly there for her—for comfort and reassurance in her new experience of insecurity and isolation.

A list, then, is a symbolic *imposition* of a particular vision upon reality.[14] If, as I contend, the vision encoded in a list of divine names is nothing short of the metaphysical order on which the Christian experience of reality rests, then such a list is a basic rhetorical tool for the symbolic production of order in Christian society.

What Is Symbolic Production of Order?

When I refer to the Christian production of order as "symbolic," I align myself with the theoretical assumption that order is a symbolic enterprise grounded in the power of language to produce social realities. This position was first articulated as a coherent theory in the 1970s by the French sociologist Pierre Bourdieu.[15] For Bourdieu, order is a "vision of social di-vision" that has been collectively recognized and sanctioned as authoritative. The process of its social recognition is a matter of rhetoric: even when supported by the reality they claim to describe, classifications can be recognized only if they are first represented in symbolic form. Such an understanding of "symbolic production" makes explicit some hidden relations between authoritative speaking and order-making that allow us to position a rhetorical discussion of lists on firmer theoretical ground.

Bourdieu's key term *symbolic capital* designates a particular relational aspect of order-making: symbolic production requires complicity between speaker and audience, a shared knowledge about the rules of the game, a shared belief in the structure of the social exchange and its stakes that allows the audience to recognize a given symbolic representation as legitimate.[16] The "symbolic" aspect of capital is its potential to be "recognized" (or indeed "misrecognized") as power—the seemingly magical power of shaping reality by words alone. Symbolic capital, then, is nothing more than a veritable credit of trust that the members of a group invest in a person, granting him the right to speak for all of them and, in so doing, to shape the reality in which they live.[17] The group typically misrecognizes this privilege as a personal power of authority instead of recognizing it properly as the "pure fiduciary value" that it is—their own very personal investment of trust and hope.

This process of public recognition hinges on *naming* rituals that Bourdieu calls "rites of institution": the ordination of a priest, the inauguration of a president, the crowning of a king, the convocation of a college graduate. Clearly, by *name* we are to understand in this context a definition of social distinction that determines the precise coordinates—the "address"—of a person in the social field. If the imposition of a name is an act of public investment of symbolic capital in a professional who thereby becomes an embodiment of power, we may say that the name itself functions in Bourdieu's model as an atom of social order—the very instrument by which order is imposed upon social reality.[18]

Having thus established an explicit connection between symbolic production and order-making, Bourdieu takes it a step further by linking the growth of symbolic capital directly to the struggle over the legitimate vision of order. Once the members of a group invest symbolic capital in a social agent, they expect him to turn a profit—to augment their investment in the form of added honor and prestige. Since his distinctive power is "the power of constituting the given through utterances, of making people see and believe [the invisible and the incredible]," the specific product expected from such a spokesperson is a visionary one: the annunciation of a vision of order.[19] And if his initial professional capital grants him the right to advertise his private vision in the market of symbolic goods, we measure his ultimate success by the willingness of the group to buy into his vision and embrace it as their own social reality.

While my concern with symbolic production is informed by Bourdieu's theory, my practice is governed by priorities that are far removed from his own. Bourdieu the sociologist is interested mostly in the potential of symbolic capital to effect social change by reinforcing social inequality. My concern is not with the social results but with the rhetorical mechanisms of this process, with *verbal strategies* such as listmaking that shape the symbolic representation of order, making it socially recognizable. Furthermore, unlike Bourdieu, who is preoccupied with the careers of the authority figures involved in producing order, I call attention to the social promotion of *texts* that embody authoritative visions of order. For a medievalist, such a preference is a matter not only of professional bias, but also of necessity: the rites, rituals, and rivalries related to the imposition of order in medieval communities have reached us only in the form of textual traces.

The Material

I focus in this book on the careers of two texts, each remarkable in its own right. The texts form an unlikely pair at first sight: one of them is a theological treatise, the other a protective amulet. What makes them equally relevant for our discussion, despite the obvious dissimilarities, is their shared interest in listing the names of the Lord. And what makes them stand out together in the long tradition of this trope in Christian culture is their ambition to offer the definitive list, to exhibit *all* the names of the Lord from a position of authority.

The very possibility of such a gesture, of course, has everything to do with successful social promotion, which is always the result of extratextual factors, of specific (though often anonymous) actors pursuing their own agendas with respect to the texts they promote. It was a triumphant career across both time and space that ensured, in each case, the public recognition of our texts as loci of religious authority and symbolic power. That is why this book begins and ends with a historical narrative about the career of a text (chapters 1 and 10). The two success stories sample well the varieties of religious experience in the field of Christian logology, for the equally intense expression of social renown in each case is rooted in opposite practices exhibiting alternative positions on the Word and the Name, and on the ways the two could shape social realities in a Christian context. The recognition of the theological treatise manifested itself as a continual hermeneutic effort, documented in a substantial body of commentaries and translations that literally produced an "out-standing" text. This text, like a burning bush, was seen as perpetually instructive, inextinguishable, forever drawing new readers into its circle of significance.[20] In the second case, recognition took the form of a devoted use of the text itself as an instrument of power. Every amulet in active use is an embodiment of the public trust in its power to make real the order it represents; and the more visibly and abundantly it is being used, the faster its symbolic capital grows.

The theological text that I have chosen as the center of analysis in the first part of this book is the well-known Greek treatise *The Divine Names*, which belongs to the historically first Christian corpus of systematic theology. The author of the corpus presented himself as St. Dionysius the Areopagite, a first-century Athenian converted by St. Paul, although the texts were evidently written much later, close to the time when they first came into the public eye in the sixth century. Due to a cluster of factors that I examine in chapter 1, the corpus (including our text) was the focus of intense exegetical labor almost from the start, and the intensity only increased with time. The result was an interpretive project that remains unique in Christian history outside of the biblical canon, a project that invested the corpus with an authority second only to that of the Bible itself. Nineteenth-century philology's definitive proof that the near-apostolic authorship of the corpus was an elaborate hoax did little to impugn its authority. If anything, it made the text's value even more obvious. For the real "authority" of the corpus is measured by the enormous intellectual energy distilled into its rereading, by the trust—the credence—with which generation upon generation of Christians have approached the beautifully opaque texts of the Pseudo-Dionysius as a mirror in which they can confront the central dilemma of their own intellectual identity: what it means to believe in a divinity beyond comprehension—in a *theos* beyond *logos*—and to make, in the face of such a radical otherness, a *theology* by which they can live as they believe.

All these familiar facts from the career of the Areopagitical Corpus present the treatise *The Divine Names* as the most authoritative formulation of the Christian theological position on the names of God. The gist of this position is the formula "God is both nameless and of every name," which I explicate both against the tradition of the Christian theology of the Name and against the comprehensive theological vision that Dionysius proposed in his work (chapters 2 and 3). What is particularly significant for me in the context of the current discussion is that Dionysius frames all principal questions about the names of God directly with respect to his overarching concern with divine order (or the "hierarchies," as he preferred to call them, thus coining one of the most powerful terms in our cultural vocabulary of order).

While the contribution of the Pseudo-Areopagite to Christian thought has been studied from every angle imaginable, there has been little reflection on the relation of his theology of the Name to Christian rhetorical practices. Even less has been done to address the interrelation of his theory with the continual Christian practice of listing the names of the unnamable Divinity. My rereading of this familiar text is intended to explore such an unfamiliar territory. What I propose in chapter 4, as the outcome of a long journey into the world of Dionysius, is that his treatise endorses the open-ended list of divine names as the "proper" name of God while regulating membership in this ideal list through biblical exegesis. The practical consequence for Christian rhetoric was what Bourdieu would call the "theory effect."[21] It made explicit practices that had typified Christian rhetoric from the start by cloaking them with theological legitimacy, which is to say that the treatise *The Divine Names* placed all its authority—the authority it had borrowed from St. Dionysius the Areopagite—behind the open-ended list of biblical terms for the Lord and, in so doing, produced this trope as a recognizable authoritative pattern for articulating the terms of Christian order. The rest, as the saying goes, is history. As the symbolic capital of the treatise grew beyond the control of its author, spectacularly magnifying the initial impact of his theory, so did the authority of the trope itself.

The text that forms the center of my second case study is a Slavonic amulet known as *The 72 Names of the Lord*, whose earliest copies date from the end of the thirteenth century. Its employment as an amulet is declared directly in the text itself: it is to be worn on the body as protection from "every evil." From the outset we can discern at the heart of this text a double contrast with Dionysius's position. In place of the open-ended list of God-terms that Dionysius promoted, the amulet offers a closed numerical series. No less conspicuously, it repositions the list of divine names from the speculative field of theology into the field of apotropaic practices, where it is mobilized not as a prop in pursuit of the Good but as a protective shield against evil.

The respective scholarly careers of the two texts reveal further distinctions. Unlike the Areopagite's treatise, the amulet is virtually unstudied, though its solid tradition through the nineteenth century makes it perhaps the best-documented Slavonic list of divine names and one of the most popular amulets of its type in Christian practice. The profusion of gaps and dark spots in our knowledge of this text imposed a rather specific set of priorities and methodological choices on my approach. As a result, the second part of this book appears to be almost incongruous with the first in its language and frame of reference, even in its disciplinary locus. On the face of it, the study is cast as a literary "microhistory" that speculates through the exploration of a single, small-scale phenomenon about a large area of cultural diffusion. Though I never pursue mythological reconstructions or aim to master quite the same scope of dispersion as Carlo Ginzburg, this study resembles, in its general thrust, Ginzburg's famous microhistorical projects and shares their heterogeneity of subject and form.[22]

My inquiry begins with a question about the number 72—the element that not only sets our talismanic list apart from the orthodox tradition, but also provides both the formal and the conceptual matrix of this list. Subscribing to the assumption that the number has a shared Judeo-Christian symbolism, I explore clusters of 72-fold concepts that abound in the written production of the Semito-Hellenic world. The goal of the quest is to recover behind the apparent heterogeneity of these concepts a common network of meaning—a unified vision of order—and to identify the particular channels through which it could have informed Slavic magic practices (chapters 5, 6, and 7).

The results of this extensive experiment become visible in the last three chapters of the book. I demonstrate, over a large body of textual traces, that *The 72 Names of the Lord* has its roots in the Gnostic Kabbalah and originates from a Kabbalo-Christian exchange that most probably took place in Provence in the twelfth century (chapters 8 and 9). Such a conclusion posits our text as one of the earliest cases of Kabbalistic influence on Christian practice, considerably predating the "discovery" of the Kabbalah by the European Humanists in the 1490s. I further prove, on the basis of indisputable textual evidence, that the Slavonic amulet was directly dependent on Provençal sources, contrary to the prevailing opinion among scholars that it was a translation from Greek (chapter 9).

Unlike my first case study, which begins by establishing the authority of Dionysius, my discussion of *The 72 Names* has the opposite trajectory: it concludes with the moment in history that pushed the amulet to the mainstream of Slavic culture and produced it as a highly recognizable Christian list of divine names (chapter 10). This most glorious chapter in the history of the text begins in Venice in 1520, when the Slavonic amulet was first set in print. The following century saw several highly successful editions of *The 72 Names* that, in effect, transformed this previously obscure magical artifact into a popular commodity on the emerging Slavic book market. The process has a number of intriguing implications, though what interests me here is chiefly the fact that it invested the amulet with significant religious authority. And even though the sociocultural context in which the promotion of the amulet took place is radically different from the context that distinguished Dionysius's treatise, the symbolic power attached to the texts in both situations is comparable.

The apparent discord between my two case studies thus collapses in the end into a unity of focus and purpose. The unlikely pairing of one of the most visible texts in Christian theology with an amulet of obscure, heterodox origin and rather provincial fame proves to illuminate a common concern at the heart of Christian culture. The two texts represent—from their respective positions of authority in the Christian field—two alternative models for listing the names of God that coexist, more or less unproblematically, in Christian practice: the open-ended list, and the closed, numerical catalogue that defines the limit of expansion by a particular number. Both of these types of listmaking presume to be exhaustive, though their distinct views of the nature of God's names determine the different teleological horizons of their shared ambition for totality. Each has its own representative locus in Christian culture. The open-ended list typifies the orthodox theological position on the limits of naming God as an interminable endeavor both reflecting upon and reflected in the official Christian rhetoric of infinity. The closed list, by contrast, represents subaltern landscapes of Christian practice—often called "magic"—where divine names are placed directly in human service to ensure protection and well-being.

The two texts, when counterpoised as a contrastive pair, not only illuminate a set of theoretical questions about making lists and making order in Christian culture, but also mutually illuminate one another, revealing in each other aspects that remain otherwise eclipsed. Without the background of *The Divine Names*, we cannot adequately understand the enormous effort distilled into redressing *The 72 Names of the Lord* as a truly Christian text by way of legitimating the names in the list according to Dionysius's standards. (The compiler of the printed version went so far as to include in the amulet itself an exegetical passage, thus incorporating biblical exegesis—prescribed by Dionysius as a requirement for the proper listing of the names—directly into the making of the list proper.) No less importantly, the explicit correlation of sacred order and divine names in the project of Dionysius conditions us to recognize the equivalents in other spheres of Christian practice where it is not necessarily as striking (including magic). Conversely, *The 72 Names of the Lord*, being itself an overdetermined list that is both closed and defined by a particular number, pushes to the forefront the list-pattern itself and forces us to identify the significance of listmaking in Dionysius's own project. The dual theoretical focus of this book—a focus on order *and* lists—thus emerges directly from the unorthodox juxtaposition of my two privileged texts.

If indeed, as I have suggested here, there is a direct relationship between the production of sacred order and the pronouncement of a list of divine names from a position of authority, our two highly visible lists should represent two alternative visions of Christian order. Moreover, since, for Christianity, order is also an ethical system, Christian cosmological imagination is always already a moral imagination. We are to expect, therefore, that the list of divine names would function in the Christian context not only as an epistemological figure but also as a motivational gesture, as a scenario for social behavior. My analyses put these conjectures to the test, treating them as open questions rather than as axioms. What does it mean to live "in the name of the Lord" when his name can be either an open-ended list or a closed numerical series? Does it make a difference which option you choose? Are the two compatible?

By posing such questions as our distant goal—our Ithaka, as Cavafy would say—we doubt not that the quest will be a long one. So, with hope for adventure and discovery, we are ready to embark.[23]

PART I

The Claim of Theology: "Nameless and of Every Name"

The language of God has no grammar. It consists only of names.
—Gershom Scholem, "Tradition und Kommentar als religiöse Kategorien im Judentum"

Bearer of all names,
How shall I name you—
You alone the unnamable?
—Gregory Nazianzen, *Hymn to God*

There was a time when God had no name, and there will be a time again when He will have none.
—Isaac the Syrian, *Homily*

CHAPTER ONE

The Divine Names and Dionysius the Areopagite

The Romans used to say that books have their own fates. Less fatalistically perhaps, we can claim that they have careers: unique trajectories of social promotion and recognition that are often distinct from those of their authors. The enduring success of a book, like that of a person, depends largely on the will and labor of others, and so it often tells more about management than about intrinsic merit. Books' careers thus make particularly illuminating cases of intellectual and social history, especially since they often span centuries and mobilize multitudes of readers across historical bounds.

There are only a few books in Christian culture that rival—in scope or impact—the fabulous career of the Greek theological works attributed to Saint Dionysius the Areopagite. These works, which have survived as a unified corpus, encompass four treatises, *The Divine Names (DN)*, *The Mystical Theology (MT)*, *The Ecclesiastical Hierarchy (EH)*, and *The Celestial Hierarchy (CH)*, as well as ten Epistles (Ep.).[1] Each of them holds a unique position of authority in the Christian canon, and the corpus as a whole has shaped Christian spirituality as few texts, outside the biblical canon, ever have. Since, however, I focus on the names of God, our particular interest turns on the treatise *The Divine Names*, which stands out in the Christian tradition as the most authoritative theological discourse on the naming of God.

Myth and Mystification

The Areopagitical corpus was written, in all probability, at the beginning of the sixth century, shortly before it first came into the public eye.[2] The man who penned it, however, clouded its origin in a thick veil of mystery

Fig. 1. St. Dionysius the Areopagite, ca. 1200, fresco from the Refectory in the Monastery of St. John the Baptist in Patmos. Courtesy of Avery Library, Columbia University.

by misrepresenting himself as Dionysius the Areopagite, who was the first Athenian converted by St. Paul's defense before the Areopagus (Acts 17:34) and who, as tradition has it, later became the first bishop of Athens, dying as a martyr in Christ.[3]

Whoever the man behind this pseudonym really was, he could not have chosen a better guise. While effectively concealing from posterity his true identity, the pen name granted his work a near-apostolic authority and placed it at the head of the patristic tradition. Luck was on his side as well, for he not only managed to fool everyone with his mystification, but even benefited from the unintended consequences of assuming the name of Dionysius. I have in mind, of course, the typical medieval conflation (and confusion) of namesakes that, in the ninth century, presented our mystery man with another fabulous extension of his biography. He was identified— by intent or by mistake—also with Saint-Denis, a third-century missionary to Gaul who became the first Bishop of Paris and then a beloved patron saint of all of France.[4] This new piece of fiction, though it obfuscated even further the truth about the Dionysian corpus, helped cement its authority and make its author one of the most popular Eastern theologians in the West.

The Exegetes

The name of Dionysius was invaluable for promoting the Areopagitical corpus across the Christian world. Yet the sustained career of this work was not so much the result of self-promotion as the fruit of a continual interpretive labor—the rich tradition of its theological commentaries and annotations that, almost from the start, became inseparable from the corpus itself. The first in a succession of medieval commentators was John of Scythopolis (d. ca. 548), who, some time between 537 and 543, augmented Dionysius's works with scholia and a prologue.[5] In the next century, Maximus the Confessor (ca. 580–662) added more scholia and further solidified the stature of the corpus by his presentation at the Lateran Council of 649, where he quoted Dionysius twice as a competent orthodox witness against Monothelitism.[6] Both John and Maximus accepted without reservation the apostolic authorship of the works and convincingly defended their orthodoxy. Thus they secured a place for the Dionysian corpus in the mainstream of the patristic tradition and opened the door for its continuing impact on later theological thought. After them, and especially after the inclusion of Dionysius in the definitive dogmatic summary, *The Orthodox Faith*, by John of Damascus (ca. 675–ca. 749), the status of the corpus was sealed as an authentic early Christian work of utmost repute and unchallenged authority.[7]

New commentaries proliferated, too many to be listed here in full, though the names of some of the authors alone command respect: Albert the Great (ca. 1200–80), Thomas Aquinas (1225–74), Bonaventure (1217– 74), Meister Eckhart (ca. 1260–1327). This interpretive zeal is unique in Christian history outside of scriptural exegesis. In fact, as Bernard McGinn suggests, the works of Dionysius were treated from the start "much like the Bible itself—as a divine message filled with inner life and mysterious meaning which could never be exhausted." Unlike some other turns in the remarkable history of the corpus, this outstanding status in the exegetical tradition is no accident. It has much to do with a certain quality of the work itself: that rich and inviting opacity (McGinn calls it "hermeneutical flexibility") that not only allows but almost demands continual exegesis.[8]

Dionysius's arguments are paradoxical, luxuriously thick, labyrinthine. And so is his language, with its incantatory rhythm, meandering syntax, and profusion of rare words and neologisms in which it is so easy to lose your way.[9] That difficulty is, I believe, deliberate, and very much part of the theological project of the corpus. The reader's effort to understand the text is meant to approximate the experience of being in God's presence, and it aims to cultivate a particular state of mind: not only receptivity, but also responsiveness—by deed as well as words—to a divinity beyond being, beyond language and comprehension. It should not surprise us, therefore, that almost every generation of Christian thinkers has felt compelled to revisit Dionysius and find new treasures of meaning and insight in his works.

The Translators

The labor of translating Dionysius is but one aspect of the same interpretive effort, being subject to all the difficulties of interpretation, compounded by a specific linguistic challenge—the resistance of Dionysius's idiosyncratic Greek to any other idiom. Daunting as it may be, however, the task has found plenty of enthusiasts over the ages, and though the results have rarely been up to the original, they have been crucial for making the Areopagitical corpus an all-Christian currency.

The earliest translation came out almost simultaneously with the corpus itself in Syriac.[10] This is hardly surprising, since Dionysius's writings first appeared in public in the context of Syrian Christianity, and most scholars today are inclined to believe that the author himself belonged to that geographical milieu. In the sixth century, however, Christianity was rapidly losing ground in Syria in the aftermath of the Council of Chalcedon.[11] The gap between Antioch and Constantinople widened greatly, paving the way for the transformation of Syria into the center of a new, mighty Arabic Empire of Islam in the seventh century.[12] Under the circumstances, the impact of the Dionysian corpus in the Syrian context was understandably limited and short-lived.

The Latin West, by contrast, produced an especially rich and consistent tradition after 827, when the Byzantine Emperor Michael the Stammerer presented a Greek manuscript of the corpus to the Frankish King Louis the Pious.[13] Louis, in turn, offered the codex as a gift to the monastery of Saint-

Denis, near Paris, where the Abbot Hilduin attempted a (rather inaccurate) translation in 838. A couple of decades later, Charles the Bald, not satisfied with Hilduin's version, commissioned another translation from the Irish monk John Scotus Eriugena (ca. 810–ca. 877). Eriugena completed his acclaimed translation in about 862 and appended to it commentaries that significantly shaped the reception of Dionysius in the West.[14]

Other Latin translations continued to appear throughout the high Middle Ages and into the Renaissance. The Italian Humanists stand out in this respect for their renewed admiration of Dionysius and zealous protection of his apostolic identity. In accordance with their general philological interests, they strove to procure better editions and translations of the corpus, which modern printing technologies allowed to circulate on a much larger scale. In 1436, Ambrogio Traversari (Camaldulensis) produced an elegant new translation that was first printed in Bruges in 1480 and became the standard Latin version for both the Humanists and the Protestant Reformers. The first Greek edition was published in 1516 by Philippe Junta of Florence, followed in 1634 by Balthasar Corderius's definitive edition, published at the Plantin presses in Antwerp (with a frontispiece by Rubens).[15]

Although the first translation of the Areopagitical corpus into Church Slavonic did not come out until the late fourteenth century, there is sufficient data to suggest that it was read in Greek by the South Slavic elite as early as the ninth century, when Slavic Christian culture was still being forged. In fact, quotations and paraphrases of passages from the corpus are found in several of the earliest Slavonic codices: *Hexaemeron* and *Heavens*, the two major compilatory works by John the Exarch of Bulgaria (d. ca. 927), and the much studied *Simeonic Florilegium* of 1073.[16]

The interest in Dionysius intensified in the fourteenth century in the context of Hesychasm (from Greek *hesychia*, "quietude"), a radical form of Eastern Orthodox mysticism that became, by the middle of that century, politically dominant both in Byzantium and in the Slavic part of the Balkans.[17] Responding to the increasing demand for the works of the Areopagite, the Serbian Metropolitan Theodosius urged a monk by the name of Isaiah from the city of Serres to translate the corpus together with the combined scholia of John and Maximus. Isaiah completed the translation in 1371, on the eve of the Ottoman invasion of the Balkans, and prefaced it with an unusually personal prologue that documents well his turbulent times.[18] His translation enjoyed an abundant manuscript tradition, despite its late date of appearance.[19] The Bulgarian hesychast Cyprian (ca. 1330–1406), who became the Metropolitan of Moscow in 1389, personally brought one copy to Russia, thus expanding further the territory of Dionysius's influence. In

1675, the Russian monk Euthymius of the Chudov Monastery prepared a new translation for a printed publication which, however, never came out, while Isaiah's version appeared in print in 1870, as part of the monumental edition of the Reading Menaion completed under the aegis of Metropolitan Makarii ([Macarius]; 1542–63).

Disputed Authorship and Indisputable Authority

The supreme authority of the Areopagitical corpus, shaped as it was by the efforts of commentators and translators across the Christian world, remained unchallenged throughout the Middle Ages. Only in the context of the sixteenth-century Reformation did the carefully designed—and zealously protected—apostolic façade of the corpus slowly begin to crumble.[20] The final blow was dealt in 1895 when Hugo Koch and Joseph Stiglmayr each demonstrated independently, though using the same textual evidence, that the author of the corpus relied heavily on the fifth-century Neoplatonist Proclus (ca. 410–485).[21] He was therefore by no means a first-century writer, but worked most probably in the early sixth century.[22] Hence, the awkward scholarly reference to him as the "Pseudo-Dionysius" which—in a manner well-suited to his own apophatic theology—says nothing of who he actually was, but only of what he was not.[23]

The reorientation of the corpus from the first to the sixth century, or better yet, its return to its native context, changes radically the landscapes—historical and theoretical—against which the reader is to consider this complex and influential work. The corpus is now stripped of the apostolic garb to which it owed much of its initial popularity and success. Yet precisely because of that, we can finally appreciate it for what it really is beneath the camouflage: the ripe fruit of a ripe age, the perfect epitome of a historical moment when Christian theology had graduated to new levels of maturity and complexity and was primed for syntheses unimaginable five centuries earlier.

As Paul Rorem and John Lamoreaux have observed, our modern vision of Greek intellectual history in the sixth century is shaped largely by two competing and equally reductionist narratives: the Post-Chalcedonian Christological controversy, and the decline and death of ancient philosophy. A common scholarly bias is to try to narrate Dionysius exclusively in the idiom of one or the other. As a result, much of the modern speculation about the mysterious Pseudo-Areopagite is plagued by a hermeneutics of suspicion and conspiracy theories.[24] Was he a Neoplatonist who paraded as a Christian and, by the Trojan horse of his writings, helped Greek thought take over the temple of Christian wisdom? Or was he, conversely, a key player in the Christian project of assimilating pagan culture, despoiling the Greeks, as it were, to enrich the Christians?[25] Luther seems to have set the tone in 1520 with his notorious remark, "Dionysius is most pernicious; he platonizes more than he Christianizes."[26] And now, half a millennium later, the oddly quantitative question "What is he *more*, Platonist or Christian" still hovers. But it is a flawed question. It presumes that Dionysius the Christian and Dionysius the Neoplatonist must be at war with one another, thus neglecting perhaps the most distinctive quality of Dionysius the thinker: his uncanny ability to synthesize where others see only irreconcilable conflicts. Dionysius himself prefers to frame plurality as a set not of alternative choices but of complementary chances, and so he dwells not in militant *either/or* questions but in more harmonizing *and*-propositions, embracing a world of antinomies where, contrary to the assumption of Aristotelian logic, negation is *not* the opposite of assertion. His very choice of a pseudonym suggests a symbolic site where Plato and Christ meet, or rather, where Plato acknowledges Christ, since in the biblical story it is the Athens of classical thought that bows down, however briefly, to the wisdom of St. Paul.[27] The sixth-century man behind the pseudonym, however, was much better positioned than his first-century prototype not only to make such a meeting a reality that lasts, but also to make it less asymmetrical. And he made the most of this opportunity when, just before the closing of the Platonic Academy (in 529), he ushered the Athens of Proclean Neoplatonism into the shrine of a Christian corpus of systematic theology—his own.[28] Whatever his true intentions, I believe the result was a double gain: he salvaged the Platonists for the Christians, and enriched them both.

In my private visions of Dionysius, I am always tempted to imagine his merger of Christianity with Proclean Neoplatonism as but a facet of a more inclusive and pervasive synthesis.[29] To turn this intuition into a scholarly hypothesis, however, goes beyond both my objectives in this chapter and my expertise. For the purpose of my current project, the synthesizing tendencies of Dionysius and the remarkable dialectical flexibility of his theological propositions interest me only with regard to his views on divine names, and I restrict my argument to this specific arena.

The central claim in what follows is that Dionysius's treatise *The Divine Names* is a creative synthesis of preexisting and often conflicting Christian theories and concomitant rhetorical practices of naming God. This longest— and arguably most reputable—treatise of Dionysius appeared at a time when the positions of the various camps in the theological disputations on divine names, as well as the general doctrinal framework in which they were

embedded, had been articulated with relative clarity. Such an opportune position in the historical trajectory of the Christian experience allowed Dionysius to have both an encompassing and a balanced view of his subject, and the
freedom to approach it directly rather than by polemics with others (though
in his own narrative, of course, his advantages are attributed not to the fact
that he came late enough, but to the fiction that he came first). I believe that
this particular quality of *The Divine Names*—which, for lack of a better term,
I call "synthesism"—is the root of its abiding authority in the Christian
tradition, and that it makes this work the natural fulcrum of my historical
survey—the most suitable text through which we may screen the entire intellectual output of Christianity on the subject of naming God.

Dionysius is a welcome figure in my narrative in still another way. His
story dramatizes in a particularly spectacular scenario the role that margins
of various kinds play in the social promotion of texts. Thus it illuminates
well an overarching concern in this book for the interdependence between
center and periphery, high and low, the privileged and the underdog. As
I have already pointed out, the Areopagitical corpus appeared initially in
the periphery of the Christian East at a time when the Christological disputes after Chalcedon were tearing the Eastern Churches apart. Furthermore, it was introduced to the public by the outsiders in the controversy,
the Monophysites, and quickly gained currency among various heretical
groups, while the Orthodox first dismissed it as spurious.[30] It must have
seemed that this provincial, idiosyncratic, and deliberately "difficult" text
was destined for obscurity, despite the clever name games that its anonymous author was playing with his audiences. But then the commentators
stepped in. The scholia of John of Scythopolis and Maximus the Confessor, often documented literally in the margins of the Dionysian corpus,
grew around the original text and fused with it into a new creation, the
Annotated Areopagite, which became for subsequent readers the definitive
Corpus Areopagiticum.[31] This symbiosis between text and exegesis was a
most productive collaboration indeed. The marginal notes not only fed on
the text of Dionysius, shaping—in acts of "limitrophic violence"—its messages according to a strictly Orthodox mold.[32] They also "garnished its margins with their lubrications," thus smoothing its communication with wary
audiences, enhancing the elasticity of its meaning, highlighting its inner
radiance.[33] Still, the major consequence was political. The continual interpretive effort of Christian thinkers who labored in the margins of the
Areopagitical corpus shifted this once "marginal" work to the center of Orthodoxy, and its unknown author was crowned for at least a millennium
with an authority second only to Scripture itself.

Fig. 2. Marginal drawing of St. Dionysius Areopagite in a Greek manuscript of the *Areopagite Corpus* from the Monastery of St. Catherine on Mt. Sinai, fourteenth-fifteenth century, fol. 46v. Reproduced by kind permission of the Library of Congress from Microfilm #5010.322 Greek, the St. Catherine's Monastery, Mount Sinai.

CHAPTER TWO

Back to the Sources

To get a more adequate view of the Dionysian synthesis in its immediate intellectual context, it helps to step back and observe the more inclusive landscape of concerns, preoccupations, and practices that constituted over time the Christian theology of divine names.

It is common to regard Christianity as a religion of the Word, though to call it "a religion of the Name" might sound like a stretch at first. Yet the status of the name—or the names—of God in the Christian idiom is not like that of any other word. About two thousand years ago, the very first Christian communities chose to define themselves as those "who invoke the name [of the Lord]" (Acts 9:14), a "name that is above every name" (Phil. 2:9). And since then, the struggle to articulate and sustain a Christian identity has always been entangled with the striving for profession, for confession and confirmation of God's name. This absorbed attention to the name of the divinity is perceptible in Christian history across speculative and devotional discourses alike. After *logos* (the Word), *onoma* (the Name) is one of the most disputable yet indispensable categories of Christian theology—as much a source of controversy as it is of gravity and inspiration. And throughout the heated debates, despite the vicissitudes of theological argumentations, respect for the name in the language of worship has never wavered, making it one of the pivots of the Christian liturgical idiom.

To be sure, such intense concern with divine names is not uniquely Christian. It is common to all Abrahamic religions and reflects a more general stance regarding language that Christianity and Islam inherited from Judaism.[1] All three religious traditions are built around a particular sacred text—the Tanakh, the Bible, the Koran—that, as a witness to the proclamatory Word of God, demands both utmost devotion and perpetual exegesis. Such radical logocentrism, or preoccupation with the Word, when paired with the premise of a single Creator, engenders a no less radical *onomato-centrism*, or preoccupation with the name, whose complexities are rooted in the idiosyncratic treatment of God's name by Scripture itself.

The Bible and the Name

It is, I believe, the Hebrew Bible that prepared the stage for the quirks and the crux of Christian onomatocentrism. It suggests—simultaneously and in an apparently non-contradictory fashion—that God has one name, no name, and a multiplicity of names, a paradoxical proposition that invites, if not necessarily trouble, certainly some prickly hermeneutics.

On the face of it, the Jewish Scripture—both in its original form and as the Christian Old Testament—makes abundant references to "the name of God," a name that, in accordance with the grammar of monotheism, is single and singular. The topos originally appeared as a ritual substitute for the ineffable name Yahweh, and thus its chief use pertained to public worship: it was associated with the altar and the Ark of the Covenant, with Mt. Sinai and Jerusalem. Most directly, the name was linked to the Temple of Solomon, where it was believed to dwell as a form of divine presence, since the Lord had declared to David, "Your son . . . shall build a house for my name" (1 Kings 8:19).[2]

Christianity readily adopted "the name of God," absorbing the topos directly from the Old Testament, and especially from those parts of it— hymns, lections, and invocations—that penetrated Christian liturgy and became models for Christianity's own language of worship. The result is a particularly rich Christian texture of references to the one name of the single divinity, where old Judaic formulas, such as the Third Commandment, "You shall not make wrongful use of the name of the Lord your God" (Exod. 20:7), or the Psalmist's exclamation, "Blessed be the name of the Lord from this time on and forevermore!" (Ps. 113:2), resound with brand new ones: from the opening of the Lord's Prayer that each and every Christian is supposed to repeat daily, "Our Father in heaven, hallowed be your name" (Matt. 6:9), to the common Trinitarian ekphonesis, "In the name of the Father, and of the Son, and of the Holy Spirit!"[3]

These constant references to the single name, however, become increasingly frustrating the deeper we get into the scriptural world and its patterns of thought, for the Bible never reveals that name. Moreover, it pointedly refuses even to discuss the issue. In fact, the three Old Testament episodes that include an open request for the name all raise the question only to rebuke it. When Jacob dares to ask the One he wrestles with, "Please tell me your name," his opponent evades the question by countering, "Why is it that you ask my name?" (Gen. 32:29). Almost the same exchange occurs between the angel of Yahweh and Manoah and his wife, but with a notable qualifier to the answer: "Why do you ask my name? It is too wonderful." (Judg. 13:18).[4] And then there is the famous dialogue between Moses and the Lord before the Covenant that provides the only positive—albeit notoriously ambiguous—answer of God to the question of his name:

> But Moses said to God, "If I come to the Israelites and say to them, 'The God of your ancestors has sent me to you' and they ask me, 'What is his name?' what shall I say to them?" God said to Moses, "I am who I am (Ehyeh asher ehyeh)." He said further, "Thus you shall say to the Israelites, 'I am has sent me to you.' . . . This is my name forever, and this my title for all generations." [Exod. 3:13–15]

This cryptic passage, one of the most discussed scriptural texts, is often interpreted in the Christian tradition as a positive ontological assertion about God, following the Septuagint translation ego eimi ho ōn ("I am the one who is").[5] Paul Ricoeur has summarized the results in the following terse observation: "This translation opened up an affirmative noetics of God's absolute being that could subsequently be transcribed into Neoplatonic and Augustinian ontology and then into Aristotelian and Thomistic metaphysics. In this way the theology of the name could pass over into an onto-theology."[6] Even at its most affirmative, however, this revelation of the name remains strikingly evasive, concealing at least as much as it reveals. When read as an ontological assertion, it encompasses being in its totality, thus going against the grain of naming itself, which is meant to identify by delimiting and excluding. Thus the name "I am" at once opens the notion of naming God to all-embracing dimensions (an all-name) and stretches it beyond the scope of human language to the realm of the ineffable (a no-name).[7] To put it another way, the only direct biblical revelation of the name elegantly dispenses with that name by making it shade into either everything or nothing.[8]

Finally, both the Hebrew and the Greek biblical texts offer a plethora of terms for God: epithets, symbols, descriptive phrases, and nominal predicates of identity statements.[9] These scriptural appellations (such as God of gods, King of kings, Good, Life, the Holy One, Truth, Vine, Lamb, the Door) fall in exactly the same category—both structurally and functionally—as do the names in the Slavonic amulet The 72 Names of God. Though they are never directly introduced as the Lord's names in their immediate biblical context, the pattern of using them as such is certainly available there, since they are often employed to refer to the divinity and even to address it. More important still, these biblical terms are commonly used as divine names in the ritual language of worship to cope with the practical problems that thrive in the absence of a direct name revelation.

Thus, on the one hand, the Bible consistently refers to a single name of God that remains mysterious, while, on the other hand, it provides an array of God-terms that are never defined explicitly as his names. The result is a salient singularity/plurality dynamics that sustains an epistemological tension in the Christian discourses with and about God, and that raises questions with no easy and clear-cut answers.[10] What *is* the name that the Christians worship and confirm? Is it, to paraphrase T. S. Eliot, an "ineffable effable," a tabooed and unknowable singular name? Or is it, as Sergei Bulgakov suggests, just an empty "ontological receptacle" for the numerous titles and epithets handed down in Scripture and the sacred tradition, a generalized category of "all-name"?[11] Is God, in other words, revealed to us as essentially anonymous, the One without a proper name? Or is he truly polynomous—a God of many names, and perhaps of every name? And, in either case, how should we relate to a divinity with such a problematic name, when we regard unambiguous naming as a must for any communication?

Such questions form the backbone of Christian *onomatology*, the domain of theoretical concerns with the name of the Lord. To simplify the picture, we may say that two queries rule over this domain, "What is a divine name?" and "Which are the (true) names of God?" We can further imagine these questions as defining two relatively autonomous projects: a purely speculative one called "name theology," and another, more pragmatic in its orientation, that we can call "name epistemology."

In reality, however, speculations on the essence of divine names and pragmatic concerns for codifying their actual application are aspects of the same pursuit. The process of formulating a systematic name theology developed parallel to the largely nonreflexive liturgical practice of using various titles and referring expressions as names for the unnamable divinity. It was the task of theology to justify this application by devising a concept of divine names that was compatible with the tenets of a unified theological vision, and to defend the very possibility of "naming" a transcendent divinity against the absence of a direct name revelation. The question *"What* is a divine name?" in other words, could never be broached successfully without considering the various terms applied to God in the Christian tradition, just as the question *"Which* are the Lord's names?" could not be answered without a relatively clear theoretical concept of the name. In short, a systematic Christian onomatology could emerge only as a negotiation between the theoretical constraints of theology and the demands of living rhetorical practice.

The Trouble with Logos

The clash of ideas on the nature and function of divine names, against which Dionysius pursued his synthesis, is highly representative of internal contradictions about language in general that have plagued Christianity since its emergence as a universal religion. Christian name theology, in other words, is subsumed in a larger theology of language.

The internal paradoxes of the Christian position on language are usually attributed to its hyphenated, Judeo-Hellenic heritage. More specifically, they stem from the need—and the struggle—to reconcile the two opposite linguistic sensibilities that come with this heritage: the Judaic doctrine of a fully transcendent God proclaimed in Scripture; and Greek philosophy, whose ever-ambiguous *logos* presupposes a connection between "discourse" and "reason." The logocentricity of the first comes across as essential and largely unproblematic; the second necessarily makes any logos project both self-reflexive and highly skeptical of itself. It is hardly surprising, therefore, that the naming of God became a focal point in this difficult process of reconciliation: the Judaic demand for unconditional, filial trust in the Living God confronted dramatically the Greek philosophical preoccupation with reason.[12]

Incidentally, it was St. Paul, the alleged mentor and teacher of Dionysius, who initiated the major shift in the history of early Christianity, generating a change with far-reaching repercussions, of which those discussed here are only a part. At its core, Christianity was transformed from a local, rabbinic movement within Judaism into a universal religion open for membership to Jews and Gentiles alike. This remarkable metamorphosis created a dialogical situation, in which the mastering of just one cultural code was no longer sufficient. It put enormous pressure on the new religion to rearticulate its message into idioms that Gentiles and their elites could not only recognize, but to which they could relate.[13] The generation of the second-century Apologists responded to this need for broader intellectual legitimacy by experimenting with a Platonic defense of Christianity—a colossal "translation" endeavor that came to fruition later in the work of the Cappadocians. The result was the birth of Christian metalanguage out of the *logos spermatikos* of Greek philosophy and the emergence of that peculiar critical inquiry that we call Christian theology and that, in David Tracy's words, began with asking Greek questions of Hebrew narratives.[14] The same process afforded the chance for Christianity to be accepted as a philosophy among philosophies and to become a major force in the intellectual life of the Roman Empire, allowing it finally to monopolize the scene with Emperor Justinian's ban on pagan education in 529.[15]

Before that landmark event, however (and under circumstances leading directly to it), Christianity had to confront one principal rival in the intellectual arena of the Imperial Age: Neoplatonism, definitively articulated between the third and the fifth centuries in the works of Plotinus (205–301), Porphyry (ca. 232–304) and Proclus (ca. 411–485). This major opponent had a sustained impact upon Christian intellectual life and its patterns of thought and discourse, or—if you prefer—upon the "logos" aspects of Christian theology.

Moreover, Neoplatonism is the school that articulated most directly the worst Hellenic suspicions about logos, thus effecting a change in the linguistic sensibilities of the Greco-Roman world that had been brewing for centuries. Discourse is unreliable, Neoplatonists claimed, because it fragments reality and creates distance and differentiation.[16] This separative power of logos makes it particularly unsuited for handling unity and unitive experiences—a major problem in the Neoplatonic scheme of things, since the premise of the entire cosmological program of Neoplatonism was the hypothesis of the One understood as both an ontological source and an epistemological goal.

Neoplatonists worked hard to find a way out of this predicament, trying to subvert the ground rules of language and to make it transcend its own limits. Their solution was a method for apprehension of the One which, to quote Vladimir Lossky, is "apprehension by supreme ignorance," the acknowledgment of intellectual failure in the face of the inconceivable.[17] This speculative technique is known as the negative method, or *apophasis* ("negation"). Its logic runs, more or less, as follows: positive predicates particularize and misrepresent the One; hence, we can only say what the One is not—that is, negate the positive predicates we attach to it. The practical result of this reasoning was a distinctive type of rhetoric of the One, avowing the inexpressible nature of the object it nonetheless strives to express, a paradoxical rhetoric of negatives and superlatives that, despite its abundant verbosity, remains always on the brink of silence.

The Neoplatonic negative method had a profound influence on Christian rhetoric, tapping right into the anxieties created by the absence of a manifest name. In Christian hands, of course, the method underwent a theological reorientation from the Neoplatonic impersonal One toward the Christian personal divinity, the Living God revealed through creation and incarnation according to the canonical witness of the Bible. It also underwent, as I hope to illustrate later in the case of Dionysius, a significant adjustment to the Christian doctrine of the Trinity and its salvation economy. Still, even though the Christian apophatic message was distinct from the Neoplatonic one, the rhetoric—from Clement and the Cappadocians to Dionysius and the later mystics—was apparently the same, and so were its linguistic assumptions.

The Two Roads, or the Nature of Divine Names

We have glimpsed the two central issues that the early Christian theology of divine names faced: the ambiguous biblical testimony of the name, and the growing mistrust in the efficacy of language that permeated the intellectual concerns of late antiquity, including those of Christianity itself. Let us now take a brief look at the early theological discourses on the names of God and consider how they chose to thematize these issues and what were the focal points of the controversy that ensued.

The Christian discussion of divine names was shaped from the outset by the tradition of the Greek philosophy of language, and specifically by semantic concerns about the relationship between names and the things they name, or their referents. As a result, its natural venue has always been what we call today semiotics, or the theory of signs and representation, focusing upon such questions as what names signify and how to interpret them properly. Epistemological concerns with divine names as potential instruments of knowledge, however, were pursued—in view of the radical transcendentalism of Christianity—within a general ontological framework where questions of knowledge were posed as questions of origin. The crux of Christian onomatology, at its minimum, is thus the question of the ontological status of divine names.

Framed in such a way, the onomatological debate exhibited from the start a distinctly Platonic character, for it developed within the old "by nature" *(kata physin)* or "by convention" *(kata thesin)* controversy initiated by Plato in *Cratylus*. The eponymous interlocutor of this dialogue, Cratylus, sustains the traditional view that names have a natural relationship with the things named, a view that was essential for ancient and medieval Judaism.[18] Contrary to Cratylus's theory of "natural correctness," his opponent, Hermogenes, proposes the conventionalist idea that names are merely of arbitrary human origin. This position proved more popular in the long run. It ultimately gained the upper hand in Hellenistic philosophy (and, by extension, in modern linguistics) when none other than Aristotle himself took it up. Unlike Plato, who committed to neither the "cratylic" nor the "hermogenic" views, Aristotle explicitly declared his position: "It is by convention and in no way by nature that nouns *(onomata)* have their meaning."[19] Still, we should not overestimate the contribution of Aristotle's linguistic relativism to Christian thought. It did manage to undermine the Cratylian longing for "true by nature" names of God, but it never actually succeeded in eradicating it. Upon reflection, the early history of Christian name theology is defined more by the competition between the camps of the name-realists and the name-relativists than by the temporary victory of one over the other.

Christian representatives of the cratylic trend gravitated toward the theory that the true divine names are given to man by God himself. Contrary to the warnings of Aristotelian logic, they claimed a genuine divine origin for all the names of God revealed in the Bible and the sacred tradition. They further rejected as "incorrect" all the other names invented by humanity, which, being ontologically secondary to the divinity, are inappropriate to it. The "correct" divine names, according to them, are ontological entities of transcendent origin and are, therefore, essentially nonreferential. They do not represent God, but automatically manifest his power regardless of the speaker's intention, for they derive ontological and performative strength directly from their transcendent source.

Echoes of this position resound through the strongest name-endorsing statements of early Greek theology, especially in the Arian claim that "The Name of the Father is the Son" and the similar views of Eunomius the Anomoean (d. 394).[20] Yet the most consistent articulation of a cratylic theory of divine names belongs admittedly to Origen (ca. 185–254?), one of the principal Christian mediators between the worlds of Hebrew and Greek culture and, despite his condemnation by the Constantinople Council in 553, a thinker of compelling influence. He openly declared in his treatise *Contra Celsum* that "names . . . are not arbitrary conventions of those who give them, as Aristotle thinks. For the languages in use among men have not a human origin."[21] If this is true of any name, it is all the more valid for the names of God, which for Origen are the efficacious words par excellence and, as such, are the pivot of any ritual language.

If we are to translate Origen's view into the language of modern (Peircean) semiotics—the discipline that tackles directly the uneasy relation between the material and the representational aspects of signification—we should say that divine names for him function as iconic signs.[22] Unlike symbols, they do not need the mediation of an interpretant (i.e., of exegesis), for their automatic power does not depend on signification but solely on their material form, especially phonic structure. The iconicity of divine names also renders them virtually untranslatable, a point of particular importance for Origen, who claimed that Hebrew was superior as a ritual language to Gentile tongues and, therefore, that Hebrew names for God had power rivaled by no other name.[23]

Such a nonreferential theory that, in its various modifications, reifies the divine names has been systematically criticized on a number of points by the Christian name-skeptics who took over Aristotle's conventionalist stance. At its most obvious, the reification of names poses a discursive problem of infinite regress. If divine names indeed have automatic powers, they cannot (and should not) be used outside of a ritual context, which means that speculative discourse requires substitutes for them. The Cappadocian Fathers raised this problem as a major argument against Eunomius's treatment of divine names.[24]

On a more pragmatic level, emphasis on the materiality of divine names made the nonreferential theory particularly vulnerable to accusations of idolatry and outright magic. By favoring the untranslatability of sacred appellations, this theory encouraged the use of unintelligible names. Thus it allowed for *nomina barbara* to crop up in Christian rituals, opening the door also to various heterodox texts and practices. This potential danger was clearly not to the taste of the Church, ever so zealously struggling to vindicate its orthodoxy and orthopraxis against heathen "corruption." Consequently, the nonreferential views on divine names have been traditionally stigmatized as heretical, and texts of sacred nomenclature that overtly advertise their automatic powers (e.g., amulets, such as the Christian phylactery *The 72 Names of the Lord*) have been deemed unorthodox, scoffed at, and pushed to the margins of ritual practice.[25]

The Christian followers of Hermogenes, by contrast, asserted that divine names, including those found in the Bible, do not share in the divine essence—they are merely conventional names that use human language for things divine. As such, they are also epistemologically impotent: we can learn the conventional rules for their application, but we cannot learn anything from them about the nature of their transcendent referent. The names of God, in other words, are essentially inadequate to God himself, who is beyond being and thus beyond language, which is of being. The final result of this (distinctly Neoplatonic) reasoning, which characteristically combined metaphysics with epistemology, was the thesis of God's unnamability, reiterated persistently by the advocates of Christian apophasis from the earliest Christian Middle Platonists, Justin Martyr (ca.100–163?) and Clement of Alexandria (ca.150–ca.215), to the Cappadocian Fathers, most notably Basil the Great (329?–79) and Gregory of Nyssa (ca. 330–95?) during their disputes with Eunomius.

Such blanket negation of God's names, however, had from the start rather disturbing overtones for practical Christianity. It threatened to force the believer into a communication cul-de-sac. Since invocation is ambivalent without the use of a proper name, the unnamability of the Lord puts in question the possibility of successfully initiating any verbal contact with him. The postulate of God's anonymity, therefore, potentially undermines from within the entire system of logocentric Christian worship, which is essentially worship of the Word by the medium of words.

That is why, parallel to acknowledgments that God is beyond words and beyond any name, even the most ardent exponents of the Christian negative way kept raising the question "How shall I name You—You alone the Unnamable?"[26] This variation of Jacob's request to the Lord, "Please tell me your name," articulates more than a dilemma of the intellect. It goes deeper than the need to know and comprehend and rationalize, which an authentic Christian experience can do without since there is always a possibility for apprehension by faith. It reads above all as a dramatic plea to God for contact and reciprocity: "How should I relate to You, and reach out to You, and worship You?" What is at stake in this plea is nothing short of salvation itself—the entire soteriological promise of Christianity. In other words, the clash between the ritual need for verbal communion with God and the doctrinal axiom of his ineffability forces the paradoxical dilemma of naming the nameless into the very heart of the Christian onomatological project.

The early advocates of Christian apophasis tried to reconcile their linguistic relativism with the ritual requirements for explicit divine names by arguing, along with Plotinus and his followers, that God can be properly articulated in negative names, most of which are formed in Greek by alpha privative, as in *a-rrheton* (in-effable) or *a-nōnomaton* (un-namable). Yet this naming by negation is hardly a practical solution, for it creates more problems than it actually solves. Negative naming is no more than an "unfortunate necessity," as Leszek Kolakowski put it, for it imposes on the divinity a reversed, anthropological perspective, taking as its measure human contingency and not the transcendent superexistence. In reality it is not that "God is not"; it is the transient being which is negative, "characterized by limitations and by participation in non-being."[27] Thus negative names address not God, but only his essential difference from man, and their ultimate result is an elaborate and amplified reiteration of the same old message about God's namelessness. Reaching not unto God himself, but treading instead around his unattainability, negative naming is bound to be rhetorically ineffective, since it fails to offer the believer the comfort of mutuality.

There is also another, more subtle pitfall involved in the idea of negative naming. Although apophatism does indeed veer toward mystical silence, negation is still a linguistic technique, grounded in language and inconceivable without discourse. The fact that every exponent of negative theology recycles the same set of positive terms in their negative garb suggests by itself that negation is a form of reiterating these concepts by other linguistic means. Raoul Mortley has a powerful image of this effect: "The aura of the positive concept remains through the negative."[28] This, in more mundane prose, translates into the suspicion that the endless rhetorical variations of "God is nameless" negatively emphasize only the importance of his name. To claim that God is nameless does not erase the concept of divine names; it merely modifies its conventional meaning. While the positive term *name* encloses, the negative term *nameless* opens endless possibilities, de-specifies, de-limits. In place of the fragmented approach to the transcendent that positive names offer, the negative proposes a new conceptual and discursive mode of encompassing the divinity in a holistic gesture.

And there's the rub. The elegant solution proves to be a problem in itself. Precisely because it liberates thought into the blurred vastness beyond the clear constraints of human discourse, the negative way undercuts the ambition of institutionalized Christianity to pronounce its doctrine in lucid terms, and thus to channel and govern the individual striving toward the Higher Principle. Implicitly stressing individual freedom, apophasis may easily assume not only generally anti-institutional but also specifically anti-ecclesiastical forms. That is why the Church could never wholeheartedly embrace the negative way, searching instead for balance between the negative (apophatic) and the positive (kataphatic) in theology.

CHAPTER THREE

The Synthesis of Dionysius

The Dionysian corpus presents us with something of a paradox. On the one hand, it is admittedly the work that most systematically introduced apophatism into Christian religious thought.[1] At the same time, it contains the most elaborate kataphatic study to date on the subject of naming God. That contradiction was hardly an accident. It was carefully designed, in fact, and thus reveals not only the inner workings of the mysterious mind behind the Areopagitical corpus, but also and above all the logic implied in the Christian theological experience. For the man who called himself Dionysius responded—purposefully, promptly—to a need emerging at the very heart of the Christian theological project: the need to balance the negative with the positive method in a way that would transcend the limitations of both. That is, I believe, the gist of his remarkable synthesis, of which his onomatological project is a significant part.

The Dionysian Vision

There is one crucial difference between *The Divine Names* of Dionysius and almost all previous Christian discourses on the naming of God: it is *not* a polemical work.[2] In accordance with the Areopagite's general disapproval of polemical engagement in theology,[3] he does not establish his onomatological position by refuting or endorsing preexisting views. Instead, he approaches his subject directly and negotiates his legitimacy by "speaking appropriately of what he knows" not in preestablished contexts of conflict and controversy, but within the frame of an autonomous, comprehensive, and largely original theological system.

The fact that the treatise is designed as part of a corpus of systematic theology is not just a formal matter of context or structure; it defines a specular as well as a speculative position. For *The Divine Names* does not concern itself only with specific onomatological issues: it also asks the meta-question about the relevance of these issues to a unified theological vision and works to resolve them with respect to all the variables that such a vision entails.

The most distinctive feature of the Dionysian vision is the premise of a universal sacred order revealed in the relation between *thearchy* and *hierarchy*. Both terms occur for the first time in the works of Dionysius and appear to be his own invention. By "thearchy" (*thearchia*), we are to understand the manifest God who reveals himself as the hidden principle of creation in the hierarchies of the created world. "Hierarchy" (*hierarchia*) is thus the specific mode of God's manifestation in the world, a manifestation that is ordered, all-pervasive, and manifold.

The hierarchical order that Dionysius lays out in his works is, as one might expect, a purposeful one. It patterns the relationship between God and the created world into a relentless teleology that is ultimately beneficial for the creation. "The goal of a hierarchy," he explains in a famous passage, "is to enable beings to be as like as possible to God and to be at one with him" (*CH* 3-165A/154). What is implied in the divinely ordained arrangement of the world, in other words, is deification: a gradual assimilation of the creature into the divine leading toward a perfect union with it. Hierarchy is thus more than an ontological proof of God's will, an imprint of the divine presence in creation which gives form to the "innate togetherness of everything" (*DN* 4-704C/77).[4] It also externalizes the innate need of all things to strive for deification, and as such is itself an epistemological pattern. That is why Dionysius calls the sacred order *epistēmē*, "a state of understanding", and *energeia*, "an activity" or "a way of action" (*CH* 3-164D/153).

Dionysius stages his vision in a vertically organized space where meaning and value are predicated upon an ontological split between "above" and "below," or between the domains of the Creator and creature. Any significant transfer within this cosmic "quality space" is seen as a movement up or down a vertical axis represented by the hierarchies that bridge invisibly the above and the below.[5] Since both the downward and the upward trajectories are equally significant in that dynamic, the Dionysian vision is distinctly "binocular," synoptically including in itself both the divine and the human perspectives.

Dionysius articulates the movement across the ontological divide in the typical Neoplatonic idioms of descent (*katabasis*) and ascent (*anabasis*), of procession (*proodos*) and return (*epistrophē*). In his hands, however, this model of an impersonal procession from a single source and an equally impersonal return back to it is transformed into a personal relationship with the Living God who "imparts being, life, wisdom, and the other gifts of [his] all-creative goodness" (*DN* 2-644A/62). He thus reinterprets Neoplatonic automatic differentiations (*diakriseis*) as personal gifts (*dōreai*) laid down as the cornerstone of a larger economy of love that intends the universe as an all-embracing gift circle.[6]

The perpetual circulation of gifts that sustains such a community of love hinges on a particular, shared, gratuitous stance that, for Dionysius, is best exemplified by Christ's *kenosis*.[7] By a kenotic dispensing of gifts (which mysteriously has no effect on the fullness and superabundance of the divinity), God bestows perpetually and personally upon each individual being the greatest gift of all—the ability to participate in him, sharing in his perfections, and being lifted upward toward him.

This chance for communion with God is open to all, but it does not automatically grant salvation, for participation (*metochos*) and uplifting (*anagōgē*) depend on the receptivity of the created beings.[8] The divine descent, in other words, invites an ascent as the creature's proper response to the divine gifts, yet every being participates freely in that interchange and only "in proportion to its capacities" (*DN* 1-588A/49). Thus the Dionysian ascent is not a matter of compulsion, but a voluntary fulfillment of destiny. It is a reciprocal act that mirrors the divine descent not only in structure as its symmetrical pair-part, but, more importantly, in intentionality, as a self-giving gesture of love that, in acknowledging the gifts of the divinity, offers a fitting response to them.

We can see how Dionysius's cosmological program outlines a specific model of Christian living. The teleological framework of this model contains within itself its own ethical "outside" (the transcendent God the Good) and envisions a specific way of reaching or interiorizing it: deification made possible by the hierarchies that are themselves the divine order of being. In this program, Dionysius designates a special place for the knowledge of God, presenting it as both implied in the hierarchies and as instrumental in deification. This is a crucial point for the entire project of the Areopagite, for it serves as its internal justification. At this juncture of his argument, his theology observes itself in its own mirror, so to speak, searching for its place in the universal order it has envisioned. And the place it allots for itself is admittedly limited, though strategic for the salvation scenario of the return. Such is the positive core of Dionysius's apophatism, the foundation of his theology of divine names.

The Theological Project

The founding principle of the Dionysian theological project is the axiom that knowledge of the divine depends on revelation: we know only as much of God as he allows us to know. Christian revelation, however, is admittedly paradoxical. The more God reveals himself in and through history, the more enigmatic he appears to be. For he is, in his essence, absolutely transcendent to creatures and can only reveal himself to them as hidden and mysterious.

Characteristically, Dionysius uses the hierarchy trope to thematize this biblical dialectic of revelation and concealment by introducing yet another dialectical pair, that of similar dissimilarities. If hierarchy is the pattern of gradual manifestation of the divine in the creature on a descending scale of proximity (or "differentiation"), depending on its position in the hierarchy, divine manifestations are—to varying degrees—both similar and dissimilar to the divinity.[9] Proper knowledge of the divine should sort out the similarities from the dissimilarities, affirming the first and negating the second. Both procedures are necessary for theology, albeit in different measure, as they are—in different measure—both adequate and inadequate to the theological goal.

That ultimate goal is thus knowledge of God as he is in himself, outside of his creative and redemptive economy and his relations with his creature; it is knowledge of the hidden God, of God the Unknowable. Clearly, to attempt to know God in this capacity is to attempt the impossible (as in the case of naming the nameless, which is but a facet of the same problem). Yet such a theological commitment is fueled by the assumption—the hope—that the act of trying itself has both an epistemological and a salvific value. This is the raison d'être of theology according to Dionysius, calling to mind T. S. Eliot's stoic resolution in *The Four Quartets*, "For us, there is only the trying. The rest is not our business." Even though the goal is unattainable, perpetually hidden, the increasingly closer approximations to it that result from the ascent are by themselves productive, progressively revealing. At the heart of Dionysius's positive theology, in other words, there lies his trust in the hierarchies, in their capacity to illuminate similarities within the dissimilar and thus to further the ascent. This trust, I believe, is the force working to redeem theology from inside a theological project that circumscribes so rigidly the human potential for knowing the divine.

What, then, is the model for a theology beyond knowledge if theology within knowledge is based on the hierarchies? As Lossky argues convincingly in his analysis of Dionysius's apophatism, the Trinity provides such a model. This is most fitting, of course, since it is the Trinitarian relationship—the relationship of God to and in himself—that constitutes the proper subject of "theology."

The Trinitarian model as envisioned by Dionysius is distinctly non-hierarchical—in sharp contrast to the standard Neoplatonic model of the primary Triad, where Mind and Soul are ontologically inferior to the One. As I have pointed out already, the Dionysian hierarchy manifests God in his creature, investing meaning into the created world by establishing distinctions within it. Hierarchy—or what humans perceive as the divine order of things—is thus solely a creationist phenomenon, which is to say that the Trinitarian relation is free of any hierarchy, exempt from the order that makes the world below a meaningful world. In God himself, as Dionysius never tires of asserting, unity predominates over differentiation.[10] If (human) meaning is contingent on distinctions, then the Trinity collapses meaning as we know it, together with all the ground rules of binary thought and hierarchical logic, and opens an epistemological space where opposites are not mutually exclusive:

> Thus, regarding the divine unity beyond being, they [those fully initiated in our theological tradition] assert that the indivisible Trinity holds within a shared undifferentiated unity its supra-essential substance, its supra-divine divinity, its supra-excellent goodness, its supremely individual identity beyond all that is, its oneness beyond the source of oneness, its ineffability, its many names, its unknowability, its wholly belonging to the conceptual realm, *the assertion of all things, the denial of all things, that which is beyond every assertion and denial.* [DN 2-641A/61; emphasis added]

Even in translation, it is impossible to miss Dionysius's emphasis on such lexical units as "beyond" and "supra," which point to the surpassing of limitations.[11] The semantic thrust is toward breaking out of bounds, toward expressing what cannot be contained in the available patterns of language and meaning. This intent to transcend, to jump over one's head, has an ontological justification. The Trinity—or the "Unitrinity," as Lossky prefers to call it[12]—encompasses opposites without being affected by them, because it holds within itself also the negation of their opposition: not only the affirmation and the denial of all things, but also that which is beyond every affirmation and denial. Such a metaphysical premise allows for the epistemological possibility of knowledge that is not exhausted by the opposition between the negative and the positive (between the yes- and the no-position), of knowledge that includes something outside of these alternatives, a remainder, a "beyond." That is how, according to Lossky, the principle of personal non-opposition within the Trinity (which is the proper theological subject) presupposes the "dialectics of affirmation and non-opposed negation" of theology properly so-called;[13] or, if you will, the epistemological object is reflected, quite literally, in the epistemological method itself.

Within this general program, the enterprise of Christian theology is envisioned by Dionysius as a triadic movement (not dissimilar structurally to the much more familiar Hegelian triad of thesis-antithesis-synthesis):

> Since [the Godhead] is the Cause of all being, we should posit and ascribe to it all the affirmations we make in regard to beings, and, more appropriately, we should negate all these affirmations, since it surpasses all being. Now we should not conclude that the negations are simply the opposites of the affirmations, but rather that the cause of all is considerably prior to this, beyond privations, beyond every denial, beyond every assertion. [*MT* 1-1000B/136]

The Areopagitical corpus itself is the perfect illustration of its own theoretical guidelines. The first stage in its tripartite scenario is affirmative or kataphatic theology, exemplified by the treatise *The Divine Names*. Apophatic theology, as represented by explications of the two hierarchies (ecclesiastical and celestial), marks the second stage of the process as the negative counterpart of the first. Both stages, however, still remain within intellection and language, within the order imposed by the hierarchies. It is only at the last stage of the project (a stage which, I should emphasize, is to be reached through the hierarchies) that Dionysius offers a way beyond hierarchical order and the artificial opposition between positive and negative theology that such an order prescribes. In the crowning treatise of the corpus, *The Mystical Theology*, the Dionysian vision finally opens itself to "the brilliant darkness of a hidden silence" (*MT* 1-997B/135) to intimate an apprehension of the divinity that surpasses the constraints of intellection, "imparting to the ignorance of what God is . . . the value of mystical knowledge."[14]

The Areopagitical corpus thus advances theoretically and exemplifies structurally a remarkably holistic notion of order—an order that already includes in itself its own transcendence, and not as its alternative, as a negation of itself, but as its condition for possibility.[15] The Dionysian order of the hierarchies is "a state of understanding" and "a way of action" that allows for an awareness of its own limitations and, precisely because of that, gives those who embrace it a chance to break out of its constraints. At the end of the journey, I believe, the lesson of the Areopagite is an anthropological one: order—and the need for order—is part of the human condition. The discovery of true humanity, however, lies in the potential to break out of the constraints of humanness—logic, language, meaning—and become like the divine, knowing not only the distinction between good and evil, but also the collapse of these distinctions in goodness itself.

United Differentiations

The Dionysian theology of divine names is engendered by the same logic of dialectical order that supports the entire Areopagitical corpus, and so its validity is thought of as contingent on its own negation. Within the epistemological space opened up by the model of the Unitrinity and cultivated by Dionysius in *The Mystical Theology*, the triple biblical opposition "one name—no name—every name," which has caused so much anxiety in Christian onomatology, is unmasked as illusionary. Once the mind is liberated from the structures of linear thinking and hierarchical logic and surrenders itself to "the truly mysterious darkness of unknowing," (*MT* 1-1001A/137), such hitherto relevant distinctions all collapse into unity. Yet in order to get there, to achieve such freedom, the mind needs those distinctions: only with the support of the hierarchies can the mind ultimately break out of their rule. Thus the epistemological (and hence, the salvific) value of divine names lies in their being a stepping stone, first for the negation of divine names in negative naming, and finally for the negation of their negation in mystical silence. Since my study of Dionysius is limited only to his contribution to the theory of Christian discourse, I am concerned here exclusively with the function of divine names as stepping stones in the ascent, setting aside for now the higher stages of the journey to which they lead.

From among the works of Dionysius that have reached us, *The Divine Names* offers, no doubt, the most complete exposition of his onomatological views. Note, however, that two lost or fictitious treatises, *The Theological Representation* and *The Symbolic Theology*, are summarized in the third chapter of *The Mystical Theology* as belonging to the same thematic domain. *The Theological Representation*, discussed at some length in chapters 1 and 2 of *The Divine Names*, is said to address the doctrine of the Trinity and the Trinitarian names and distinctions. *The Symbolic Theology*, in turn, was to address scriptural anthropomorphism and the symbolic God-terms as opposed to the conceptual appellations treated in *The Divine Names*. The idea that Dionysius's kataphatic theology was indeed expounded in a tripartite form appeals to some authors as fitting the general triadic structure of his order-system, and is found plausible on that ground.[16] Since our knowledge of these additional onomatological texts—whether they are hypothetical or not—is extremely limited, I focus my discussion mainly on *The Divine Names*.

The initial premise of *The Divine Names* is kataphatic through and through: God "is not absolutely incommunicable" to creation (*DN* 1-588C/50), and therefore one may speak of names for the Unnamable. The premise, however, involves a pivotal qualification: as the cause of all things that transcends them all, God may be praised only by the things caused ("[T]o praise this divinely beneficent Providence you must turn to all of creation" [*DN* 1-593D/54]). We must, in other words, face the plurality of the created being in order to face, by analogy, the united differentiations within the Godhead. The divisive, particularizing aspect of logos may work to our advantage only insofar as discourse is applied to divine differentiations. And, as Dionysius defines it in a terse statement, "The differentiations within the [unified] Godhead have to do with the benign processions and revelations of God" (*DN* 2-640D/61).

This double bond of differentiations to processions and revelations is a highly significant point of departure for the Dionysian onomatology and for the general linguistic theory it implies. Understood as processions, differentiations concern the divine economy, the creative work of God that results in the hierarchical multiplicity of being.[17] When seen as revelations, on the other hand, they concern above all the incarnation of the Logos (and the Bible, as the Divine Logos itself) that alone grants the created world the possibility of recognizing God as its Creator. Within this general framework, divine names represent for Dionysius the nexus where the interdependence between the revelatory and economic aspects of the "common and united differentiations . . . of the entire Godhead" is especially manifest (cf. *DN* 2-652A/67).

According to the Areopagite, the numerous names for the single Creator are disclosed in the Bible and are therefore part of the revelation. This is clearly a key thesis for Dionysius, since he never tires of reiterating that the only legitimate divine names are those found in Scripture. From the outset of his treatise, he states firmly, "We must not dare to resort to words or conceptions concerning that hidden divinity which transcends being, apart from what the sacred scriptures have divinely revealed" (*DN* 1-588A/49). He returns to this point many times, repeatedly referring to "the Scripture writers" (*theologoi*) and "the wise men of God" (*theosophoi*) as the only authoritative source of divine appellations.[18] Furthermore, all the divine names that he samples in a comprehensive list in chapter 1, "good, beautiful, wise, beloved, God of gods, Lord of Lords, Holy of Holies . . . " (*DN* 1-596A–C/55–56), and which he later explicates by means of scriptural exegesis, are exclusively biblical terms.[19]

Although all of these are names for "God in his entirety" (*DN* 2-636C/ 58), they do not refer to him directly, but only through the medium of creation, and as such are partial to the divine economy. "[W]hat the Scripture writers have to say regarding the divine names," Dionysius emphasizes with utmost precision, "refers, in revealing praises, to the beneficent processions of God" (*DN* 1-589D/51). In other words, every single name designates a specific aspect of the differentiated being, a particular bountiful act, while the source of the gift remains beyond the scope of designation. "When, for instance, we give the name of 'God' to that transcendent hiddenness, when we call it 'life' or 'being' or 'light' or 'Word,' what our minds lay hold of is in fact nothing other than certain activities apparent to us, activities which deify, cause being, bear life, give wisdom" (*DN* 2-645A/63–64). The names for God, one may say at the risk of simplifying Dionysius's condensed and sophisticated reasoning, are the names of his differentiated bounty.

In summary, we can refer to God by numerous biblical terms, all of which designate his "differentiations in unity." This is vintage Dionysian dialectics at work. The unifying aspect of divine names shines through their apparent diversity. And unity resides at the heart of differentiation to collapse logical impasses into (paradoxical) breakthroughs, where all divine names point unproblematically toward the divinity in its entirety precisely because each name designates only a separate gift of God, a single attribute, one particular energy. The bounteous differentiations of the divinity are "common and united" because God remains one, complete and identical to Himself "amid the emptying act of differentiation" (*DN* 2-649B/66). Therefore, if a name represents one gift, it is then intrinsically related to all other divine names without being, at the same time, interchangeable with them. Put in semiotic terms, if every name denotes a particular gift, it connotes all the others in their totality. In this sense each name, without signifying God directly, "stands for" the entire divinity.[20]

The application of each individual name to God is thus validated by Dionysius only on the grounds of its coextensiveness with all the other names, on the grounds of the holistic vision of the one and united Godhead it renders despite its apparent fragmentariness: "For the unnamed goodness is not just the cause of cohesion or life or perfection so that it is from this or that providential gesture that it earns a name, but it actually contains everything beforehand within itself. . . . Hence the songs of praise and the names for it are fittingly derived from the sum total of creation" (*DN* 1-596D–597A/56).

This revealing argument deserves to be restated in still another way. The names for God disclosed in the Bible present the multiplicity of being as the bounteous differentiations of a single Creator. And it is the unifying differentiation revealed by these names that allows them to assist our return to God, the "ascent" that is the essence of both deification *(theosis)*, the desired ontological state, and of knowledge of God *(theognosis)*, its epistemological counterpart.[21]

A Hierarchy of Names

Following his concept of divine names as "meaningful" terms, Dionysius proposes a classificatory grid that enables us to handle systematically the diversity of biblical terms for the Lord with respect to their meanings. The major dichotomy in Dionysius's taxonomy is drawn between conceptual and symbolic names.

It is unfortunate that Dionysius's views on the two classes of divine names are not equally well documented. As noted earlier, Dionysius planned to discuss symbolic names in another kataphatic treatise, *The Symbolic Theology*, which—if ever written—has been subsequently lost or destroyed. In any event, the available evidence of it today consists only of a few references, the most revealing of which is a lengthy passage in a letter to Titus the hierarch.[22]

I should emphasize from the start that Dionysius's distinction between conceptual and symbolic names is not relevant from the standpoint of standard linguistics. More important, it was not intended as a linguistic distinction. It does not address the grammatical and the semantic heterogeneity of divine names. Instead, it regroups the vocabulary of natural languages from a theological perspective by dividing God-terms with respect to the different ontological status of the realia they designate. It thus classifies not the words (or the verbal signs) but the intelligible entities they designate, rearranging them hierarchically in accordance with the general hierarchical framework of the Dionysian corpus.

The upper stratum of the Areopagitical hierarchy of names belongs to the conceptual names that designate God's united differentiations, his "emanations," or "perfections," or "attributes," conceived of and articulated as his gifts. Good, Beauty, Truth, Wisdom—to name just a few—are not human abstractions for Dionysius, as they might appear to us. They are ontological entities, incomparably more concrete than anything belonging to the realm of the senses, because they are aspects of the divine, differentiated being by means of which all beings came to be.[23] That is why they are not part of the creation, but only manifest themselves through it and, as such, have essentially a superior ontological status to the created world that partakes in them. Like God himself, the perfections are unaffected by the mutability of the finite and transient physical reality. Put in slightly different terms, all these gifts designated by conceptual names are ontological constants. And it is because of them that the created beings can be viewed as identical to themselves (as "beautiful," or "good," or "wise," or "true") throughout the vicissitudes of their fragmented existence. In this sense we may say that, from the standpoint of the created being, the conceptual names of the Lord function as axiological categories, by means of which we can identify and evaluate human experience.

Although these categories are drawn from different semantic domains, they share one characteristic: they all represent the ultimately positive pole of their respective domains of selection. Following James Fernandez's topographic model of culture as a "quality space defined by n dimensions or continua,"[24] we may claim that Dionysius's model of Christian quality space is defined by as many dimensions as there are divine gifts, and that each continuum is represented and identified by a particular gift. Thus Christian culture is ordered by the domains of Goodness, Truth, Beauty, and Wisdom, and all things in it are evaluated with respect to the position they occupy in any of these continua.

Unlike the dimensions in the quality space of our modern culture, however, the continua in the model of Dionysius are not based on antipodal notions. The pole of Goodness does not presuppose, as its diametrical opposite, a pole of evil. (This assumption would allow for the existence of a second Cause, hierarchically equal to that of Good, and would be incompatible with both orthodox Christianity and orthodox Neoplatonism.) In chapter 4 of *The Divine Names*, which deals with the name "Good," Dionysius discusses at length how only Good, and not evil, is a creative cause.[25] The difference between what we call "good" and what we call "evil" is one of degree and not of essence. They both are defined by their share in the Good; only the share of what we call "evil" is minimal. Thus the dispersion of the Good throughout the creation is bound for Dionysius within a unified continuum of Goodness, where "[a] lesser good is not the opposite of the greater good" (*DN* 4-717A/85)—they are only ranked hierarchically according to their participation in the divine that is the supreme and absolute Goodness. And the same principle of non-opposition applies to any other continuum.

Grammatically speaking, these gifts can be articulated both as abstract nouns—such as Beauty—and as qualifying adjectives—such as Beautiful. The distinction between the nominal and the adjectival form of the names, however, is not essential for Dionysius.[26] He differentiates between qualities and objects only in the realm of individual beings. Only in the phenomenal world can objects be evaluated according to their share in Beauty and "beauty" be viewed as the ingredient (or quality) that renders objects more or less beautiful. Such distinctions, however, do not apply to God, who does not share in beauty but is Beauty itself in its fullness. Beauty, as the source of everything beautiful, is identical with God, although God is not identical only with Beauty. He is also Wisdom in its fullness, Power in its completeness, and any other gift in its superabundant totality. And because of that He alone can be called both Beauty and Beautiful, both Wisdom and Wise, both Power and Powerful, these labels functioning not as qualitative descriptions, which are subjective and relative, but as God's strict designators in the superlative sense that he is the Most Beautiful One, the One Most Wise, the One Most Powerful, the One Most Perfect in any respect imaginable and beyond. That is why scholars of Dionysius often call God's gifts his "perfections."

The symbolic names of the Lord are treated by Dionysius as secondary God-terms, hierarchically subordinate to conceptual names. Drawn from the realm of sense perception, they designate not the divine gifts themselves, but only physical objects created by virtue of these gifts (such as vine, or lamb, or shepherd, or king). While conceptual names are oriented toward the ontologically superior level of God's creative faculties, symbolic names concern the lower ranks of created beings—the ultimate downward differentiation of the divinity that brings about an ever-increasing multiplication of matter. Thus symbolic names are at once more numerous and less effective in the general framework of human "return" than are the conceptual names of the Lord.[27]

But how can the designation of a physical thing—be it a vine, or a lamb, or a shepherd—serve as the name of God? Dionysius's answer is rooted in his theory of symbols, which is inseparable from his general theory of participation. Since all created beings participate in God, they all manifest, in their own limited capacity, his perfections, or gifts.[28] Thus physical objects can be defined as "visible images" or "revealing depictions" of the abstract categories designated by conceptual names in the same way that "Light" and "Sun" are for Dionysius visible representations of the Good.[29] Put in another way, while conceptual names denote directly the gifts of the Lord, symbolic names represent the same gifts by analogy: they are "analogies of God drawn from what we perceive" (MT 3-1033A/139). They are "sacred pictures boldly used to represent God, so that what is hidden may be brought out into the open and multiplied, what is unique and undivided may be divided up, and multiple shapes and forms be given to what has neither shape nor form" (Ep. 9-1105B–C/282–83). Virtually everything in the created world is in itself a symbol of the Creator. Some are similar symbols, some dissimilar; some are more "appropriate" than others. Yet all of them represent in a material form "the divine realities they are unable to contain."[30] That is why "the names for [God] are fittingly derived from the sum total of creation" (*DN* 1-597A/56), and we are free to "use whatever appropriate symbols we can for the things of God" (*DN* 1-592C/53).

Because a symbolic name is most often the atom of a biblical event, it functions as an index to the biblical narrative of its origin and, hence, to the whole narrative network in which this episode partakes. The name "Lamb," to give but one example, contains in itself the Old Testament story of Abraham's sacrifice which, in turn, prefigures both Jesus's redemptive death on the cross and his resurrection.[31] We may say that, if conceptual names are the central categories of Christian doctrine, symbolic names are the building blocks of what Jean-François Lyotard would call "the grand Christian narrative."[32] Furthermore, by evoking historical precedents, symbolic names offer scenarios for ritual performance and for social behavior in general. They excite and persuade; they create solidarities and cement communal or individual identities. In other words, they are the organizing images of the Christian experience, the core of the Christian moral imagination. As such, the symbolic names are rhetorically much more effective than the conceptual names, whose operation is limited mainly to the sphere of speculative discourse.

Nameless and of Every Name

The Areopagite's interpretation of divine names sets him apart from the representatives of both the natural and the conventional trends. For the naturalists, like Origen, the divine names were above all ontic entities: they concerned the divine economy but had no relevance to the knowledge of God. For the conventionalists, like the Cappadocians, on the contrary, the names of God were only instruments of knowledge, though highly imperfect and limited. All they could reveal were the various attributes of God, but they were unable to reach the transcendent One, who remained fully concealed and unnamable. Dionysius conceives of divine names as relevant to both creation and revelation. For him, the names of God are instruments for the revelation of God's economy—in the very process of creation, from the medium of the creation, and for the benefit of the creation.

Within the framework of creation, divine names refer to the divine processions understood as united differentiations of the divinity. Within the framework of theology, which "extricates notions of God from all the cosmological implications proper to economy," divine names point to the transcendent.[33] They assist the human ascent and thus lead to higher levels of

knowing God. Out of his unlimited goodness, the transcendent and hidden
God has revealed himself as the Creator of all things in "forms and images
of the formless and unimaginable," providing man with numerous names to
accommodate the notion of what God is to the human level of comprehension.[34] The multiplicity of names corresponds to the multiplicity of being.
Yet all the various names, like all the various aspects of being, are united
in their differentiation as teleologically oriented toward the single source of
being that is God.

The epistemological capacity of divine names, however, is only partially based on comprehension. Christian theognosis relies in a very limited
manner on the positive knowledge that the names provide and that can
be explicated from them through exegesis. This idiosyncrasy is based on
the paradoxical Christian concept of revelation. As Lossky so aptly puts it,
"the transcendent God becomes immanent in the world, but in the very
immanence of His economy, which leads to incarnation and to death on
the cross, He reveals Himself as transcendent, as ontologically independent
of all created being."[35] Therefore the knowledge that divine names provide
of God cannot be anything more than knowing in the unknowing (cf. *DN*
1-593A/53), an insight about the concealment of God's revelation within
the very revelation of his concealment. For he who is the source of being
and is revealed through being remains beyond being, truly hidden. And he
who, as the source of everything that is, appropriately "has the names of
everything that is" (*DN* 1-596C/56), remains within the multiplicity of his
names beyond any name, truly nameless. "Realizing all this," Dionysius
recapitulates, "the theologians praise [Him] by every name (*ek pantos
onomatos*)—and as the Nameless One (*anōnymon*)" (*DN* 1-596A/54).

This formula—nameless and of every name—is probably the most succinct articulation of Dionysius's onomatological synthesis that, by means
of a paradox, masterfully resolves the paradoxical Christian dilemma of
"naming the nameless." The non-representationists before him claimed
that God is polynomous because of the "natural" relationship of his names
to the transcendent being, whereas their opponents asserted that all these
names were only human conventions and that, consequently, God was in his
essence truly anonymous. Dionysius rendered their conflicting standpoints
non-contradictory by contending that God is simultaneously polynomous and
anonymous. He is the anonymous First Cause, and because of that he rightly
bears the names of all things caused.

CHAPTER FOUR

Theory and Practice

The entire edifice of Dionysius's elegant synthesis on the subject of divine names rests on four propositions:

1. the essentially unnameable divinity can be referred to by numerous names;
2. they are all to be found in Scripture;
3. all these names are meaningful terms;
4. they are coextensive with one another since they designate the united differentiations of the divinity.

What kind of a practice of the name does such a theory envision? What are its main pragmatic implications and its practical consequences? How does it relate to the actual rhetorical practices of Christian communities? In concluding my study of Dionysius, I reexamine his theory with an eye to such questions, being led by the general assumption that practice informs the production of speculative models, which in turn transform, more or less radically, the practices they purport to reflect.[1]

Biblical Exegesis

Dionysius's position, that divine names are exclusively biblical, envisions practical onomatology as an extensive hermeneutical project—a particular, in-depth rereading of the scriptural texts in search of names for the unnamable divinity. Dionysius is most explicit on this subject. He demonstrates the advantages of such a method in action by engaging in a series of exegetical studies that occupy the major part of *The Divine Names* (chapters 4–13).

What are the parameters of this extensive exegetical project? It includes both identifying terms for the divinity within the biblical texts and justifying their name-status through explication of their contextual meaning. It is not surprising that the kind of exegesis that Dionysius both prescribes and practices focuses specifically on meaning, since he argues emphatically throughout that the names of God are all meaningful.[2] The overarching goal of this hermeneutical exploration is to explicate the "innate togetherness" of the individual God-terms, which alone allows us to treat them as "united differentiations." Only through exegesis can the apparently centrifugal proliferation of divine names be ordered into a unified system of coextensive terms pointing invariably to the Lord despite the diversity of their lexical meanings. And only then can the plurality of names be seen not as a disadvantage of language vis-à-vis the One (as Dionysius's fellow Neoplatonists viewed it), but instead as an advantage granted by revelation, a gift in itself that allows us to address God's unity from within the multiplicity he generates.

Instead of viewing the plurality of divine names as a numerical multitude, Dionysius proposes to treat them as a unit of numbers or an idea of unity, much like the concept of *one* in the Neoplatonic mathematical monotheism.[3] It is revealing that he qualifies the name One as "the most enduring name" of God. It is the name that is both a name and a number, without being *sensu stricto* either a name or a number. It is the non-number that potentially contains every number, just as the color white contains every color. And it is also the least identifying name of all (almost the indefinite pronoun underpinning every name, the universal antonomasia for any singular entity), potentially containing the entire array of possible names. Just as behind each name of God there lurks a multiplicity of names, and any divine name yields many, behind their number lurks the name One, which encompasses, underpins, and transcends God's polynomy.

That is why, I believe, the discussion of the term *One* appears at the Areopagitical corpus's most significant juncture: it concludes the treatise *The Divine Names*, thus marking the ultimate frontier of kataphatic discourse, beyond which lies Dionysius's most radically apophatic work, *The Mystical Theology*, with its unitive experience of mystical silence beyond either name or namelessness.[4] The ultimate objective of name exegesis, in other words, is to explicate the mystical import of all biblical terms for the divine, using their literal meaning as a vehicle for a trip upward, beyond the realm of the senses, comprehension, and language, toward God himself. "With eyes that look beyond the world," the Areopagite writes elsewhere, summarizing his exegetical project, "I must behold the sacred forms attributed to it by the scriptures, so that we may be uplifted by way of these mysterious representations to their divine simplicity" (*CH* 4-177C/156).

By entrenching the Christian epistemology of divine names deeply in biblical hermeneutics, the Areopagite also ascribes to it a particular teleological horizon. The general Dionysian formula "God is nameless and of *every* name" seems to evade deliberately the important practical question about the number of these names. If the number of God's names is hidden from us behind assertions of an all-encompassing plurality, when can we consider the project of identifying all his names complete? Indeed, can such a project be completed? Dionysius's definitive assertion that all divine names are contained in the Bible, which means within a fixed text with well-defined boundaries, suggests that their number is also limited.[5]

If the names for the Lord did form a finite class, it would be very good news for Christian epistemology. While the knowledge of God is infinite and unattainable to us (so unfortunately trapped in the confines of our own finitude), at least the knowledge of God's names seems perfectly compatible with the limitations of human knowledge. Nothing, however, is ever that simple for Dionysius. The multitude of divine names may be restricted, though it is not numerically fixed, because the number of God's names is neither defined nor deemed in any way definable. The possibility of identifying still another name within the dense texture of the Bible can never be considered exhausted. That is why, though the project of disclosing all the names of God in the biblical texts is potentially circumscribed, in reality it remains perpetually open-ended. The horizon of Christian epistemology of the name, in other words, constantly escapes those who reach out to it, pushing them to probe ever more deeply into the infinite complexities of Scripture.

The Proper Name of God Is a List

If the telos of the hermeneutical project underlying Dionysius's onomatology is always one step ahead of us as we pursue it, endlessly feeding our epistemological desire by its unattainability, all the partial results of the project have a very well-defined and predictable shape. They are all lists: open-ended lists of biblical terms for the Lord, perfect specimens of the trope that Foucault once called "the endless figure of desire."[6] The evidence is again present in *The Divine Names*. Dionysius opens his argument with a list of more than forty God-terms that, despite its imposing size, leaves the reader with the distinct impression of having merely scratched the surface:

And yet on the other hand they [the Scripture writers] give it [the unnamable divinity] many names, such as "I am being," "life," "light," "God," the "truth." These same wise writers, when praising the Cause of everything that is, use names drawn from all the things caused: good, beautiful, wise, beloved, God of gods, Lord of Lords, Holy of Holies, eternal, existent, Cause of the ages. They call him source of life, wisdom, mind, word, knower, possessor beforehand of all the treasures of knowledge, power, powerful, and King of Kings, ancient of days, the unaging and unchanging, salvation, righteousness and sanctification, redemption, greatest of all and yet the one in the still breeze. They say he is in our minds, in our souls, and in our bodies, in heaven and on earth, that while remaining ever within himself he is also in and around and above the world, that he is above heaven and above all being, that he is sun, star, and fire, water, wind, and dew, cloud, archetypal stone, and rock, that he is all, that he is no thing. [*DN* 1-596A–C/55–56]

The goal of the treatise is this abundant crop of names. Dionysius eagerly displays it to us right away as an incentive—or as subsistence—before schooling us in the extensive exegetical labors that produce such a yield.

Is this list, however, merely an external form, a receptacle that holds the indeterminate multiplicity of God's names? Or is there an essential link between the nature of the divine name, as envisioned by Dionysius, and lists? To begin to answer this question, let me first negotiate some general characteristics of the list trope.

I have already claimed in the introduction that a list is a verbal model of serial arrangement: it circumscribes a group of lexical units—names, in our case—and displays them in a fixed, syntactic sequence.[7] The most visible effect of this arrangement is that the list (mis)represents a set of lexical elements as equivalent terms. It provides a site for the cohabitation of words and in that capacity alone predicates a kinship upon the words' referents. Stubbornly ignoring everything that makes its members different, a list is fixed upon the one thing that makes them alike, even if that is only their presence in the list, "the simple crime of contingency."[8] Thus a list institutes an equivalence among its elements, no matter whether it reiterates conventional classes (the Twelve Apostles) or constructs them *ad hoc* ("a few of my favorite things").[9]

While a list creates solidarities, it never really loses sight of its members' individual identities. Lists both separate and connect, being delicately poised between continuity and fragmentation, the particular and the general, the grand and the microscopic. Their visions are always synoptic, at once particularizing a given domain and displaying it as a totality. In this sense a list is a "differentiation-in-unity" trope par excellence, the perfect rhetorical equivalent to Dionysius's theory of divine names. If the many terms for God are indeed his names because they designate his united differentiations, the most adequate name of the Lord is not one but all of them in their totality. In a word, the "proper name" of God is a list.

There is yet another characteristic of the list that makes it appropriate to the Dionysian project: its capacity to accommodate visions of order well. An affinity for order is inherent in listmaking. A list does more than merely fix information and make it available ("these are the students of the class," "these are a few of my favorite things"). It also structures this information, *orders* it, by imposing upon it a grid of spatial coherence, so that a cumulative enumeration, itself a continuous temporal sequence, becomes a figure of spatial contiguity. A list, at its bare minimum, is a serial arrangement of *words*. By ordering words, however, it also imposes an orderly pattern upon the *referents* of these words and, in so doing, organizes both our perception of reality and our interactions with it.[10]

The list's ordering or disciplining capacity goes hand in hand with its ability to display. Lists not only confine an inchoate lot of objects to a manageable few, but also exhibit them for everyone to see—translate them, as it were, into a set of "visibles."[11] A list, we may say, resembles an exhibition, a pageant, a parade, or any other project of serial display that engenders a Borgesian imagination and a Foucauldian critique: the Museum, the Library, the Encyclopedia.[12] It is this double affinity for the orderly and the visible that makes the list the perfect rhetorical vehicle for visions of order.

Dionysius's reliance on lists, therefore, does not merely serve the purpose of presenting rhetorically the multiplicity of God's names. Listmaking is also especially effective for explicating the continuity that he posits between the hierarchy of names and the hierarchical divine order. As I have already established, the names of God designate for Dionysius not a divine identity, but a table of differentiations within the created world, or, as Bourdieu might say, the coordinates for evaluating one's position in the social sphere. Divine names are hierarchically organized according to the same scale of gradual approximation of the divine essence that underpins the entire cosmological program of the Areopagitical corpus. While symbolic names, being indices of biblical narratives and ritual acts, represent specific scenarios for social behavior, the hierarchically superior conceptual names designate the ultimately positive values of Christian society and serve as axiological norms of conduct, be they ethical or aesthetic. In the general triadic model of Dionysius's dialectics, these names are, of course, to be transcended, first through negation in negative naming, and finally by the negation of their negation in mystical silence. Yet, as the only positive terms that ground the human striving toward God in language and being, they are indispensable for the Christian experience of both meaning and purpose. As such, they are the only terms of Christian order that are truly made to human measure. The list of these terms thus represents the single most economical and effective articulation of the Dionysian vision of order.

Listing the Names of God

How does Dionysius's theory of practice relate to actual Christian practices of the name? The short answer is that his theory was steeped in a long-standing and viable tradition of listing biblical terms for the Lord, a tradition that Dionysius aimed not so much to transform as to endorse, by vesting it with theological legitimacy, and to codify, by firmly grounding it on scriptural exegesis.[13] Both before and after Dionysius advanced his theology of the name, lists of biblical terms for the Lord and inventories of names that followed biblical models had been put together and put to use in Christian praxis. I do not attempt here any systematic presentation of this listmaking tradition or its various functions in Christian life; such a demanding project deserves a study of its own. My purpose is much more limited: to illustrate with a handful of examples the perfect agreement between the Areopagite's theory of the name and the abundant Christian practice of listing the names of God, and the mutual validation they confer on one another.

The territory of Christian listmaking is rich in detail and sufficiently amorphous to resist easy generalizations. As an orientation, however, it might be useful to reduce its complexity to a simple model by positing two major centers of listmaking activity in Christian culture. I shall call them provisionally "academic" and "ritual" (and qualify the respective lists they produce with the same terms), for the first is dedicated primarily to knowledge of the name, and the second to its ritual glorification.

In the Christian academic context, the habitual locus of listing the names of God was the *florilegium* or, more generally, the encyclopedic miscellany that functioned as a common reference book of medieval knowledge. The strategy of storing positive knowledge about the proper terms for the Lord in lists was part of a more general preference of Christian *florilegia* (and perhaps of Christian medieval episteme as a whole) for exhaustive listmaking, the list being the major medieval tool for preserving, retrieving, and communicating valuable information.[14]

This extensive listmaking practice, and the didactic and cognitive practices related to it, followed in the footsteps of a rich, ancient tradition. Its roots reached to the religious life of the ancient Near East, where Christianity first sprouted. Perhaps the earliest models for Christian listmaking were the Mesopotamian and Egyptian onomastica. These monumental compilations, which often rivaled modern encyclopedias in scope, represent, according to Wolfram von Soden, the first scientific project of mankind: the ambition of putting together the words for all the things in the world and exhibiting them in a list for everyone to see.[15] The premise, as well as the purpose, of this "list-science" *(Listenwissenschaft)*, von Soden is quick to point out, was essentially religious: the collections "endeavored to order [visible reality] from a particular point of view that was ultimately rooted in theological ideas."[16] That is why lists of sacred names represented the semantic core of every onomasticon and, as such, were always placed before any other group of names. By verbally displaying the pantheon that governed the polytheistic imagination of the ancient Near East, sacronymic lists made visible the principle of universal order on which a polytheistic society rests, that "particular point of view" from which such a society could perceive itself as comprehensive as well as comprehensible. The lists of gods, in other words, were the ultimate order lists of the ancient world.

The transfer of this ancient Near Eastern practice to Christianity, though significant in its results, was neither straightforward nor uncomplicated, since it was often transformed beyond recognition by the mediation of Judaic monotheism.[17] In the Sumerian and Egyptian onomastica, the practice yielded polytheistic lists that named a vast array of deities—presumably all the gods there are—each in charge of a particular aspect of the cosmos. In the Judeo-Christian context, it took the form of a list of many names for the one God who rules the universe in its entirety. I should emphasize that the shift involved more than just a conceptual transformation. Compiling a list of the pantheon of gods and goddesses is a practice concerned more with the deities themselves than with their names; the clear-cut correspondence of one name for one god renders the concept of the divine name relatively unproblematic. The accumulation of numerous terms for a single divinity, on the other hand, is already an exercise in metalinguistic competence, an attempt to master the code of verbal communication, which suggests an awareness of the problematic nature of language itself. As a result, the concerns and the priorities of discourse change. The question "Which are our gods?" is replaced by "What are the names of our God that is single and one?" Or, if you prefer, the onomastic catalogue, which for millennia had been the standard for mapping out the sacrum and for articulating the principle of sacred order, was reinvented as an *antonomastic* list.[18]

The inherent goal of the Christian variety of these antonomastic reference lists is impossible to achieve: they are supposed to exhaust the inexhaustible by collecting a numberless lot of names for a God "of every name." The result is a compilation of gigantic proportions that recalls the general structural rule of ancient onomastica: "Plenty is better, more is best," or, to borrow Woody Allen's mantra in *Manhattan* (1979), "Many is my favorite number." The examples are numerous,[19] but a Greek list of 187 divine names, first documented in a seventh-century Byzantine *florilegium* as part of the anonymous treatise *Doctrina Patrum de Incarnatione Verbi* (Patristic doctrine for the incarnation of the word), will suffice as an illustration:

Wisdom. Word. Son of God. God Word. Light of the world. True Light. Resurrection. Way. Truth. Life. Door. Shepherd. Messiah. Christ. Jesus. Lord. Master. Word. King. Just One. True Vine. Bread of life. The First and the Last. The One Who Lives *even after becoming dead*.[20] The Alpha and the Omega, the Beginning and the End. He-Who-Is. He-Who-Was. He-Who-Comes. The Faithful One. The True One. Chosen Arrow. Servant of God. Light of the nations. Lamb without malice. Lamb of God. The Man. Advocate. Expiation. Power of God. Wisdom of God. Means of Expiation. Consuming Fire. Sanctification. Redemption. Justice. High Priest. Judah. Lion Cub. Lion. Jacob ["the heel"]. Israel. David ["beloved"]. Holy One. Root. Sprout. Flower. Bud. Stone. Rock. Unicorn. Star. Prophet. Prince of the host. Priest. Sacrifice. Altar. Beloved like the young of the unicorn. Redeemer. A man. Most High. A worm. Name of the Lord. Poor youth. A poor wise man. Bridegroom. Panther. Leader. Master of All. Hand. The Right Hand. Arm. The Holy One. Power of God. Name of God. Messenger. Sun of Justice. Lamb. Cloud of Justice. "Rising Sun" is His name. Son of man. Law. Just Judge. Emmanuel ["God is with us"]. Wonderful Counselor. Marvelous. Counselor. Mighty God. Master. Prince of Peace. Father of the world to come. Cloud. Beloved. Witness. Salvation. Justice. Glory of the Lord. Majesty of God. Salvation. Covenant of the people. Servant whom I have chosen. God of Israel. Savior. Exultation. Image of God. Form. Brightness. Effigy. Firstborn. Bridegroom. Beloved. Nard. Sachet of myrrh. Flower of the plain. Lily. Apple tree. Gazelle. Stag. Beloved. Solomon ["perfect"]. Shepherd. Cluster of henna. Palm tree. Tree of life. Apostle. Good. Beloved Son. The Child. Newborn. Stumbling stone. Rock of scandal. Peace. Power of God. Master of All. Only Son. Bread. Drink. Source. Door. Sun. Light. Lamb. [Little] Lamb. Door. Offering. Ransom.

Counselor. David. Jeremiah ["grandeur of God"]. Paul ["worker"]. Isaiah ["salvation of the Lord"]. Daniel ["judgment of God"]. Simeon ["the one who hears or is heard"]. Malah ["a melodious song"]. Mark ["shining"]. Luke ["luminous"]. John ["the grace of God"]. Solomon. Effigy. Hair. Rising Sun. Meek. Savior. Humble. Witness. Just One. Curse. Blessing. Way. Truth. Balaam ["sorcerer"]. Fall and Rise. Advocate. Intercessor. Spirit. Water of Life.[21]

Even though the reference list is well-known in the Slavonic tradition as a functional text-type, lists of divine names are almost never exclusively relegated to reference purposes in the extant Slavonic sources.[22] The predominant function of such inventories is magical, as we will see in detail in the next part of this study. Moreover, the Slavonic material often transforms a traditional reference list of God terms by reorienting it toward magic employment.

The Slavonic version of the list entitled "The Ten Names of God" is a good case in point. This well-known Christian text is a compilation of the Hebrew divine names used in the Old Testament: "El, Eloim, Eloe, Sabaoth, Elion, Ieie eser Ieie, Adonai, Ia, Iao, Saddai." It originates from a Latin treatise, *De decem Dei nominibus* (On the ten names of God), by St. Jerome, the chief author of the Vulgate translation of the Bible (ca. 393), whose version of the Old Testament is much closer to the Hebrew original than was the old Latin version based on the Septuagint translation.[23] The treatise had an overtly philological purpose. By explicating the Hebrew meaning of the names used in the Torah, Jerome aimed to assist their translations, so he provided not only the Latin but also the Greek equivalents of the Hebrew terms, thus producing a trilingual catalogue.[24]

The list appears in shifting contexts across Christian culture, both as an independent text and as part of larger compilations. A non-numerical Greek list of more than ninety divine names, for example, opens with a series of ten names (explicitly labeled "Hebrew" in a subtitle) that generally agrees with the list in Jerome's treatise.[25] The monumental, encyclopedic *Etymologies* by Isidore of Seville (ca. 560–636) includes a similar version of the list.[26] The catalogue of the ten Hebrew names, rendered in transliteration only, was also widely used in Christian magical practices, as its presence in a number of magic handbooks attests.[27] The Slavonic version, extant in only a handful of copies, in which the Hebrew names are corrupted beyond recognition, appears to be part of that same tradition.[28]

This example alone suggests that our provisional distinction between "academic" and "ritual" lists is merely conventional. The same list could perform with equal success in either group, and, more significantly, the ritual and academic objectives of listmaking are largely overlapping and interconnected. Since the earliest times in Christian history, the building of a repertoire of God-terms through biblical exegesis and extensive listmaking has been part of Christianity's continual effort to find its own ritual vocabulary. The perpetual recycling of these terms in a variety of ritualized contexts had a dual orientation from the start: apart from the devotional goals of invoking and professing the names of God, it also sought to cultivate a specifically Christian metalinguistic competence.[29] This logological enterprise had a logic and a course of its own, distinct from—and largely independent of—the meandering trajectory of name theology. Like the theology of divine names, however, its gradual establishment into a corpus of written texts depended upon the consolidation of the Christian liturgy and the definitive formulation of the Church's dogmatic principles.[30]

In that respect it is important to note that Dionysius's time was an age of maturity not only for Christian intellectual thought, but also for Christian ritual worship.[31] Drawing on the contributions of the Church Fathers, especially St. Basil the Great (ca. 329–379) and St. John Chrysostom (ca. 347–407), who composed the basic texts of the liturgy still used in the Eastern Orthodox world, the ecclesiastical writers of the sixth and seventh centuries developed further the solemnity of the ritual and the richness of the liturgical idiom. Roman Melodos, a Syrian who came to Constantinople during the reign of Emperor Anastasius I (491–518), was a key figure in this process, particularly in the development of new, sophisticated hymnographic forms. He invented the basic hymnodal genre, *kontakion* (a metrical sermon on a selected subject from biblical history or Christian hagiography). He is also credited with composing the famous *Akathistos Hymn of the Theotokos*, which broke new ground for hymnography in general, and specifically for the extensive liturgical use of antonomastic lists of sacred nomenclature.[32]

The *Akathistos Hymn* is a complex composition consisting of one or two introductory stanzas *(prooemia)* and a *kontakion* of twenty-four stanzas. Its prooemia and odd-numbered stanzas *(oikoi)* all end with a refrain of thirteen salutations to the Virgin *(chairetismoi)*, of which the last one, "Rejoice, bride unwedded," remains unchanged throughout the text.[33] The hymn is thus an elaborate reprise of the archetypal *chairetismos* from the Gospel of St. Luke ("Greetings, favored one! The Lord is with you" [1:28]), its complex hymnographic texture of repetitions and variations incorporating more than 250 different epithets of the Most Holy Theotokos.

The genre of the *akathistos* proved not only highly popular, but also highly productive in Eastern Orthodox practice. The subsequent hymnographic tradition in the Byzantine world introduced other compositions based on the same generic model. Especially relevant for our discussion is the thirteenth-century *Akathistos of the Most Sweet Jesus*, whose origin is usually linked to Byzantine Hesychasm, and which was translated into Slavonic as early as the fourteenth century. Following closely the hymnographic structure of the Theotokian *akathistos*, the hymn reiterates a respectable repertoire of Christological titles around the basic formula of the Jesus prayer, "Jesus, Son of God, have mercy on me."[34]

The *akathistos* genre is perhaps the most illustrious site of Christian liturgical listmaking, but it is by no means an exception. Christian ecclesiastical rhetoric, in all its generic diversity, has always depended on lists of divine names to resolve the tension between the *singularia tantum* of God and the *pluralia tantum* of his scriptural and ritual appellations. Encomia and panegyrics, hymns and prayers all abound in lists of pleonastic addresses to the Lord. These lists can be relatively short and straightforward ("One Lord Jesus Christ, the Son of God, the only-begotten, begotten of the Father before all ages, Light of Light, true God of true God, begotten, not made, of one essence with the Father, by Whom all things were made").[35] Often, however, they are organized around complex paratactic patterns in which divine names fill in the variable of a given liturgical formula or an array of God terms is played out as a hesitant naming sequence that derives authority from biblical references.[36] A passage from an exegetical homily on Ps. 45 [Slav. 44]:10, a text falsely attributed to St. John Chrysostom and widely used in Orthodox ecclesiastical practice, represents the more complex variety of such liturgical lists:

> Why did he call himself the Way? To teach that by means of Him we come to the Father. Why did he call himself Stone? To teach a firm and steadfast faith. Why did he call himself Foundation? To teach that he supports everything. Why did he call himself Root? For we flourish in Him. Why did he call himself Shepherd? For he tends us. Why did he call himself Ram? For he sacrificed himself for us and became our purification. Why did he call himself Life? For he resurrected us, the living dead. Why did he call himself Light? For he changed us from darkness [to light]. Why did he call himself Food? For he is of one essence with the Father. Why did he call himself Word? As he was begotten of the Father: as a word is begotten of the soul, so was the Son of the Father.

Why did he call himself Garment? For when we were baptized we were clothed in him. Why did he call himself Meal? For we eat him when we accept the Mystery [i.e., during the Holy Communion]. Why did he call himself House? For I live in him.[37] Why did he call himself Caretaker? For I am his temple. Why did he call himself Head? I am part of his body. Why did he call himself Bridegroom? For he betrothed me as a bride. Why did he call himself Pure? For He made me a virgin. Why did he call himself Ruler? To teach me that I am His servant.[38]

The significance of antonomastic lists for Christian God-talk grants this pattern a privileged status in hagiography, understood broadly as texts about sacred figures, from the Lord and the Theotokos to all saints. Any saint, being a follower of Christ, emulates some of Christ's representative virtues and can therefore be predicated and addressed by a selection of his names. This doctrinal rationale for applying lists of divine names to a saint is often openly stated in hagiographic texts. Only God has many names, claims, for example, Deacon Photius in his *Encomium of St. Luke the Evangelist*, but he has entitled his disciples to bear his names according to their deeds. That is why we would not be mistaken to name St. Luke the Tree of Life, the Door of Salvation, or the Vineyard, following the typology of God's polynomy.[39]

A particularly intricate product of Christian listmaking is the figurative list of divine names that functions by itself as a devotional "figure poem."[40] The names in such lists are arranged in a graphic design that reproduces a recognizable figure, usually a combination of viable Christian symbols, whose meaning is superimposed on the list to enrich its semantic complexity.

The minor English eighth-century poet Josephus Scottus was a master of such figurative lists. One of his more interesting compositions is a poem woven entirely of epithets for Christ and entitled *De nominibus Iesu* (On the names of Jesus), whose rectangular graphic design recalls a book with a cross inscribed on it.[41] The figure is formed by thirty-seven lines, each consisting of thirty-seven letters, and the letters that outline its contours are rubricated (marked out in red ink) for visual emphasis. Two horizontal and vertical lines of letters, also written in red, form the central cross image of the poem that divides the rectangle into four identical segments (seventeen lines by seventeen letters each). The symmetrical design thus recalls not merely a book, but the Good News itself, with the cross inscribed on it to divide it symbolically into the four individual Gospels. In other words, the poem visually represents two central Christological symbols that dominate the Christian liturgical experience, which reinforces the Christocentrism of the list itself.

VITASALUSUIRTUSUERBUMSAPIENTIASPONSUS
I ANUAPASTOROUISPR O L I SQUEPARENTISIMAG O
R ECTACOLUMNALAPIS Tu RRISESLUCIFERETSO L
G RATIAPLENAPATRISA u G MENTUMLUCISABORT V
A LTITRONUSIESSUSL Ex O PTIMAFACTOROLIMP I
C ONSILIUMPRINCEPS Re P LETUSFRUCTUSOLIU A
O MNIPOTENSUITISRE Ct O RENUNCTORETUNCTU S
L EGIFERAETHERIUST Es T ISDUXSERMOPROFET A
U ICTORUBIQUETREMI Tt E CAELIREGIAPRAESU L
M AXIMUSETMINIMUSS Ig N UMUENERABILECULT U
B UTRUSESINCY.PROMO Rs S ERUUSUICTIMAMANN A
A RBITERAETERNUSNI Mb V SQUOTERRAUIRESCA T
L AMPASESAUTPANISS Vp E RUSCOMMISUSABALT O
E XITUSINTROITUSSO Rs R EGNUMSIUEREDEMTO R
O RBISESENMEDICUSP On E NSPIGMENTASALUTI S
S IGNIFERINCLEPEIS Tu V INCISSEMPERETARC U
E MPTORADEPTUSERAS Cl A RODESTIPITEMUNDU M
REXREGUMDOMINUSCUNCTISLUXALMAPERORBEM
P RINCIPIUMFINISLOCUPLESETPAUPERAMICT U
ENPUERETSENIORFONSFLUMENPASTORETAGNUS
N OMENHABENSORIENS Ve X ILLUMLUCISESORTU M
S IMPLICITERMITISM Ir A NDUSESOREPROFUSS O
F ORTISSEUINFIRMUS Tu P LENISSENSIBUSARO N
I USTUSESETIUDEXTU As O LUMSANCTAUOLUNTA S
R EGNABEATATENENSD Es T ERCORESUMISEGENO S
M URUSESINUALIDISP Vt E USQUEMFEMINAPOTA T
I GNISINHUNCORBEMM Is S ITQUEMUERUSABARC E
S UPREMUSQUEPARENS Tr I TUSTUPASSUSESABE L
S CRIBAESTUCERUUSC Ap R EADECESPITEBETHE L
I NCLYTAPORTABONIS Pl A NAETTUSEMITARECT A
M URSUSESINFERNIOR Ex C UIUSCELSATRIBUNA L
A STRAPOLISUPERATP Ri O RACONSORTIBUSEST U
P ACIFICUSSALOMONU Er U SQUEOBLATUSESISA C
E NHOMOTUQUEDEUSPE Ns A SQUIPROEMIACUIQU E
T USTASDAMNANSOMNE Ne F ASDEFENSORETULTO R
R EXPIEUIRTUTUMTIB Ig L ORIAMYSTICESAMSO N
AUXILIAREDECUSFLOSCAMPISUMMAQUEDEXTRA

Fig. 3. Graphics reproduction of Josephus Scottus's figure poem, *Iesu ad Carolum regem*, eighth century. Ernst Dümmler, *Poetae Latini aevi Carolini*, vol. 1 (Berlin: Weidmann, 1881), 156-57.

A simple horizontal reading of the text decodes a devotional list-poem of thirty-seven lines that consist solely of more than ninety divine epithets strung together ("Life, salvation, virtue, word, wisdom, bridegroom, door, shepherd, sheep . . . "). The poem, however, does not end there. If we track the rubricated passages that outline the two basic images, the book and the cross, moving from left to right and then up or down, depending on the pattern, we decode, in this labyrinth of letters, a concluding stanza of eight lines. This poetic acrostic fits perfectly the rigid formal pattern of the principal poem and reads again as a lengthy list of divine names.

Decoding this list of names for the Lord is by itself a devotional act, a meditation or a prayer, much like the tracing of a labyrinth was a form of meditative practice in Western medieval monasteries. Yet prayers proper are not strangers to lists of divine names. The usual position of such lists is the initial invocation in prayers: "O heavenly King, the Comforter, the Spirit of Truth, Who are everywhere present and fillest all things, the Treasure of blessings and the Giver of life."[42] In some rare cases, however, the entire prayer may be built around a list of such names.

An example of this kind is a prayer attributed to St. John of Kronstadt (1829–1908), one of the most influential spiritual leaders in modern Russian history, whose teaching of the divine names proved crucial for the renewed interest in the theology of the name among Russian religious thinkers in the early twentieth century. In his well-known diary, *My Life in Christ*, Father John included the following passage, whose backbone is a list of five Christological titles, "Love, Power, Light, Peace, and Mercy": "Lord! Thy name is Love: do not cast me away, erring as I am! Thy name is Power: strengthen me, who so often grow weak and fall! Thy name is Light: enlighten my soul, darkened by earthly passions! Thy name is Peace: appease my troubled soul! Thy name is Mercy: do not cease to forgive me!"[43] Although this passage is but a fragment from a larger meditation on the name, it has the intensity and the lyrical pathos of a spontaneous prayer. It is not surprising, therefore, that the saint's followers came to treat his personal plea as a special prayer, and that its ritual repetition became one of the central practices of the most visible religious movement associated with the saint's name, the Ioannites.[44]

One curious Ioannite document offers interesting evidence to this effect. The document—an address to the Russian people published in 1930 under the title "God's Miracle"—claims that Father John before his death had personally ordered that this prayer be read in every home where Ioannites found themselves welcome.[45] (The movement was severely persecuted under the

Soviet regime as was, more generally, the entire spiritual legacy of the saint.) The document also includes the text of the prayer itself, though with significant changes from the initial version in Father John's diary. The personal plea is reinvented here as a communal prayer, with an added political urgency that befits the radically transformed spiritual context to which this prayer is now addressed:

> Lord! Your name is Love: with brotherly love kindle and inflame our hearts grown cold.
>
> Lord! Your name is Strength: with the power of the Cross fortify us in the fight for Your Truth.
>
> Lord! Your name is Light: with Your Truth illuminate our thoughts, with repentance enlighten our souls, and direct our will toward Your Light.
>
> Lord! Your name is Peace: pacify our troubled souls, extinguish the squabbles and discords in the Russian Land.
>
> Lord! Your name is Mercy: forgive our sins and iniquities, have mercy on us, and save Russia.

⋅∞⋅

This rich and extensive tradition of listing the names of God, which both preceded and followed the time of Dionysius, is the backdrop against which the Areopagitical theology of the name took its shape. Dionysius's onomatological views, as we might expect, were rooted in existing listmaking practices and in the biblical exegesis of the name that was inseparable from those practices. If the production of the Areopagitical corpus as the highly authoritative formulation of the Christian theological vision was in any way consequential for the practical knowledge and employment of God's names, it was not because it introduced anything new, but because it reaffirmed what was already there by furnishing it with theological legitimacy. Drawing on the onomatological experience of Christianity, Dionysius succeeded in devising a theological framework that was ultimately aimed back at this experience: to validate its objectives, to justify conceptually its contingent procedures, and to endorse their results as existentially significant for each and every Christian. For, in Dionysius's view, the intellectual exercise of mastering divine names, made possible through biblical exegesis and extensive antonomastic listmaking, is not an end in itself. It grants positive, though limited, knowledge of the divine processions. It recognizes the benevolent revelation of names in which God has "clothed his transcendence" to provide mankind with appropriate terms in which to worship him. It ultimately assists the human mind to rise from the world of matter up toward the higher domain of concepts, and then, abandoning every name, to enjoy the collapse of all human knowledge in the experience of a mystical union with the Nameless One.

PART 2

A Magical Alternative: The 72 Names of God

Question: How many are the names of Christ? Answer: 72. And [the names] of the Theotokos are just as many; and just as many are the apostles, and the great islands in the sea, and the languages on earth, and the members [of the human body], and the diseases in men.
—Slavonic manuscript, 18th century

These are the names of the Lord, 72 in number. Whoever has them and carries them on his person cleanly, will be saved from every evil.
—Slavic *Miscellany for Travelers*, published in Venice, 1520

The world is simply the universal "convenience" of things; there are the same number of fishes in the water as there are animals, or objects produced by nature or man, on the land (are there not fishes called *Episcopus*, others called *Catena*, and others called *Priapus*?); the same number of beings in the water and on the surface of the earth as there are in the sky, the inhabitants of the former corresponding with those of the latter; and lastly, there are the same number of beings in the whole of creation as may be found eminently contained in God himself, "the Sower of Existence, of Power, of Knowledge and of Love."
—Michel Foucault, *The Order of Things*

CHAPTER FIVE

How Many Are the Names of God?

"How many are the names of God?" In the world of Dionysius and his intellectual peers, such a question would appear naive and inadequate, or rhetorical at best. If God—who has no proper name—can be called by every name, to ask *how many* are those names would be no better than asking how many are the grains of sand in the desert, or drops of water in the ocean, or the stars in the sky—not a question that looks for an answer, but a mere cry of awe and amazement in the face of phenomena that overwhelm the imagination and puzzle the will: "O Lord, how manifold are your works!" (Ps. 104:24) and "How majestic is your name in all the earth!" (Ps. 8:1).

We know better, though, than to imagine Christian culture, even in its more homogenous medieval varieties, as uniformly governed by Dionysius's theological system of order. The Areopagite—and those who identify with his vision—represent only the ideological center of a rather nebulous universe. This center, despite its privileged position and all the power concentrated in it, is still a minority in its own realm—as representative of its margins as is the palace or cloister of the world outside the walls. This means, among other things, that we ought to take the lessons of theology with a grain of salt whenever we take them out of the cloister into "the world."

The text that I have chosen as the first epigraph to this part of the book offers a good case in point. All lessons of theology aside, it inquires about the number of God's names both unapologetically and with no sign of rhetorical flair. It is a matter-of-fact question that presumes—and expects—a straightforward answer. The context of the query itself suggests such serious intent. The text stems from the strong tradition of Christian *erotapocriseis*, or the genre of questions and—that is, *with*—answers: a *sui generis* heterodox catechesis. The immediate source of this text is an eighteenth-century Slavonic version of the *Discourse of the Three Hierarchs*, the best-known apocryphal collection of its type that is staged as a dogmatic disputation between St. Basil, St. Gregory the Theologian, and St. John Chrysostom.[1] Although its patristic attribution is, of course, spurious, this rich tapestry of religious fact, fantasy, and fiction shares the ambition of any canonical catechesis: to identify the acceptable religious questions and the correct answers to them.

The Number of God's Names

If merely asking about the number of God's names may offend outright our theological sensibility, the answer that goes with it only makes matters worse. I am familiar with two different Slavonic erotapocritical corpora that feature our question, and both of them, apparently pointing back to a common source, give the same prompt and definitive answer: 72.[2]

The same answer is echoed in another text that presents a list of divine epithets under the rubric "The 72 names of the Lord":

> These are the Names of the Lord, 72 in number. Whoever has them and carries them on his person honestly, will be saved from every evil, and from insolent death, and from the devil. Power, Strength, Word, Life, Grace, Love, Wisdom, *Sother* [Gr., "Savior"], *Pantokrator* [Gr., "Omnipotent"], *Paraklit* [Gr., "Intercessor"], the Light, Meal, Shepherd, Ram, Stone, the Way, House, Garment, Blossom, Foundation, Head, the Pure, Bridegroom, Ruler, Truth, Son of Man, Immanuel [Heb., "the Lord is with us"], the Beginning, Firstborn, Messiah [Heb., "the Anointed One"], the Highest King, Jesus, Bread, Father, Creator, Sabaoth, *Kyrios* [Gr., "Lord"], the Holy Spirit, Mercy, Intercessor, Leader, Sun, Christ, Healer, Of the Good Womb, Merciful, Primordial, *Athanatos* [Gr., "Immortal"], Maker, Lamb, Lion, Bull, Effigy, Glory, I Am the One Who Is, Justice, Source, the True Mouth, Joy, Senior, *Eleon* [possibly from Heb., *Elion*, "the Most High" or from Gr., *Eleos*, "Mercy"], Priest, Prophet, Eternal Door, Justification, God, Indivisible Trinity, the King of Kings. These names to be of help and for the health of the servant of God Michael.

This text, which scholars usually classify as a false prayer, is the best documented list of divine names in the entire Slavonic tradition.[3] Compared to the erotapocritical entry about the 72 names, it is both older and has a much wider distribution. Its earliest extant copy is found in the famous *Berlin Codex*, a miscellany from the end of the thirteenth century.[4] From that time onward, and especially after the text's first printed publication in 1520, this list enjoyed a long and viable tradition, both in script and in print, all the way to the nineteenth century.[5] Judging by the extant evidence, the tradition appears to be exclusively South Slavic, which is to say, specific to the cultural area of the Balkans.[6]

At first sight, the names in the list seem to fit perfectly the framework of Dionysius's onomatology, since they are selected mostly from the biblical repertoire of symbols and titles for the divinity and are no different from the names in the catalogues that populate Christian *florilegia*. Yet the fact that they are restricted here to a particular number is by itself an index to the unorthodox status of this text. The proviso that usually goes with the names makes the ideological gap between the list of 72 names and Dionysius even more explicit. The names are to be worn in their written form to ward off evil forces; in other words, they are to be used as an amulet.[7] In accordance with these instructions, the available sources of the text suggest that it was distributed mainly through the medium of phylacteries: either scrolls or small-format personalized prayer books that were worn as magical objects for healing and protection. Similarly, the printed editions of the text reveal that they were often treated as personal amulets. The nonverbal employment of a verbal text as a talisman, a practice widespread across confessional bounds, is rooted in an overtly nonreferential treatment of language that contradicts the very essence of Dionysius's theology of the name. According to this view, any word, and especially a divine name as the most potent of all words, has automatic power that is inherent in the materiality of its scribal texture. Hence, written amulets are viewed as magical objects whose performative power is manifest graphically and can be transferred to the owner of the amulet through continual contact with his body.[8] Such a prescribed use of the list of divine names clearly removes it as far as possible from the privileged center of Christian orthodoxy, redirecting it toward an obscure corner of heteropraxis that is usually called protective or preventive magic.[9]

The proviso also defines the particular effect to be achieved if the names are properly used. In accordance with the instructions for amulet application, the names are assigned an exclusively defensive function: they are to be used only to protect from evil, not to coerce or induce the demonic powers. Within these limitations of preventive magic, however, the amulet claims to have almost unlimited power. "Whoever wears these names purely, will be saved from every evil," read most of the instructions for the list. Some of the copies elaborate further on the power of the names by unpacking the presuppositions behind "every evil." The Lord's names are claimed to secure a long and healthy life, to cleanse from all kinds of corruption, to deliver from suffering even in the world-to-come, and to secure protection not only from the devil, but also from evil men and from various malevolent assaults in the form of disease, sudden death, and attack by visible and invisible enemies. This powerful self-promotion secures, no doubt, the popularity of the amulet, especially at times when danger seems imminent and the fragility of human fortune is too conspicuous to miss.

But what makes this list so powerful? In the inner logic of the amulet practice, the answer is simple: power comes from the names. Yet we have already observed that the names are essentially no different from names in other, strictly orthodox catalogues of divine names that, needless to say, would never make such claims about themselves. What allows our list to present itself as a superpowerful amulet is the number that closes the list. The unorthodox ethos of this text (and by extension its apotropaic employment) thus hinges on the number 72. It is important to note also that, despite the apparent equivalence between the list and the erotapocritical answer about the number of God's names, the semantic gesture of the answer is more radical and theologically problematic. While the amulet never explicitly claims that its "72 names" are the only valid divine names, the erotapocritical text reduces all names of God to that particular number.[10] It thus assumes an openly unorthodox stance, something the amulet seems careful to camouflage, if not to avoid.

The number itself is an unlikely and almost disappointing alternative to the infinity of names proposed by Dionysius. We expect the number of God's names to impress us. If the number is not large enough to suggest infinity by approximation, as it does in Arthur C. Clarke's *The Nine Billion Names of God*, it should certainly be round, the epitome of completeness and perfection, as are the 10 names of Yahweh, or the 100 names of Allah, of which the most mysterious one keeps the other 99 bound in a comprehensive unity. And, at the very least, the number of God's names should always be symbolically significant. At first blush, 72 appears to be none of those things, though appearances can be deceiving.

The number 72 is indeed unremarkable within our habitual decimal system of calculation. If we switch to the duodecimal point of view, however, we gain a new perspective of its status as a "round" number and can fully appreciate its long tradition of symbolic application.[11] The switch is hardly frivolous. Counting to base 12 proved historically the most persistent obstacle along the way to decimal supremacy,[12] and the most fecund period in the history of the number's symbolism points exactly to the time of competition between the two systems.

In the duodecimal universe, 72 has the status of a round number: as the product of a dozen and a half-dozen ($12 \times 6 = 72$), it is equivalent to fifty in the decimal system, the product of the base 10 and its half ($10 \times 5 = 50$).

Furthermore, 72 is the only duodecimal number in the centum that has as many as ten divisors (2, 3, 4, 6, 8, 9, 12, 18, 24, and 36), which means that it can be presented as the product of various combinations of factors. Since all of these numbers also have customary cross-cultural symbolic meanings, those meanings are always already implied in the semantic halo of 72 and constantly amplify one another by metonymic transfer. This special status of 72 in the centum singles it out as a significant number at the intersection of the decimal and the duodecimal systems and makes it the logical candidate among the two-digit numbers to signify contained plurality and comprehensive multitude.

Our erotapocritical entry itself is a useful introduction to the rich symbolic load of 72, since the restriction of the names of God to that number is only a point of departure for the text. The answer goes on, passing in quick succession through several classes of objects that are equally 72-fold, embracing the number—not the names—as its real focus: "And just as many are the names of the Mother of God, and just as many are the apostles, and just as many are the great islands in the sea, and just as many are the languages on earth, and just as many are the members [of the human body],[13] and just as many are the diseases in men." The effect of this short text is as vertiginous as its ambition is all-encompassing. In the span of a single sentence, it transports us from sacred history to the political geography of the human world and, dwelling for a moment on the surface of the earth with its vast expanses of land and water, completes its journey in the depths of the human body. The number 72, that peculiar number of the divine names, seems inscribed in the very texture of creation—a structural code that harmonizes the visible and the invisible, the above and the below, the universal and the merely human. The macrocosm and the microcosm thus meet each other in an elegant design of numerical correspondences, underscored by the refrain "and just as many." And although the items listed in it are only seven, we are left with the impression that, in such a world of perfect symmetry, everything must be 72 in number.

All this contributes to a very optimistic epistemological proposition. The answer to our question, we may infer, presupposes a unified cosmology that is strikingly at odds with the vision of Dionysius the Areopagite. According to this new vision, the creation consists of finite and structurally homologous classes that share as a common numerical denominator the finite number of the Creator's names. The number 72, in other words, is the limit of universal expansion, so that positive and negative forces alike are as many as God's names and can therefore be kept in check and subordination in a marvelously predictable and controllable universe.

If we imagine for a moment a universe organized along such lines of perfect numerical symmetry, it is not hard to see how, in such a world, an amulet with the 72 names of the Lord could be construed as the ultimate tool of prophylactic magic. By juxtaposing one omnipotent divine name to each of the 72 agents of disease, destruction, and death, such an amulet delivers, as it claims, unbeatable defense against every evil.

The question is, Would it be prudent of us to give so much credit to an accidental text, reading into it a complete cosmological system? And even if this text is indeed the tip of a conceptual iceberg rooted in the number 72, can we conjecture a locus in life where such a vision of a 72-fold universe might have mobilized the imagination of larger religious communities to organize both their perception and interactions with reality?

The Larger Context

Hypothesizing unified visions of order behind scattered remnants of old discourses is always a tricky business, and it gets trickier the more one moves away from ideological centers of any kind. The particular brand of *ad hoc* religious eclecticism that I call "heteropraxis" marks the ultimate margin of organized religious life where all rules and distinctions are negotiable at best.

Always oriented toward a particular need of the moment, heteropraxis draws indiscriminately from ideologically incompatible systems, never developing a "theory" of its own. It is thus a form of religious life without an overarching principle, an eclectic mixture of practices that has no explicit theoretical counterpart. As such, heteropraxis is not only opposed to orthodoxy and orthopraxis, the "right doctrine" and its rightful application in life, but it is also distinct from the various heterodoxies (the heresies) that always purport to be systematic alternatives to the dominant religious ideology. *Erotapocriseis*, as a genre that thrives in the expansive heteropractical provinces of Christian culture, is characteristically omnivorous in its curiosity and promiscuous in its exchanges and, as a result, is generally prone to inconsistencies, "occasionalisms," and great variability in individual articulations. We should be especially cautious, therefore—and healthily minimalist—when evaluating erotapocritical postulates or any data of similar origin.

To what degree is our erotapocritical text an exception? We may say for certain that it is hardly unique, since several individual entries from other Slavonic collections of questions and answers support its cosmological implications with similar conceptual summaries keyed to the number 72.

Some of them duplicate classes already familiar to us; others further enrich our image of a 72-fold universe with new, though analogous, data. Consider, for example, the following text, which, while spinning its cosmological proposition around the 72 islands in the sea, substantiates it with several zoological and botanical classes of 72 members that are all entirely new to us: "John asked, 'How many are the big islands?' Basil said, '72, and just as many are the different languages, and just as many are the different kinds of fish, and just as many are the different kinds of birds, and just as many are the different kinds of trees'" (emphasis added).[14] I. A. Bychkov, in a description of a seventeenth-century codex that has been subsequently lost or misplaced, quotes a heading that suggests the same numerical homology, for it directly equates the number of the nations, or classes of people, with the number of the kinds of animals: "The number of the human languages on earth, and also of the [animal] genera: four-footed [beasts], fish, and reptiles."[15]

The most compelling evidence in support of a hypothetical 72-fold universe, however, does not come from the erotapocritical tradition but from the tradition of *The 72 Names of the Lord*. This amulet was associated almost from the beginning with a similar sacronymic list called *The 72 Names of the Theotokos*, a twin amulet that is apparently modeled after the list of the Lord's names as its gender counterpart.[16] The earliest codex known to document their collocation is an apocryphal *Book of Hours* from 1498.[17] In this source, the list of the 72 divine names is immediately followed by the names of the Mother of God, and then the contextual bonds and the inner affinities between the two symmetrical texts are strengthened additionally by a common closure: "The same is the number of the islands in the sea, 72. And the same [is the number] of the languages on earth, 72. And the same [is the number] of the disciples, 72. And the same [is the number] of deaths, 72."[18]

This remarkable evidence suggests that the early conjunction of *The 72 Names of the Lord* and *The 72 Names of the Theotokos* was designed as part of a larger textual unit. Just like the erotapocritical entry about the names of God, this macro-text (predating it by almost three centuries) put forward a global vision of a 72-fold world based on the number of divine names. The resemblance between the two articulations of the vision is striking. The amulet cluster introduces virtually the same six classes included in the question-and-answer text.[19] It only lists them in a slightly different order and, instead of the 72 diseases, features a similar anthropological topos addressing the contingency of human existence, "the 72 deaths."

If there is a distinction between the two texts, it is purely modal, a matter of the preferred discursive mode. While the erotapocritical text articulates its operative classes by numerical topoi alone, the amulet corpus combines numeration with enumeration by expanding some of these topoi into numerical lists. The ease with which the articulations of the same vision shift back and forth between the two discursive modes suggests that numeration and enumeration are treated in this context as functionally equivalent idioms. A numerical topos can be expanded into a numerical list, and a list, in turn, can be shrunk laconically to a single topos. The choice between the two seems to depend largely on the pragmatic goal of each locution, with *erotapocriseis* apparently opting for succinct numeration, and preventive magic leaning in the opposite direction, toward extensive listmaking. This preliminary observation—if it could be generalized indeed over a larger body of texts—raises interesting theoretical questions about the interrelation between a discursive mode and a pragmatic site.

Here, however, what interests me is the possibility of positing a vision of a 72-fold universe that could have informed the constitution and the performance of *The 72 Names of the Lord* in the Slavic context. Let me repeat the facts that support such a hypothesis. First, there is a fairly popular, late-medieval Slavonic list of 72 divine names that claims to be a most potent amulet. Second, several entries in Slavic collections of questions and answers propose the idea that the 72 names of the Lord are the structural code of the universe that defines its pattern of numerical correspondences. Third, a peculiar amulet corpus attested in *Jerusalem 22* reveals a link between the two traditions that suggests a common source behind them.

We can add a fourth, largely circumstantial piece of evidence—the preponderance of isolated topoi based on the number 72. Various classes of 72 members crop up almost everywhere in the extant repertoires of Slavonic texts, from magical formulas and incantations to canonical historical narratives, and from the fabulous—and fabulously permissive—world of biblical apocrypha to the rigidly regulated texts of the Bible itself. Some of the concepts (the 72 peoples and languages, the 72 disciples) are all-pervasive; others (the 72 diseases, the 72 names of the Lord and the Virgin) thrive mainly in the margins of the official culture. All of them, however, present the number 72 as a most fertile figure for the Slavic religious imagination.

Is this tradition restricted to *Slavia Orthodoxa*? Not by any means, for every single 72-based topos that is registered in the Slavic context has abundant cross-cultural equivalents. A large spectrum of Hebrew, Greek, Latin, Coptic, Syriac, Georgian, Armenian, and Arabic sources documents the persistent appearance of the same 72-based matrix on a much larger scale and over the span of nearly three millennia. The Slavonic repertoire, we may conjecture, reflects only part of an older and much more complex tradition that is rooted in the number 72. The inner logic of this tradition is often lost in the unrelated fragments that have reached the written culture of the Slavs, and we catch our first glimpses of its richness and significance only when we consider the full scope of the available data.

The Synonymy of 72 and 70

That last statement requires, however, a crucial qualification. In order to consider the full scope of the potentially relevant material, we must bear in mind that in the cultural traditions of the Helleno-Semitic world, 72 is completely synonymous with several other numerical symbols. The available written sources reveal that in Judaism and Christianity alike, 72 is often used interchangeably with the numbers 77 and 73, and most often with the number 70. How did this peculiar equivalence come about?

The synonymy of 72 with both 77 and 73 could be explained as the result of a secondary substitution. It is almost certain that in both cases 72 was the primary number and the other variants developed later under the pressure of external changes. In the case of the symmetrical number 77, the substitution is most likely motivated semantically. Being a reduplication of the magnificent 7, this number is immediately meaningful for the Judeo-Christian imagination, unlike the relatively more opaque 72. This circumstance must have made it a welcome substitute, particularly in contexts where the rich symbolic import of 72 had been reduced or lost in transition. The replacement of 72 by 73, on the other hand, appears to be a matter of pure convention. It is rooted in the general tendency of Semitic cultures to avoid even numbers because they are deemed unlucky. (That is why in the Muslim tradition Allah has 99 + 1 names instead of the even 100, and the number of Arabian Nights is not 1,000 but an odd 1,001).

As for the synonymy of 70 and 72, the picture is more complex, most probably the result of conflation and confusion between two independent traditions rather than a simple unidirectional substitution. The process, which is impossible to trace in strict historical terms (as are all cases of cultural diffusion), reflects the prolonged competition between the base-12 and base-10 systems of computation. The aggressive presence of 70 in territories where 72 has previously ruled unchallenged reflects the ultimate victory of the decimal system in those cultural landscapes, since for the decimal minds of Jews and Christians alike, 70 is not only "more round" than 72, but—being the superlative tenfold of the most sacred 7—it also has a far superior status. Yet we can assume that the opposite influence has also taken place, that 72 has absorbed in the process some of the meanings that 70 had before the time of mixture and confusion.

In any event, what we can observe today in the written sources is a case of perfect functional equivalence between the two numerical symbols, so much so that virtually every 72-related topos that we encounter is equally documented as a group of 70. The most striking case, no doubt, is the number of Christ's disciples, for its fluctuation is registered directly in the Bible (Luke 10:1, 17), both in copies of the Greek original of Luke's Gospel and in its versional evidence. For the practical purposes of this study, therefore, we can safely augment our 72-related data with material in which the number 70 is registered instead.

⁊∞⁊

Both the erotapocritical entry and the amulet corpus in the codex *Jerusalem 22* single out three major domains that harbor classes of 72 objects: divine nomenclature (the names of the Lord and of his Mother), geopolitics (portions of inhabitable land, the nations and languages on earth, and the disciples of Christ who brought the Good News to all the world), and anthropology (the parts of the human body and the diseases that lurk in them). In the chapters that follow, I adopt these categories as my own operative tools to organize the relevant 72-related data in a more or less coherent narrative that brings to the fore the conceptual links behind the scattered individual locutions. To reflect the peculiar teleology of my own quest, I take up these categories in reverse order, from the human body to the divine names, thus aiming the entire narrative at the meeting between the number 72 and the names of God.

᪥

CHAPTER SIX

A Body of 72 Parts and
the 72 Diseases

The concept of 72 diseases in man and its correlative notion of a human body made of 72 parts harboring illness and decay belong to the domain of anthropological imagination. In the local cosmologies that we are tracing through remnants of old texts, these concepts relate directly to practices of faith healing and to the imaginative structures that have formed and informed them over time.[1]

A central concern for faith medicine is the question of how diseases came about. This is not just a matter of simple curiosity, but of existential consequence bearing directly on personal well-being. Religious epistemology, as is well known, correlates genesis and essence, so that knowledge of a phenomenon's origins is thought to offer epistemological insight into the phenomenon itself. Hence the great emphasis in religious culture on narratives about beginnings and on etiology in general.

The tale of how human ailments came to be begins, quite literally, with Adam.[2] There are two alternative versions of the story about the origin of human maladies, and they both take us back to the beginning of human history. The oldest of the two narratives links disease directly to the Fall. The source text is the apocryphal cycle known as *The Books of Adam and Eve*. This is the collective designation for the oldest nonbiblical Adam stories that have survived in Greek, Latin, Slavonic, Georgian, Armenian, and Coptic versions.[3] All versions contain a common narrative about the Lord's infliction on Adam of 72 (or 70) diseases as a punishment for his disobedience in the Garden of Eden. The corresponding Slavonic passage reads as follows:

> Then the Lord came and set the Lord's throne in the center of Paradise, and called out in a formidable voice, "Adam, Adam, where are you." And I [Adam] declared, "I am naked, o Lord, and cannot come out." And the

79

Lord said, "Never before have you so hidden away from me. If you hide
from me, you have transgressed my commandment. I will inflict numerous wounds on your body and diseases on your heart. The first ailment
will be cholic, the second ailment—eye-disease and deafness, and then
all the ailments will follow, 72 [in number]."[4]

Embroidering on the familiar biblical text, the story weaves together
the ability to give life and the inevitability of death as mutually dependent
and inseparable aspects of the human condition. If the initial act of creation
opened to Adam and Eve the divine promise of eternal life in the Garden,
the discovery of their sexuality ("I am naked, o Lord!")—or of their power to
procreate, which is the same thing—was a willful rejection of that promise.
It was a choice to be able to give life at the cost of having to die. That is
how man traded eternity for mortality. The 72 ailments with which the
Lord cursed the human race that originate from this "original sin" (as it was
infamously labeled by St. Augustine) are no more than agents and omens of
death. It is death, not disease, that is the true punishment in the apocryphal
narrative, just as death, not pain and toil, is the core of the Lord's curse in
Genesis 3. The 72 diseases thus represent in our story the new fallen state
of man in which he is already subject to death. And if disease itself is an index
to human mortality, so, by association, is the total number of its various
manifestations, 72. Note that the emphasis on finitude is additionally high-
lighted in the same apocryphon by its particular narrative setting: the narra-
tor is Adam himself, who is telling the story to his son Seth on his deathbed,
at the very moment when the precedent of natural death (as opposed to the
violent death of Abel) is to be set in human history.

The same idea is explicated even more directly in another apocryphon,
The Testament of Abraham.[5] The long Greek version of the text contains
the following notable exchange between Abraham and the Angel of Death:
"Then said Abraham, 'I beseech thee tell me: is there untimely death?' Death
said, 'Verily, verily I say unto thee as God's truth there are seventy-two
deaths. One is the just death that has its allotted time. And many men suddenly [literally, 'within one hour'] go to death, and are consigned to the
grave.'"[6] The concept of 72 deaths, which the passage propagates as "God's
truth," is evidently analogous to the concept of 72 ailments from the Adam
apocryphon in terms of cause and effect. There is, however, something new
in this text that sheds light on a broader imaginative structure behind these
numerical concepts. The information about the 72 deaths comes up in the dialogue in response to Abraham's question about "untimely death." As background I should add that the entire story is about the death of Abraham, who

is not ready to die yet, although his hour has already come. Because he is in great favor with the Lord, he is treated with exceptional kindness: the Archangel Michael and the Angel of Death both have colloquia with him on the subject of dying, attempting to make his transition as easy as possible. Nothing, however—neither great repute nor divine favor—can cancel out his imminent end, for the death that is upon him is a "timely" one.

We can see that the concept of 72 deaths is not homogenous: it branches into 71 + 1. There are 71 "untimely" deaths that may strike at any time and in various forms. They are all premature and unseasonable. As deviations from the norm, they are improper deaths, unbefitting the order of things. We call them "accidents" and treat them as disaster and tragedy, lamenting the people struck by them as "unlucky" (a young person who has passed away unmarried or childless, a child who is survived by a parent). Such anomalous deaths, all 71 of them, can be avoided; and protective magic has precisely that purpose. The last, the 72nd death, however, is just and timely: it marks the end of the days allotted to each of us. This last and "orderly" death no one can avoid. And the lesson of *The Testament of Abraham* is that such death is not a tragedy. It should be neither feared nor lamented, but accepted and honored as God's will.

The immediate linking of the number 72 to death surfaces in several Judeo-Christian texts as yet another image of the end: it is the number of the years in a human life, the same allotted time that is completed by a timely death.[7] Thus Psalm 90:10 explicitly states that the span of a human life is measured by 70 years (Ps. 90:10),[8] the age known in Slavic cultures as "the biblical age" (Russian, *bibleiskii vozrast*) or "the David limit" (Bulgarian, *Davidov predel*). Similarly, the prophet Isaiah claims that 70 are the numbered years of any king (Is. 23:15). The same figure recurs in both canonical and apocryphal texts, leaving its mark even on poetry of the highest order. In his *Convivio*, Dante Alighieri (1265–1321) unequivocally fixed the midpoint of the human life at age 35.[9] In a similar vein, his famous opening of *The Divine Comedy*, "When I had journeyed half of our life's way" (canto 1.1), refers to the night of April 7 in the year 1300 when Dante—exactly 35 years of age at the time—was supposed to have set out on his journey to the Other World.[10] Less famously, though no less to the point, late Slavonic variations on *The Book of Adam and Eve* assert that Adam died at the age of 70,[11] while the Mother of God is said to have lived for 72 years in the *Vita of the Theotokos* by Epiphanius of Jerusalem.[12] The finite number of human diseases, we may conclude, functions more broadly as a numerical symbol of a biological limit, designating both death—that ultimate bound of human biology—and the very notion of human finitude.

The alternative story of how diseases came about is also an Adam tale but with an entirely new spin. As we have seen, *The Books of Adam and Eve* rationalize the existence of disease by a modified version of the biblical narrative about the Fall and attribute the 72 ailments directly to human sinfulness. Much more recent Adam-related narratives, known to me only in Slavonic sources, shift the narrative focus from the Fall to the Creation of man and revisit the issue from the point of view of a dualistic cosmogony. These texts turn away from the former ethical interpretations of disease and health to present human ailments not as God's punishment, but as the spiteful work of his nemesis, the devil.

One such narrative was made available by Pypin from a seventeenth-century Slavonic manuscript.[13] It testifies to how the devil, envious of God's flawless work, secretly pierced the body of Adam at 70 places and planted in it 70 ailments. According to more elaborate variants of the same plot, which circulate to this date in Balkan Slavic folk milieux, when God found out that his creation had been corrupted, he filled in the holes with the same number of curative herbs, and that is how herbal medicine was born. Much in the spirit of the *Testament of Abraham* and its notion of one timely death among the 72, a variant of the same Adam legend specifies that the Lord left the last hole open so that the soul could go away through it when death comes.[14]

This cycle of dualistic narratives advances a polarized vision of the human body as a battleground between the devil's forces of disease and God, the Healer—an imaginative structure much more suitable for magical manipulation than the ultimately abstract opposition between sin and retribution. It has the advantage of singling out one archetypal external adversary, the cause of all ailments, whose powers are, by definition, limited and inferior to the divine powers of health. Furthermore, the legend ideates a numerical symmetry where the number of all diseases corresponds not only to the number of vulnerable spots in the human body (a version, no doubt, of the familiar topos "a body of 72 parts") but also to the total number of existing remedies. Such a symmetrical design, based on order and equivalence, suggests a universal balance between health and disease. Within such a conceptual framework, the task of curative magic becomes simple and manageable. To heal an ailing body, magic need not thwart the divine order of things but can support it, since healing—not disease—comes from God. All that magic needs to do is restore the primordial balance between disease and health by reenacting the sacred precedent of healing harmony that God established in the final act of Creation.

It is not surprising, therefore, that Slavic practices of faith healing and the texts accompanying them readily draw from this dualistic story about the origin of disease, while the older, "ethical" version has almost no influence on them. One Carpatho-Rusyn curative exorcism, documented in an eighteenth-century manuscript, explicates the connection directly in a short paraphrase of the master narrative (with a characteristic substitution of the number's "symmetrical" equivalent, 77): "And the devil, who rose against God and created the 77 diseases, infected [with them] Adam the first man."[15]

Another, more extensive composition that combines a prayer to all saints with an exorcism of all human diseases is evidently informed by the same or similar dualistic sources. This text is documented in the Balkan manuscript tradition in several Greek and Slavonic sources, including a Greek personal amulet from 1774 that was witnessed by Abbott at the beginning of the twentieth century in the town of Melnik (in present-day Bulgaria).[16] All the versions of the text feature a common formula: "I conjure you up, 72 ailments that are in every man; go away from the servant of God N."[17] This formula alone clearly places the exorcism in the orbit of the same 72-based vision of human biology that the Adam stories lay out in detail. The Slavonic version complements this formula by a reference to the devil as to the "creator" of all the diseases in man, thus indisputably orienting the text to the dualistic branch of the etiological narratives.[18]

In addition, the extant Byzantino-Slavic repertoire of medicinal magic presents us with numerous individual topoi based on the number 72 or a close equivalent (mostly the "round" number 70 or the "symmetrical" number 77).[19] Both written texts and records of folk incantations persistently refer not only to 72 diseases and 72 parts in the human body, but also to 72 bones, joints and tendons, presumably connecting the 72 parts and, as interstices, providing weak points in the body's defense where diseases may strike and take over. No less frequent are mentions of 72 remedies or prophylactic tools (herbs, protective magic seals, sacred names, or names of evil spirits which, when pronounced, render the spirits harmless).[20] Whether having an explicit dualistic underpinning or not, each of these scattered textual fragments consolidates the status of 72 as a number of human finitude. Together they reinforce the entire mythological justification of this status by reiterating the symmetrical vision of human biology promoted by the Adam narratives and echoing the more general cosmological implications of the erotapocritical texts.

CHAPTER SEVEN

An Apostle for Every Nation

"To designate the *orbis terrarum* they draw a cynocephalus." These words belong to the authoritative ancient source on Egyptian symbolism, Horus Apollo's *Book on the Hieroglyphics*. The subject is the symbolic logic behind the Egyptian script. The passage itself introduces the peculiar cultural association between the world in its entirety and the sacred Cynocephalus Hamadryas, the dog-headed baboon whom the Egyptians associated with the underworld, the spirits of the dead, and Thoth, the patron god of wisdom, magic, and writing. The common ground on which this unexpected association rests, is—yet again—the number 72. Horus Apollo is most specific on this point: "[B]ecause they say that the world has numbered seventy-two inhabited divisions from of old [and] the cynocephali, when nurtured in the temples with care, do not die on one day the same as do other animals: Rather a certain part of the animal continues to perform its function until seventy-two days are completed; only then does the animal die entirely."[1]

The passage is a perfect illustration of an imagination that feeds on resemblance and similitude. On the one hand, we have the myth of the cynocephalus and its idiosyncratic death over the course of 72 days; on the other, a belief that the inhabitable portions of the world are 72.[2] The only thing that the two images—the cynocephalus and the world—have in common is the number 72. Moreover, the analogy does not immediately lend itself to perfect homology: 72 is a measure of time in the cynocephalus myth, while it serves clearly as a spatial matrix for the division of the world. Yet, shaky as it might appear to us with our tendency to rational ordering of categories and our emphasis on distinctions rather than similarities, this correspondence was essential to the Egyptians, so much so that they based on it one of their central hieroglyphs for writing the cosmos.

The significance of this passage for my project, however, lies elsewhere. It points to existing cultural links between the usage of 72 as a symbol of human mortality and its much more public role in the geopolitical imagination of the ancient world, a role which has already been hinted at by the topos "the 72 peoples or languages on earth" from the erotapocritical text on the names of God.

The Division of the Languages at Babel

"There are 72 languages in the world, and as an obvious corollary there are 72 lands to correspond to that number," claims Wolfram von Eschenbach in his narrative poem "Willenhalm" (ca. 1220).[3] The suggestion that 72 is the number of all human languages may appear as absurd to modern linguists as the notion of 72 diseases seems to modern physicians. Yet the same idea was accepted as a basic, axiomatic truth in medieval Europe, and it remained perhaps the most popular of all the 72-related commonplaces of Christian culture long after the Middle Ages.[4]

The classical text behind this notion is the myth of the Tower of Babel from Gen. 11:1–9. This familiar story about the division of languages is related to the biblical story that occupied us in the previous chapter, the story of the Fall. It is yet another narrative of human hubris and divine punishment, one that translates the individual rebellion of Adam and Eve onto a universal plane. By building a tower with its top in the heavens, the human race attempted to transcend its divinely ordained limitations. The punishment was division and dispersion, or "confusion," in the preferred biblical trope: "Come, let us go down and confuse their language there, so that they will not understand one another's speech."[5] Such is the Abrahamic master narrative of the birth of nations: they were born out of confusion, to bring about discord and misunderstanding.

To be sure, the standard text in the Hebrew Bible never specifies the number of the languages and nations resulting from Babel, but the number 70/72 was readily attached to them by numerous alternative sources. It fits the general symmetry between the story of Adam and that of Babel. The punishment for the transgression of human boundaries in both cases is a new set of limitations: diseases as agents of death in the first case, languages as a source of misunderstanding in the second. It seems only appropriate that those sets would be coextensive, countable by the same number. Furthermore, as with the apocryphal variations on Genesis 3, here too the limitations are articulated by several functionally equivalent metonyms: languages, nations distinguished by the languages they speak, and the lands that those nations inhabit.[6]

The number itself is usually derived from the lists of Noah's descendants after the Flood in Genesis 10. It is habitually 70 in Jewish exegetical commentaries on the genealogies, as it is elsewhere in the rabbinic tradition.[7] Following this standard interpretation, the Talmud contends that every commandment revealed to Moses on Mount Sinai "divided itself and could be heard in all seventy languages." In the same vein, the mystical treatise from early post-Talmudic times, *The Alphabet of Rabbi Akiba*, declares that "during the forty days that Moses spent [on Sinai] he was taught the Torah in the seventy aspects of the seventy languages."[8] The ninth-century Aramaic translation of Genesis in *Targum Pseudo-Jonathan* offers an even more complex numerical elaboration of the Babel story keyed to the number 70:

> And the Lord said: "Behold they are one people and they have all one language, and they have planned to do this! And now, nothing they plan to do can be withheld from them." And the Lord said to the seventy angels that stand before him: "Come then, let us go down, and confuse their language there, so that they will not understand one another's language." The Memra of the Lord was revealed against the city, and with it seventy angels corresponding to seventy nations, each having the language of his people and the characters of its writing in his hand. He scattered them thence upon the face of all the earth into seventy languages, so that one did not know what the other said, and they killed one another." [Gen. 11:6–13][9]

While there are occasional mentions of 72 languages in Hebrew and Aramaic sources, the preferred number in the Judaic visions of political division in the world is clearly the "round" number 70.[10] For Christian culture, conversely, the languages, the nations, and the lands they inhabit have been 72 from the beginning. Arno Borst, in his monumental four-volume study of the Tower of Babel, contends that the first direct articulation of the idea of 72 languages appeared in the second half of the second century in a treatise by Irenaeus entitled *Adversus haereses* (3.22.3)[11] Thereafter, the same interpretation was reiterated by scores of early Christian authors, from Clement of Alexandria (150–220) and Eusebius of Caesarea (ca. 260–ca. 340) to Epiphanius of Constance (315–403).[12] The best-known and most elaborate of these interpretive efforts was the exegetical labor of Augustine (354–430) to arrive at the number 72 through creative computations of the genealogies of Noah after the Flood.[13]

Once clothed with exegetical authority, the topos disseminated freely across the Christian lands, leaving its mark on both written texts and the oral lore.[14] The Slavic lands and lore are no exception. Slavic medieval chronicles, when they include the Tower of Babel episode, usually designate the number of resulting languages as 72. *Codex Laurentianus* (1377), the oldest representative text of the Kievan chronicle, sets the precedent for this practice: "And the Lord God descended, seeing the city and the tower. And said the Lord, 'This is one tribe and one language.' And God confused the languages, and divided them into 72, and dispersed them across the earth."[15]

The popular apocryphon *Discourse of Sybil*, a prophesy about the coming of Christ and the resultant rise and fall of nations, contains the following divine commandment: "Whatever you have received from me, divide among the 72 peoples."[16] We have already encountered the same topos—together with its spatial corollary, the 72 big islands—in the erotapocritical entry, "How many are the names of God," that appears in late Slavonic versions of the *Discourse of the Three Hierarchs*. Entries from other Slavonic collections of questions and answers provide additional examples. Consider, for example, the following text, which spins its cosmological proposition around the 72 islands in the sea:

> John asked, "How many are the big islands?"
>
> Basil said, "72, and just as many are the different languages, and just as many are the different kinds of fish, and just as many are the different kinds of birds, and just as many are the different kinds of trees."[17]

A shorter version of the same entry reads laconically, "How many are the big islands?"—"72, and in those islands, the different languages are 72."[18]

The topos, however, is not restricted to this specific erotapocritical context. The *Discourse of Our Lord Jesus Christ*, a different collection of questions and answers that was compiled most probably in thirteenth-century Bulgaria, declares directly, "So that you know: there are only 72 languages in the world,"[19] and the *Razumnik-Ukáz*, another popular erotapocritical compilation possibly of the same provenance, echoes this message no less emphatically: "Tell me, how do we count the languages? . . . All languages are 72."[20] Finally, the topos lends itself to a number of magical formulas, which abound in Slavic apocryphal prayers. A popular prayer associated with the name of the Holy Martyr Cyprian of Carthage contains the following formula for exorcising evil spirits: "As it has been written in the 72 languages, be loosed!"[21] The standard locution that enlists a superior authority, "as it has been written," is extended here by the topos "the 72 languages" as if to multiply that transcendent authority 72 times, expanding it over all corners of the human world. This tendency toward complete coverage, by the way, is one of the signatures of magical discourse, as both the amulet *The 72 Names of God* and the exorcism of the 72 diseases reveal much more extensively.

The Septuagint

The idea about the 72 languages underlies also the popular legend about the Greek translation of the Hebrew Bible. The chief source of the legend is the *Letter of Aristeas*, an account from the first or second century BCE (though it purports to have been written soon after the narrated events, in the mid-third century BCE).[22] The legend takes us to the Alexandrian court of King Ptolemy Philadelphus (285–47 BCE). As part of a grand initiative to collect all the books in the world, Ptolemy turned to the High Priest of Jerusalem, Eleazar, for assistance in translating the Jewish Law into Greek. Eleazar selected 72 learned men, 6 from each Israelite tribe,[23] and dispatched them together with a copy of the Torah to Alexandria, where they quickly accomplished their task. The result was a superb translation that in the following centuries became the standard for the Christian world.[24]

The translation came down in history by a peculiar name that is in fact a number: *Septuaginta Duo* (literally, "the seventy-two"), or simply *Septuaginta* (as in the English Septuagint), whenever the "round" number 70 is favored.[25] The fact that the translation is named after the number of its translators is hardly surprising, however, in the context of the original legendary account, for Aristeas deliberately impresses that number on us. The *Letter* includes a list of the translators' names that pointedly concludes with the formula, "all of them 72."[26] Still more emphatically, it claims that the number of the translators was matched by the length of the translation process which lasted exactly 72 days. The text thus characteristically transposes onto time the 72-partiteness of its central corporeal concept (the group of the 72 translators), not unlike the cynocephalus myth, where a body of 72 parts is said to die in the course of 72 days. And, as in the Egyptian myth, the numerical coincidence is considered both meaningful and revelatory. The text intimates the workings of a providential design: "And so it happened, that the work of translation was finished in 72 days, just *as if it had been planned that way.*"[27]

Aristeas's emphasis on the number was evidently not lost on his readers: later sources drawing on his account extend his symmetrical design even further. Most significant in this respect is the elaboration of Irenaeus, the Bishop of Lyons (ca. 115–ca. 202). In an attempt to shift to the center of the legend the divine nature of the translation, an idea that is only secondary in the *Letter*, Irenaeus claims in *Adversus haereses* (3.21.2) that the translators worked not in counsel with one another but in complete isolation. Having worked for 72 days in 72 separate cells, they delivered in the end 72 perfectly identical Greek texts. Thus they proved to be not philologists (like Aristeas's "learned men") but prophets, channels through whom the Lord spoke his will, expanding the Mosaic covenant at Sinai over those who do not know the tongue of Moses.[28]

It is also significant that the Septuagint legend deliberately cultivates a symbolic aura around the number 72. It appears in the story not by chance but by intent, as it is already projected in the letter of Ptolemy to Eleazar "requesting that he send six elders from each of the tribes."[29] The fact that Ptolemy (which is to say Aristeas, whoever he was) chose to configure 72 as the product of 12 and 6 fixes its contextual symbolism in a very particular way. Twelve is the number of the Israelite tribes that descended from the sons of Jacob, and, since God created the world in six days (Genesis 1), six is thought of as the perfect number of creation.[30] Thus the number of translators serves as an index to the universalistic ambition behind the translation itself: to make the Law of the Jewish people available to all Creation.

The belief that there are exactly 72 human languages in the world, though never explicated in the source narratives, must have reinforced the same ecumenical message from the background. When read with that interpretive key in mind, the legend suggests that each of the translators stands not only for one sixth of each Israelite tribe, but also for one of all the languages and nations in the world. The 72 translators, in other words, can be seen as representing both all Israelites and all of humanity.

The 72 Disciples of Christ

The case of the Septuagint translation illustrates how the number 72, traditionally symbolizing a limit or boundary for Jews and Christians, could imply also a comprehensive multitude ("many" or "all"). Like the translators of the Hebrew Bible, any group of 72, being structurally homologous to the populated world, could not only become a representative body of mankind, but could, by extension, signify the very idea of totality. These classes thus form a chain of equivalencies, for they share—albeit on a different scale—the 72-fold matrix of mankind, and this structural identity allows them to function not only as a synecdoche of the human world (its *pars pro toto* representation), but also as functional equivalents of one another in representing totality. (Note that the potential of this "representation" mechanism is already present in the cynocephalus myth, especially in the version that explicitly divides the body of the animal into 72 parts.)

This second meaning of 72 is, in a manner of speaking, corporate: it has to do with composite bodies, with bodies in parts. The human body—or the body of the cynocephalus—consists of 72 members; 72 peoples make up the human race; 72 translators of the Bible are selected in half dozens from each of the 12 tribes of Israel to match the number of human languages. This internal differentiation, sometimes articulated as grouping or nesting within the list, sets the groups of 72 apart from other, undistinguished multitudes as symbolized, for example, by the number fifty.[31] We may say that 72 thus quantifies the idea of totality or exhaustive plenitude, and functions as the numerical symbol of the definitive flock, the archetypal clan, the ideal quorum.

Of particular interest to us here are those aggregates of 72 separate individuals that embody what Pierre Bourdieu calls "the social power of representation."[32] By a *fictitio juris* typical of social magic, these groups of 72 representatives exist as social bodies that transcend the biological bodies of which they are made. Thus the group of Septuagint translators consists of 72 biological bodies, but they stand for, act for, speak for all the members of the 12 tribes of Israel who have delegated them to their task. Bourdieu dubs such a representational body *"corpus corporatum in corpore corporatio,"*[33] foregrounding in a playful pun what I have called above the corporate aspect of the traditional Judeo-Christian allegoresis of the number 72.

The 72 disciples of Christ, who form the central representative body of this type in Christian culture, are set apart from the rest of the 72-fold classes by virtue of their superior status. While the other 72-based topoi employed by Christian culture are only "successful immigrants" in it, the class of the 72 disciples is Christian par excellence, being personally legitimated by Christ in the New Testament: "After this the Lord appointed seventy[-two] others and sent them on ahead of Him in pairs to every town and place where he himself intended to go.... The seventy[-two] returned with joy, saying, 'Lord, in your name even the demons submit to us!'" (Luke 10:1, 17).

As I pointed out above, the early Greek evidence and the subsequent vernacular versions of Luke use interchangeably the "precise" number 72 and the "round" number 70, which is hardly surprising given the cultural synonymy of the two numbers. This otherwise habitual fluctuation is highly unusual, however, as part of the scriptural tradition, and the anomaly has intrigued biblical scholars for decades, giving rise to various speculations.[34]

In an open polemic with Bruce Metzger in 1960, Sidney Jellicoe offered a rather plausible hypothesis that ties together several lines of our own investigation.[35] His premise is that the possible sources of the number in the

Gospel of Luke should be sought among the texts that were relevant and authoritative for his contemporary Christian-oriented Hellenistic milieu (first century CE). Among such texts, Jellicoe singles out the *Letter of Aristeas*. He argues that the solid authority of this document at the time, coupled with the well-attested affection of Luke for the Septuagint text, makes it a likely intertext, from which it follows that the number of disciples in Luke's original was probably 72.[36] He goes on to suggest that the numerical parallelism between the Septuagint translators and Christ's disciples is justified by the comparable soteriological significance of their respective endeavors: "Just as the seventy-two emissaries of Aristeas had, by their translation, brought the knowledge of the Law to the Greek-speaking world, so the Seventy (-two) are divinely commissioned to proclaim its fulfillment in the Gospel message" (321).

Such an assumption is in accord with the patristic reading of Luke in the universalistic vein of Jesus's final charge to the apostles according to the Gospel of Matthew: "And Jesus came and said to them, 'All authority in heaven and on earth has been given to me. Go therefore and make disciples of all nations, baptizing them in the name of the Father and of the Son and of the Holy Spirit, and teaching them to obey everything that I have commanded you'" (Matt. 28:18–20).[37] Matthew singles out the evangelization of "all nations" as the central apostolic mission after the Resurrection. The standard patristic interpretation of Luke 10 brings out the underlying numerical symmetry between the extended apostolic body of the 72 and "all nations" to which they are commissioned. Whatever was divided at Babel, in other words, is to be put together in Christ through continual apostolic work, until the day of Final Judgment, when the initial unity of the human race will be restored in full. Such is the soteriological promise of the Christian Church of which the 12 and the 72 followers of Christ are both models and makers.[38]

Whereas the names of the 12 apostles are given in the Gospels of Matthew and Mark,[39] the Gospel of Luke provides only the number of the disciples, unstable as it is. As a result, various lists identifying the seventy (-two) by name have been compiled to fill in that conspicuous gap. The first such list appears in the *Chronicon Paschale*, a historiographic text written about the year 650 CE. It opens with the names of Matthias (Acts 1:23–26), Sosthenes, Cephas, Linus (2 Tim. 4:21), and Cleopas (Luke 24:18), then includes the names of the twenty-six to whom Paul sent his salutations in Romans 16:3–23, and concludes with thirty-nine other names selected from the Acts and some other Pauline letters.[40] The principal Greek catalogues of this type enumerate 70 disciples and are attributed in their headings to Dorotheus, Epiphanius, or Hyppolytus.[41] Bruce Metzger documents an alternative tradition, recorded also in an anonymous Graeco-Syrian index and attributed either to Hyppolytus or Logothetes, which lists 72 disciples.[42]

Such lists were widespread throughout the Christian world. As we would expect, the Slavonic tradition documents only catalogues of 72 disciples, in accord with the standard Slavonic translation of Luke 10. The earliest Slavic example of this text is found in the famous *Symeonic Florilegium* from 1073 and represents a Slavonic version of the Greek text attributed to Hippolytus. The text appears in the context of several chronological lists representing the major events of sacred history through names of emblematic people from Adam to the latest Byzantine emperors. This indexical corpus also includes two lists of Old Testament prophets, both attributed to Epiphanius of Cyprus (fols. 254r–254v; fols. 254v–261r), as well as another pseudo-Hippolytus list of the 12 apostles with a brief summary of their exploits (fols. 261r–262r).

The Slavonic list of the disciples appears with relative frequency in varied textual surroundings. *Florilegia* and iconographic manuals are its most usual sites, though the text is appended to liturgical codices with the same ease with which it appears as a building block in the amulet corpora of sacronymic lists. Three of the nine copies familiar to me are anonymous; in the others the attribution fluctuates between Hippolytus and Dorotheus of Tyre. Put together, the three versions of the text present a rather unstable repertory of names.[43]

The Ideal Quorum

In one of the most conceptually dense and factually rich articles on the Judeo-Christian symbolism of 72, Joseph Baumgarten argues that the representative judicial bodies of the ancient Israelites were all structured on a duodecimal principle.[44] His conclusions illuminate the assembly of the 72 disciples from an unexpected angle, revealing that its structure is modeled directly on the principles of political representation in ancient Judea and, specifically, the structure of the acting Israelite court from the time of the historical Jesus. This structural symmetry is hardly surprising, of course, since it reflects a functional similarity. The mission of the 72 was not only to evangelize all nations (cf. Luke 10:8–9: "Whenever you enter a town and its people welcome you, . . . say to them, 'The Kingdom of God has come near to you'"), but also to pronounce judgment *(krisis)* upon those who refused to receive the Good News from them:

But whenever you enter a town and they do not welcome you, go out into the streets and say, "Even the dust of your town that clings to your feet, we wipe off in protest against you. Yet know this: the kingdom of God has come near." I tell you, on that day it will be more tolerable for Sodom than for that town.

Woe to you, Chorazin! Woe to you, Bethsaida! For if the deeds of power done in you had been done in Tyre and Sidon, they would have repented long ago, sitting in sackcloth and ashes. But at the judgment it will be more tolerable for Tyre and Sidon than for you. And you, Capernaum, will you be exalted to heaven? No, you will be brought down to Hades.

Whoever listens to you listens to me, and whoever rejects you, rejects me, and whoever rejects me rejects the one who sent me. [Luke 10:10–16]

This eschatological function of the 72 disciples makes it a representative body of a distinctly judicial type. It should not surprise us, therefore, that its structure reflects existing legal models in the Israelite world.

According to Baumgarten's argument, the duodecimal structure of the Israelite courts is motivated both by the number of the Israelite tribes and by the idea of proportional representation. In order to represent proportionally the 12 tribes of Israel, any advisory body has to be composed of one or more panels of 12 members each. Thus both the council of the Qumran community (according to the *pesher* on Isa. 54:11–12) and the elders in Revelation 21 consist of two groups of 12 members. The Qumran elders include, first, 12 priests who represent the spiritual authority of the community and, second, 12 heads of tribes who embody earthly power. Similarly, the eschatological court of the last days in Revelation 21 comprises the 12 angels of the tribes and the 12 apostles.[45] The doubling of the representative panel invests the institution with a specific symbolic meaning in each case: the conflation of secular and sacred power in the first; the unity of the old and the new "people of the Lord" in the second. Yet in both cases this reduplication reflects a clear-cut structural symmetry between the organization of the heavenly and earthly orders, a significant chiasmic principle of the Judaic cosmological imagination that finds its most succinct formula in the rabbinic maxim "As above, so below."[46]

The two levels of rabbinical courts, the Small and the Great Sanhedrin, are structured by the same principle, contends Baumgarten.[47] He posits behind the local Sanhedrin's traditional quorum of 23 an original quorum of 24, which was reduced by one member, presumably to avoid a tie. In a similar manner, Baumgarten argues that the supreme judicial body of the

Israelites, the Great Sanhedrin, originally held 72 members, though it was reduced to the more practical odd-numbered quorum of 71.

Positing 72 as the original quorum of the Sanhedrin contradicts, on the face of it, the traditional assumption that it was in fact 70, since it was based on the number of the Elders of Moses who were as many as the descendants of Israel.[48] Baumgarten, however, unmasks an ambiguity right at the heart of the rabbinic tradition about the number of the Elders. A weighty body of rabbinic evidence sets the number at 72 instead, thus opening the door for speculation that the origin of the duodecimal principle of representation could be pushed even further back in the Judaic past, all the way to the time of the Ten Commandments. The compact presentation of Baumgarten's evidence deserves to be quoted here in full:

> Simeon b. Azzai recalled a gathering of seventy-two sages at Yabneh. R. Joshua, in his interpretation of Exodus 18:18, portrayed the court of Moses as consisting of seventy-two members, including Moses and Aaron. Elsewhere the seventy elders themselves are seen as representing the twelve tribes, with an original quorum of seventy-two, six from each tribe, but with the subsequent elimination of the two by lot. This was suggested to the rabbis by the story of Eldad and Medad in Numbers 11[:26], who were originally inscribed among the elders. It is also noteworthy that in Exodus 24:14 Aaron and Hur were assigned to preside over the seventy elders during the ascent of Moses to Mt. Sinai, thus assuring a quorum of seventy-two.[49]

Baumgarten places the quorum of the Great Sanhedrin along the same tradition and interprets its duodecimal structure as composed of six panels of representatives from each tribe, a formula of proportional representation already familiar to us from *The Letter of Aristeas*.[50] The logic behind the principle "six from each of the twelve," however, is not immediately obvious, and Baumgarten is not concerned with it, though the formula itself seems to be commonplace in a number of contexts, not all of them directly related to political representation. Apart from *The Letter of Aristeas* and the rabbinic source about the 72 elders quoted by Baumgarten, both Judaic and Christian exegetes apply the same formula to the relation between the 12 precious stones on the breastplate (Exod. 28:15–21) and the bells on the robe of the high priest that are said to be 72, six bells for each stone (Exod. 28:33). For the Christian hermeneutical tradition, the stones and the bells prefigure the two groups of Christ's emissaries, the 12 apostles and the 72 disciples,[51] while for the Kabbalistic *Book of Bahir* the 12 stones that are also 72 [bells]—as many as the 72 names of God—represent the 12 leaders of the 72 human languages:

> [There are therefore] 12 stones [each containing six names] making total of 72. These parallel the 72 names of the Blessed Holy One.
>
> Why do they begin with twelve? This teaches us that God has twelve Directors. Each of these has six Powers [making the total of 72].
>
> What are they? The 72 languages."[52]

In all these cases, we have a group of 72 members that represents a group of twelve. How are we to account for such a six-fold representation? What is misleading in this case is the fact that 6 is half of 12, which prompts us to assume that the quotient of representation (6) is somehow dependent on the number of the represented units (12). (Baumgarten's placement of the 12-tribe structure at the core of his duodecimal vision of political representation seems to follow the same logic.) Contrary to this assumption, I suggest that the representation by six has little to do with the number of the tribes or stones or apostles. Rather, it is directly dependent on the cultural dominance of the duodecimal system of calculation (which was probably responsible, in turn, for the proliferation of all those groups of 12 as well, though that should not concern us for the moment).

What are the practical implications of such a shift? It implies that in all the cases that interest us the coefficient of representation is a power of the base 12 (instead of our customary base 10). For the first order of representation, the coefficient is the base to power zero, which is one. In the case of the 12 tribes of Israel, such a level of minimal representation requires one representative from each tribe, or a quorum of 12 members. For the second order, the coefficient will be the base 12 to the first power, or 144 members total, 12 from each tribe. Instead of this maximal representation, however, the Jewish political bodies of late antiquity apparently required as sufficient quorum half of this number (or 50 percent of this assembly, if you prefer). Now, put in such terms, the principle "six from each tribe" does not appear so strange to us anymore, since the quorum of 50 percent of the assembly (plus or minus one, to avoid a tie) is still the standard for a simple majority in our modern culture and the basis of operation for many political institutions.

We may conclude that the number 12 was significant for Judaic political culture in two distinct ways. First and foremost, it was the base of calculation in the duodecimal code that provided the basic matrix for ordering. Second, it was the base number of the political division of the Israelites who envisioned their ideal polis as comprising 12 tribes. Because of this double significance of 12, Baumgarten's argument about the centrality of the duo-decimal code for Judeo-Christian political representation runs deeper than he perhaps imagined.

All of this interests us here, however, from a very specific angle and in a very limited sense. As I have tried to demonstrate above, the absolute quorum for a political assembly of a second order of representation in this cultural context should be 12 × 12, or 144. Instead of this number, however, we consistently encounter its half, 72, as the quorum of various political bodies. This practice suggests that 50 percent of the ideal assembly (an equivalent to our simple majority) was considered sufficient, provided that the principle of proportional representation ("six from each tribe") was being observed. The number 72 thus assumed the function of the ideal quorum in (at least one version of) the Judeo-Christian vision of order, an order that governed in late antiquity both functional political bodies, such as the rabbinic courts, and symbolic assemblies, such as the tribunal of the Christ for the Last Day of Judgment.[53]

CHAPTER EIGHT

The Peculiar Codex *Jerusalem 22*

We began our exploration of the number 72 from the Slavonic erotapocritical text "How many are the names of God?" To this text we now return to address some of our earlier conjectures and concerns. Let us recall the available facts. The idea that the Lord has 72 names appears in the Slavic material in two seemingly independent contexts. The first is the erotapocritical entry itself, a highly informative conceptual summary that is extant, unfortunately for us, only in two eighteenth-century copies. The second is the amulet "These are the names of the Lord, 72 in number," whose extant traces are older, going back as far as the late thirteenth century, and much more numerous. Both texts place a strong emphasis on the concept of the 72 names. While the question-and-answer text proposes an entire cosmological program of perfect symmetrical order that is based on the number of the names, the amulet advertises the names themselves as a potent protection against every evil.

The point where the two contexts come together and suggest a possible direct relationship is the extremely peculiar codex MS Slav *Jerusalem 22* from 1498.[1] A section in this codex seems to represent a mixed or transitional form of the erotapocritical summary that features the first two topoi, the 72 names of the Lord and the 72 names of the Theotokos, in the form of lists.[2] Since, in the material familiar to us, the amulet text precedes the question-and-answer entry by almost three centuries, we cannot safely posit its direct dependence on the erotapocritical material. Instead, we could treat *Jerusalem 22*, if not necessarily as a plausible source for the question and its answer, then at least as an earlier offshoot from the same genealogical line, an offshoot that is closer to the putative common source and, because of that, more revealing of it.

The Facts

It is unfortunate that we know very little about the immediate context in which *Jerusalem 22* was compiled and used. Not only is the provenance of the codex unknown, but all scholars who have worked with it pointedly restrain themselves from proposing hypotheses about its origin.[3] All we know for certain is that the manuscript was apparently put together in 1498, as it was dated by the scribe in the colophon.[4] Our other reliable clue is the fact that by 1887, when the Russian philologist Nikolai Krasnosel'tsev first described the monument for scholarly purposes, it had made its way to the Library of the Greek Orthodox Patriarchate in Jerusalem from Jerusalem's Monastery of the Holy Cross.[5]

In the absence of any more specific information, our most reliable clue to the history of this monument comes from its language, which points if not necessarily to the origin of the codex itself then certainly to the origin of its scribe (or scribes).[6] The codex documents, earlier than does any other written source, a very specific dialectal feature of South Slavic: the replacement of etymological *u* by *o* in all positions, including under stress (e.g., *postine* for *poustine*, fol. 282v; *nedozi* for *nedouzi*, fol. 131r). This feature, which occurs sporadically in such important early modern monuments as the *Tikhonravov Damaskin* and the famous nineteenth-century *Kulakia Gospel*, has been linked by dialectologists to only a handful of settlements in Macedonia. Those places include several villages between Gotse Delchev (Southwestern Bulgaria) and Drama (Northern Greece), the town Tría Élata (Slav. Leskovo) in the Meglen district, and several key towns along the old Via Egnatia in Northern Greece: Edhessa (Slav., Voden), Yianitsá (Slav., Enidzhe Vardar), and Khalastra (Slav., Kulakia), near Salonica.[7]

Based on this fairly reliable linguistic index, we may safely assume that wherever the codex was actually written, its scribes must have originated from that particular part of Slavic Macedonia. This leaves us with two rather distant geographic coordinates for our text, Salonica and Jerusalem, which, at the end of the fifteenth century, did not lie as far apart on the socioeconomic and cultural map as we might imagine today. Via Egnatia remained the most important artery in the Balkan Peninsula throughout the Middle Ages, a road that connected not only Constantinople to the Adriatic coast and Rome, but also the heart of the Balkans to Salonica. And Salonica itself had emerged in the fifteenth century as a major port of the Ottoman Empire in Europe, which made it a gathering point for Balkan pilgrims to the Holy Land and a place of departure for many secular travelers to Palestine. Our codex originated somewhere in the general area determined by these two coordinates and by the cultural dynamic that characterized the communication between them.

If the dialectal features of the manuscript point to the place of the scribes' origin, the peculiar body of texts that they left behind reveals much about the context that shaped their cultural and religious sensibilities, and, presumably, those of their intended audience. We can tell right away, just by looking at the book, that the scribes were neither well-trained in book copying nor particularly careful about the task at hand. The codex is sloppily written, crudely decorated, and rubricated only minimally with cheap (copper-based) ink. The often illegible handwriting, the inconsistent orthography, and the numerous errors and nonsensical passages all point to a rather inexperienced hand. Yet there is one area in which our scribes appear to be almost experts of sorts, and that is heteropraxis. They seem to be not only very well-informed about noncanonical religious practices that border on magic, but also particularly interested in amassing texts that document them. The codex is unanimously considered one of the oldest and richest Slavonic sources of "false prayers" and outright magical texts that, if known at all from other sources, are usually documented elsewhere from a much later time.[8]

The codex is routinely described as an incomplete Book of Hours, though the strictly horological part constitutes only one-fifth of the manuscript. About a quarter of the codex consists of noncanonical prayers, incantations, apotropaic formulas, and magical figures, as well as various books of divination, sometimes represented by more than one version of each.[9] The entire selection of texts in this part reveals an overwhelming concern with health and general household well-being. The context is clearly domestic (most probably urban) life, and the medium of choice is preventive and curative magic. All of this suggests a nonmonastic context for both the origin of the codex and its intended use.

A Kabbalistic Hypothesis

In his description of the codex, Krasnosel'tsev mentions in passing that it exhibits Kabbalistic traits.[10] *Kabbalah* (literally meaning "tradition" in Hebrew), is usually used as a cover term for the esoteric teachings of Jewish mysticism, and especially the forms they assumed from the twelfth century onward within the Diaspora in Europe.[11] It is highly unlikely, however, that Krasnosel'tsev meant to suggest an early influence of the Kabbalistic *doctrine* on the Orthodox Slavs. As a doctrine, the Kabbalah remained practically unknown outside the insulated circles of the Kabbalistic elite until the very end of the fifteenth century, when, as a result of events contemporaneous with our codex but evolving in an entirely different cultural universe, it was "discovered" by the Italian humanists and gradually transformed into a common intellectual currency of Christian Europe. I assume that Krasnosel'tsev was referring instead to the so-called practical Kabbalah.[12]

What exactly is this "practical" branch of the Judaic tradition? Apart from mystical instructions and speculative propositions, the Kabbalah commands an unusually large spectrum of heterogeneous elements, including a rather old stratum of magical practices that considerably predate the speculative superstructure above them. In fact, the first historical uses of the term *Kabbalah* were related specifically to those magical practices that later came to be known as the *practical* Kabbalah.[13] The focus of this Kabbalistic realm of magic is the protective power of God's esoteric names, and its representative form is the written amulet. That is why its specialists were called "masters of the name," men who knew how to make amulets that list all the right names to ward off evil. The cosmological program that frames these practices is in many respects akin to Gnosticism, with a strong dualistic undercurrent and a taste for polar oppositions and gender-based symmetry. It is in this realm that the distinctly Kabbalistic feeling for the reality of evil and the horror of the demonic takes center stage, an element that, according to Scholem, is most responsible for the mass appeal of this otherwise hermetic, esoteric, and elitist doctrine.[14] And, expectedly, being the most permissive among the forms of Kabbalistic practices, it is also the least exclusive of them, letting in and out through its relatively porous boundaries enough traffic to make transconfessional exchange—wherever external conditions allow it—more than a merely theoretical possibility. I presume that Krasnosel'tsev's claim about a possible Kabbalistic background for our codex suggests an exchange of that particular kind.

Such a reading is supported by the general orientation of *Jerusalem 22* toward protective and prognostic magic. It also agrees with the presumable provenance of the codex, since the zone between the Balkans (Salonica) and Palestine (Jerusalem) points precisely to the cultural territory that Moses Gaster characterizes as the center of the practical Kabbalah.[15] Moreover, the situation of the Balkans at the end of the fifteenth century not only provided numerous opportunities for cultural contacts between Slavs and Jews, but also particularly encouraged the production and consumption of amulets.

The Balkan Context

Jerusalem 22 was compiled at a time of profound and traumatic changes for the Balkans. By the end of the fifteenth century, most of the peninsula was already engulfed by the Ottoman Empire. In less than a century after 1354, when the Ottoman Turks first established themselves on the European mainland at Gallipoli, the region experienced an endless succession of military losses and political catastrophes. In 1389, the Ottoman sultan Murad I defeated the united Christian forces led by the Serbian prince Lazar at Kossovo. The Bulgarian capital Turnovo was sacked in 1393, and the fall of Vidin three years later put an end to the Bulgarian kingdom. The strategic port of Salonica was captured after a fierce battle in 1430. Another defeat of the united Christian armies followed at Varna in 1444. Then, in 1453, came the greatest Ottoman victory in Europe: the fall of Constantinople. Mehmed II (1451–81), known as The Conqueror, placed a Muslim crescent on the central dome of Hagia Sophia and proclaimed himself the heir of the Byzantine emperors. Constantinople became a capital of a very different kind under the new name of Istanbul, and both the Eastern Roman Empire and the Middle Ages effectively came to a close.[16]

Under the new political conditions, the religious life of the Eastern Orthodox Balkan communities was turned completely upside-down. From a dominant religious group in a relatively homogeneous confessional environment, they were transformed into one of the several religious minorities within a cosmopolitan Islamic empire. A number of autocephalous Eastern Orthodox churches were brought to an end under the new *millet* system of administration, implemented by Mehmed after the fall of Constantinople to centralize the political power of the Empire against the threat of its rapidly growing non-Islamic population.[17] According to the new system, all religious minorities in the Empire were organized into semiautonomous administrative units called *millets* (nations) based on a confessional principle.[18] Thus all the disparate Eastern Orthodox communities were lumped together as the millet of Rum (from *Romaioi*, literally "Romans," but "Greek" in Byzantine usage) under the jurisdiction of the Greek ecumenical patriarch.[19] In a similar way, the representatives of all Oriental Churches were united under the Armenian patriarch who, like the Greek patriarch and the chief rabbi for all the Jews in the empire, resided within the city walls of the Ottoman capital in close proximity to the Islamic authorities of the ulema. We can imagine that this reform, though designed in the spirit of religious tolerance and formally providing enough room for relative religious freedom, had a number of disruptive consequences for the actual religious life of the Empire's Christians.[20] The artificial lumping together of formerly autonomous churches and of variegated Orthodox communities who worshiped in different languages inevitably lead to the decline of ecclesiastical power, the deterioration of existing networks of communication and control, and the general slackening of doctrinal and sacramental norms.[21]

While the lives of the Balkan Slavs were being turned upside down by the Ottoman invasion, the Jews in the Balkans were dealing with a cataclysm of their own. A series of expulsions of Sephardic Jews had been going on in Western Europe since the fourteenth century, and the Ottoman Empire, renowned for its relative religious tolerance and its particularly favorable attitude toward the Jews, had become the preferred destination for the refugees.[22] The exodus reached its peak after 1492 when the banishment edict of Ferdinand and Isabella of Spain was followed by the expulsion of Jews from almost all Western European states and principalities. Most of the Sephardim settled in the Balkan part of the empire, and many of them went to Salonica, a city with a traditionally large and stable Jewish population.[23] This "new Jerusalem," as the grateful newcomers dubbed the city, soon became the fastest growing Jewish center in the empire (by 1520 Jews made up more than 50 percent of its population), and one of the most vibrant European centers of Sephardic culture, which flourished there in all its forms, including the Kabbalah.

We should bear in mind that, even though the saga of the Sephardic exodus found an overall happy ending in the Ottoman lands, exile is always a wrenching ordeal, a jump into the unknown that is heavy with fear, pain, nostalgia, and a sense of displacement and isolation. When exile is radical, an expulsion of the entire community, the personal tragedy is magnified by a collective trauma that takes generations to heal. We should remember as well that every cataclysm of this proportion brings about numerous small, isolated collisions on a local scale. In this case, the potential for local conflicts was rich: between the newcomers and the "old" Jews in the Balkans, between the local Christians and their new Jewish neighbors, among all the Jews, growing in number, and the Islamic establishment, even among the different Sephardic groups that came from disparate parts of Europe, bringing along their own baggage of local customs and ways of life.

In a word, for both Jews and Slavs in the Balkans, the end of the fifteenth century was a time of crisis, of drastic and traumatic changes that fostered a general atmosphere of chaos, uncertainty, and doom. That prevalent mood was reinforced by a millennialism that exploded because of the coincidence of the projected end of the world in 1492 (the end of the seventh millennium according to the old Babylonian calendar) and the events in Spain.[24]

The Balkan scene at the time was also perfect for transcultural and interreligious contact. The religious authorities in each *millet* were much more concerned with the survival of the religion (especially in the face of the latent but continual danger of Islamization) than with the letter of the law. "There was far less theological policing under the Ottomans than there was in Christendom at this time," remarks historian Mark Mazower, "and this laxity of atmosphere and absence of heresy-hunters fostered the emergence of a popular religion which more than anything else in the early modern period united [the region's] diverse faiths around a common sense of the sacred and divine."[25] This tendency was reinforced by the complex demographic changes that had rearranged all traditional boundaries, putting in uncomfortable proximity disparate ethnic, linguistic, and confessional groups, and providing opportunities not only for political and economic clashes, but also for cultural transfer. We can infer that the Jews were most likely to get involved in such a dialogue, being not only the most mobile and economically active ethnic group in the sphere of exchange (the merchants, the money lenders), but also the born interpreters of the empire. "The Jews who live in Turkey ordinarily speak four or five languages," quotes Fernand Braudel from a sixteenth-century source, "and there are several who know ten or twelve. . . . Those of them who left Spain, Germany, Hungary, and Bohemia have taught the languages [of those countries] to their children; and their children have learnt the languages of the nations in which they have to live and speak, it might be Greek, Slavonic, Turkish, Arabic, Armenian, or Italian."[26]

In such turbulent times of contact and confusion, heteropraxis is by far the most logical site for religious cross-pollination. Unapologetically eclectic in its pragmatism and unchecked by a theory of its own, heteropraxis is by nature wide open to interreligious transactions. It does not discriminate among available ritual options. Its operative logic is cumulative and redundant: more of the same is better, and everything goes as long as it does the trick. In a typical "heteropractical" scenario, the parents of a gravely sick child do not feel compelled to choose between the witch-doctor, the priest, the rabbi, or the *hoja*; they try them all "just in case." This predisposition to cross-practices naturally peaks at a moment of crisis when all resources are mobilized to thwart danger and set fears to rest. Heteropraxis is thus the perfect fit for any critical situation. It thrives on adversity and misfortune, since establishing control over the crisis at hand is its main priority.

One would expect, therefore, that heteropraxis not only flourished in the fifteenth-century Balkan communities, but also provided numerous opportunities for fruitful religious exchange. We add to this picture the traditional reputation of the Jew in medieval Europe as the magician *par excellence*,[27] and the result is a religious scene where the Balkan Orthodox Slavs had at once the motive, the means, and the opportunity to procure secret, magical weapons from their Jewish neighbors. Thus, the kind of cultural transfer that

would enable elements from the practical Kabbalah to surface in the Slavonic codex *Jerusalem 22* could easily have happened in the Balkans precisely around the time of the codex's compilation.

Three Possible Kabbalistic Indices

A closer look at the noncanonical parts of the codex, and particularly those
surrounding *The 72 Names of the Lord*, confirms and specifies this conjecture. I address in some detail three possible Jewish indices in this material:
(1) the unusual proviso of our target text, *The 72 Names of the Lord*, which
recalls the original Jewish *mezuzah*; (2) the tendency to accumulate divine
and angelic names under the amuletic rubric "against every evil"; and (3) the
presence of magical figures that are characteristic of Jewish and specifically
Kabbalistic amulets.

The version of *The 72 Names of the Lord* that appears in this codex[28] includes a unique proviso: "Whoever has these divine names at home or carries
them on his person on the road or in the desert, will be saved from every evil,
and from the devil, and from evil men" (fol. 194v).[29] As I have mentioned
earlier, most copies of this amulet text explicitly require that physical contact with the names be maintained "at all times." Here, physical contact is
recommended only in situations that anthropologists call "inchoate": when
"on the road" or "in the desert"—in other words, when people are stripped of
any familiar protection that makes them feel safe.[30] Under normal conditions, the owner of the amulet should keep it "at home," presumably for the
extended protection of his or her family as well as the space they inhabit.
This untypical employment of *The 72 Names* as a "house amulet" presents
it as akin to the Jewish *mezuzah* tradition.

A *mezuzah*, in the narrow sense of the term, is a strip of parchment
inscribed with biblical verses (Deut. 6:4–19, 11:13–20) that is traditionally
placed at the doorpost of a Jewish house to ward off evil forces. Though
initially strictly "rabbinic" in both form and employment, by the fifteenth
century it had acquired a variable entourage of magical names, formulas, and
figures, and had thus become practically indistinguishable from phylacteries
proper.[31] In this contaminated form, the rabbinic ritual object migrated easily to the Gentile world, where its reputation had already titillated the popular imagination long enough to make many receptive to its charms. Joshua
Trachtenberg's book on Jewish magic offers several amusing examples of religious cross-breeding that characterize the Christian appropriation of Jewish *mezuzot*.[32] That mutation, in turn, allowed for some characteristics of
the *mezuzot* (such as their association with the doorpost and the protection

of the house) to surface in other written amulets, thus blurring the genre distinctions from the other side. With all this in mind, we may take the emphasis on protecting the home in the proviso of the Jerusalem copy as a clue that the actual performance of the Slavonic *72 Names of the Lord* was shaped in a mixed Judeo-Slavic milieu.

The codex also includes the oldest known Slavonic copy of the popular apocryphon *Nomina Angelorum*, yet another list of sacronyms delegated specifically to magical protection.[33] It is common knowledge that, whatever their exact origin, angels entered the Christian world as a Jewish family and that, no matter how well they assimilated into the Christian context, no Gentile culture ever assumed the extravagant profusion and creativity of Jewish angelology.[34] The copious production and cataloguing of angelic nomenclature, in particular, has always remained one of the trademarks of Jewish religious culture.[35] Recognizably Semitic as they might be in origin and name, however, angels stopped being an exclusively Jewish currency as early as Hellenistic times, and by the Middle Ages Judaic angelological terms and ideas had been diffused over such a vast territory that it is now close to impossible to trace the specific sources for any Slavic compilation of angelic names. The selection of angel terms in *Jerusalem 22* is no exception in this respect, being a combination of names for universally known and respected archangels such as Michael, Gabriel, Uriel, and Raphael, and cryptically corrupted terms that lead us nowhere because we can place them wherever we wish.[36]

A much more promising lead is offered by the proviso of the list and its position in the codex. Instead of its usual pragmatic instruction "against fear," *Nomina Angelorum* is prefaced here by the proviso: "Carry these names on your person and you will be saved from every evil." This instruction recalls the most recognizable formula of *The 72 Names of the Lord*, a text, incidentally, that appears right after the list of angelic names in this codex. We may assume that in this early appearance the two lists were thought of as bound together in a common amulet block that provides a particularly potent magic defense.

The overt linking together of angelic and divine names in a common apotropaic gesture has a long-standing tradition in Jewish religious praxis, where angels function as envoys through whom God lets humans know and experience his will.[37] As inhabitants of the "middle world" between the divine and the human, angels are far more accessible than the divinity, and so communication with the upper sphere often goes through them. A key requirement for easy access to an angel, however, is the knowledge of his name, for the name, as Trachtenberg notes, is "the controlling factor."[38]

Names of angels, in other words, function as a remote control of the divine: by invoking the names, humans push, in a manner of speaking, different buttons on high to make their wishes come true. And this explains the particular zeal with which scribes pursued the task of amassing names of angels in extravagant proportions, and why practitioners use them generously in any form of protective magic, including written amulets.

There is one peculiarity about the names of angels in Judaic practice, though: they are not a clear cult category. Already in the *hekhalot* tradition of early Jewish mysticism, the names of angels and those of God himself blended with ease and almost without barriers because, as the popular formula went, "the servants are adjured with their king's name."[39] That is why the literature of Jewish magic consists almost entirely of divine and angelic names lumped together. There is only a scholastic distinction between the two, with hardly any practical significance. And in the real practices, as witnessed by the extant texts, those names are always consolidated into a common front against the powers of evil. In fact, the one mandatory component of the profanized *mezuzah* is a cluster of divine and angelic names.[40] All these practices are reflected in the codex *Jerusalem 22*, which not only establishes a Slavonic precedent for ascribing a list of angelic names to amuletic use, but also links this list directly to a list of divine names that is itself relegated to the same magic ends.

Incidentally, the codex's propensity for magical nomenclature goes beyond these two lists-amulets. Apart from *The 72 Names of the Lord*, it contains two more lists of divine names that have a similar magic application. The first follows immediately after *The 72 Names* and is marked out by the rather prohibitive heading "And these [names] you are not supposed to say except for fear of dying" (fol. 196r). It is almost identical with the heading of the text that follows *The 72 Names* in the only extant copy predating that of *Jerusalem 22* (the thirteenth-century Berlin copy), and the names themselves are related. The *Berlin Codex* lists only three names, the result of evident corruption that has transformed them into *nomina barbara*: "Anektonosh, Atanosh, Shusheg[a]dash."[41] The list in *Jerusalem 22* is longer, though the first three have a familiar ring: "Akthosh, Athalani, Shushash."

The second list appears near the end of the codex and is immediately surrounded by the magical recipes that Krasnosel'tsev explicitly relates to the Kabbalah.[42] Since the text has not been previously published or even identified, I quote it here in full:

> And these ten names of Christ in the Greek language are for battle, so
> that you are not afraid, or for a woman when she does not bear children

or when she suffers at childbirth, or for man's impotence, or for troubles of the heart, write [so as] to drink, and when going to court, write and drink and carry on your person. First name is *elfa deo*, second *pselon*, third *pelok*, fourth *savot*, fifth *psmiokh*, sixth *nomon phsesar*, seventh *pelai*, eighth *samba taniz*, ninth *alir*, tenth *psethor psebane*.[43]

This version of the popular Christian adaptation of the Judaic list of Yahweh's Ten Names is unique in the material that I know and markedly different from the version that appears as a third list of divine names in the *Berlin Codex*.[44] For one, the names are designated as Greek, while the Berlin list, in keeping with the tradition of both East and West, claims to list Hebrew names. The names in the two lists are strikingly dissimilar, though one at least could be identified as pointing to the same original title (viz. Sabaoth). The fact that the Jerusalem copy does not translate the names and at the same time renders them in a corrupted form, suggests that the antegraph, and possibly even the original source, was not Greek. The use of the name *Alpha* (*elpha deo*), one of the most commonly used Greek "names" in Jewish magic,[45] might be a clue that the original was Hebrew. Since positing a direct genealogical line based on sacred nomenclature alone is never a sure proposition, however, we can take this clue seriously only if it is heavily supported by other data.

The most interesting clue comes again from the proviso. It is built entirely on prescriptions for "drinking" the names, a magical practice that is exceedingly rare in the Slavonic repertoire of amulet texts. By contrast, we often encounter it in Jewish magic: the *Sword of Moses*, discovered and published by Moses Gaster, abounds in examples of this kind, and so do a number of early Aramaic amulets and charms.[46] In most of these cases, the text, which usually consists entirely of names, is "inscribed on a leaf and dissolved in water, which is to be drunk, or may simply be whispered over the liquid and thus imbibed."[47] And *The Ten Names of Christ* is not alone in its unusual role as "magic potion"—most of the texts that surround it in *Jerusalem 22* are magical recipes that contain similar instructions for drinking written words.[48]

The fact that a preponderance of elements in MS *Jerusalem 22* points to Jewish texts and practices of preventive magic already creates the impression that the codex might have a Jewish background. This impression is further strengthened by the presence in the codex of numerous magical figures. Incidentally, all of them are located in the part of the codex that contains *The Ten Names of Christ* and are directly related to some of the recipes that call for the ingestion of magic words. In at least one case, a recipe "for those

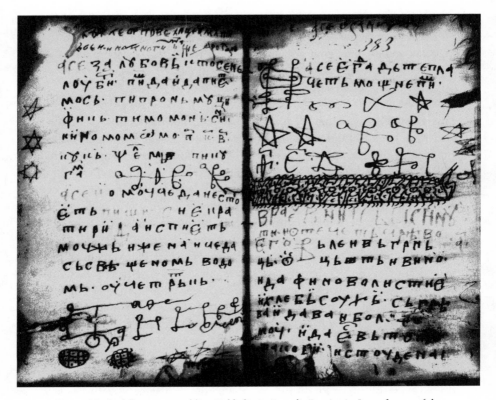

Fig. 4. Magical figures resembling Kabbalistic "angelic" script in *Jerusalem 22*, fols.
382v–383r. Reproduced by kind permission of the Library of Congress from Microfilm
#5017 Slav 22, the Libraries of the Greek and Armenian Patriarchies in Jerusalem.

whose children do not last" (fol. 382v), the figures themselves constitute the
text to be drunk as a remedy. These figures comprise not only the pentagram
("Seal of Solomon") and the hexagram ("Shield of David") that are relatively
more common in Christian magic, but also "a series of figures constructed
by joining straight and curved lines with [small] circles," particularly characteristic of Kabbalistic amulets.[49]

In summary, two text clusters in the codex abound in what I call "Jewish
indices." The first cluster (fols. 194v–197r) is a corpus of sacronymic texts
relegated to amulet use. Those texts include a list of angelic names (the earliest copy of the Slavonic apocryphon *Nomina Angelorum*); *The 72 Names
of the Lord*, with an appendix of a list of divine names that you are not supposed to say unless you fear death; and *The 72 Names of the Theotokos* (the

earliest Slavonic copy of this list-amulet), with its curious addendum about the number 72 that attracted us to the codex in the first place. A peculiar passage in the proviso of the 72 divine names tells how to use it as a "house amulet," linking it to the Jewish *mezuzah,* and its functional association with the angelic names that precede it equally points to Jewish amuletic practices. The second cluster (fols. 381r–383r) is a group of magical recipes that include a unique Slavonic version of the Ten Names entitled *The Ten Names of Christ.* These recipes incorporate a number of magical (Kabbalistic) figures and often have instructions for text ingestion that are rare in the Slavic magical repertoire but fairly common in Jewish magical texts. While one piece of evidence is by itself sufficient to link the codex (or at least these two parts) to a specifically Jewish background, the sheer preponderance of clues more than suggests such a possibility.

The Emphasis on 72

Curiously, the two parts of *Jerusalem 22* that point to a possible Jewish background of the codex exhibit an emphasis on the number 72. The first cluster introduces *The 72 Names of the Theotokos*—a text previously unattested in Slavonic sources, which is evidently modeled after *The 72 Names of the Lord.* Moreover, it concludes with the conceptual summary about the number 72 that brought us to this codex, directly recalling the 72-fold cosmological vision from the erotapocritical entry, "How many are the names of God." The second cluster, though not keyed to that number itself, is followed by a "doctor-book," a collection of medical (and often overtly magical) recipes that are conspicuously numbered in the margin as 72—a possible reference to the 72 diseases, following the familiar symmetrical pattern of one remedy for each malady (fols. 383r–399v). We have established already that the rich symbolism of 72 in the Abrahamic religions is largely Judaic in origin. If the earliest Slavonic text arranging various traditional classes of 72 members into a universal vision of order appears in a codex leading back to Judaic (and possibly Kabbalistic) magical practices, then the vision itself could have been borrowed from the same or similar Jewish sources.

This general conjecture is further supported by specific intertextual correspondences. The closest parallel to the Slavonic cosmological vision keyed to 72 that I know is a passage from the famous Renaissance compendium of magic and occult science, Cornelius Agrippa's *De occulta philosophia* (1533). The passage introduces the Kabbalistic notion of *shem ha-mephorash,* Yahweh's most powerful name of 72 combinations:

Then each of the three letters being subordinate to one another, make up one name, which are seventy-two names, which the Hebrews call *Schem-hamphorae*, to which if the divine names El or Jah be added, they produce seventy-two trisyllable divine names of angels, whereof every one carries the great name of God, as it is written "My angel shall go before thee; observe him, for my name is with him."[50] And there are those that set over the seventy-two celestial quinaries, and so many nations and tongues, and joints of man's body, and cooperate with the seventy-two seniors of the Synagogue, and so many disciples of Christ.[51]

What exactly is "*shem ha-mephorash*?" In Hebrew it literally means "the explicit name," and in mystical Judaism its status is outstanding. It is believed to be both the most powerful and the most dangerous among the esoteric names of God. This was the name by which God created the world, and there is no limit to what it can accomplish. "Whoever pronounces this name against a demon, it will vanish; at a conflagration, it will be quenched; over an invalid, he will be healed; against impure thoughts, they will be expelled; if it is directed against an enemy, he will die, and if it is uttered before a ruler, his favors will be won." But a heavy warning protects its secrets, for "whoever pronounces this name while he is in a state of uncleanness and impurity will surely be struck dead."[52]

The idea that *shem ha-mephorash* is a name of 72 parts reportedly goes back to Talmudic times.[53] It was no coincidence that the Kabbalah—as the branch of mystical Judaism that developed both the most radical theory of divine names and the most daring practice of scriptural name exegesis—would take special interest in the name of 72. And it was equally predictable that the Kabbalah's radical onomatocentrism would prove especially germane to the development of this concept into a coherent mystical doctrine. Three interrelated aspects of the Kabbalah are important in this respect. First is the link between the divine Name and the creative power of God by means of which "the universe is contained within its limits."[54] Second, there is the daring new treatment of the Torah as a mystical texture whose letters, when divided and grouped in nonconventional ways, already read not as narratives, but as series of esoteric names.[55] Third is the advancement of new types of exegesis, based on structure rather than on signification, which target the esoteric depths of the Torah and the divine order encoded in them.

Judaic lore claimed that the Name of 72 was revealed to Moses at the burning bush and that he used it to part the Red Sea during the exodus from Egypt. Since the three verses in the Torah that describe this miracle (Exod. 14:19–21) have exactly 72 Hebrew letters each, the passage was seen as a key to the mystery of the name itself. The earliest extant text that documents a reconstruction of *shem ha-mephorash* on the basis of this passage is the classical Kabbalistic work *Sefer ha-Bahir* (Book of Bahir), first made known in manuscript form in Provence between 1150 and 1200.[56] This central text of what Scholem calls the Gnostic Kabbalah is shaped as an ancient biblical commentary *(midrash)* that is focused on the divine attributes. *Bahir*'s reconstruction of the name by the *notarikon* method is a perfect illustration of Kabbalistic onomatology in action. We are to divide the passage into 72 triads of letters. The first triad is formed by the first letter of the first verse, the last letter of the second verse, and the first letter of the third verse. All the other triads follow the same pattern, using the letter of the first verse in direct order, those of the second in reverse order, and those of the third in direct order again. These 72 triads constitute the 72 combinations of the *shem ha-mephorash*.[57] The result is a very peculiar name indeed. *Bahir* calls it both "one name" and "72 names," pointing to an ambivalence about the name's morphology that remains unresolved.[58] Moreover, being a cluster of 72 consonantal triads (since ancient Hebrew script has no vowels), it not only has no linguistic meaning but is also impossible to pronounce and use discursively in ritual worship.[59] Thus it resembles a cryptogram more than anything we—or Dionysius the Areopagite—would ordinarily call a "name."[60]

Agrippa's summary in *Occulta philosophia* places this Kabbalistic name of 72 parts, with all proper references to its source passage in the Torah and its peculiar triadic structure, at the center of a cosmic vision of multiple symmetries. The 72 quinaries, or rays of the sun (6 for each of the 12 principal houses of the Zodiac), function as an astral corporate body.[61] Its 72-fold structure is reflected in the organization of the human sphere that corresponds to the 72 parts of mankind (the collective human "body" of 72 peoples or languages) and to the 72 parts of the individual human body, united by the 72 joints. In a similar way, the rulers of these quinaries, the 72 angels, prefigure the spiritual leaders of the nations: first the elders of the synagogue, and then the disciples of Christ. The entire vision is thus based on an elaborate structural symmetry between the heavenly and the earthly orders, following the good old Judaic principle for cosmological imagination, "As above, so below." And, as in the Slavonic erotapocritical text, the structural symmetry is 72-fold *because* it follows the one great name of God that is "set apart."

Agrippa's project was part of a massive intellectual effort within certain circles in Renaissance Europe to rehabilitate magic as a form of religious *sapientia*, thus producing the peculiar Renaissance invention that

Keith Thomas calls "magic in the exalted sense."[62] This project, based on reinvention of classical traditions, partially overlapped with the enthusiastic Christian "discovery" of the Kabbalah. Agrippa's own acquaintance with this branch of Jewish mysticism was almost always mediated—and conditioned—by Latin translations and Christian syntheses of the Hebrew sources.[63] The summaries presented in *De Occulta Philosophia*, therefore, are often more revealing of Agrippa's own agenda and intellectual milieu than of the Kabbalah itself. The notion of *harmonia mundi*, so prominent in our passage, is particularly suspect, for it was central in Agrippa's metaphysics.[64] Still, a number of Kabbalistic texts support Agrippa's vision of the cosmos enough to suggest that the process of organizing disparate 72-related topoi around the divine name of 72 parts may have originated within the Kabbalah.

Kabbalah and the World of 72 Parts

Sepher ha-Bahir offers again a proof text that points directly to the numerical dependence among the 72 names of God, the 72 celestial powers, and the 72 languages on earth. The passage in question (partially quoted in chapter 5 for a different purpose) refers to the 12 precious stones on the high priest's breastplate (Exod. 28:15–21) and their relation to the 72 bells at the skirts of his robe (Exod. 28:33):

> This teaches us that the Blessed Holy One has 72 names.
>
> All of them were placed in the Tribes [of Israel]. It is thus written (*Exodus 28:10*). "Six of their names on one stone, and the names of the other six on the other stone, according to their generations."
>
> It is also written (*Joshua 4:9*), "He raised up twelve stones." Just like the first are (*Exodus 28:12*), "stones of memorial," so these are (*Joshua 4:7*), "stones of memorial."
>
> [There are therefore] 12 stones [each containing six names] making a total of 72. These parallel the 72 names of the Blessed Holy One.
>
> Why do they begin with twelve? This teaches us that God has twelve Directors. Each of these has six Powers [making the total of 72].
>
> What are they? The 72 languages.[65]

The 12 stones that are also 72 [bells] are directly linked in this passage to the Name of 72, since it is said that the name is engraved on the 12 stones in groups of six letters.[66] As with Agrippa's astrological concept of the quinaries, here too, the number 72 is derived from 12: each of the 12 heavenly leaders of God has six powers, which results in 72 celestial powers (or angels), not unlike the mechanism by which the 12 precious stones determine the total of 72 bells.

In his erudite study *Œdipus Ægyptiacus* (1652), the seventeenth-century Jesuit scholar Athanasius Kircher includes a reportedly Kabbalistic figure that is even closer to the astrological imagination reflected in Agrippa's passage.[67] Under the rubric of 72 names of God in the Jewish Kabbalah, Kircher offers a diagrammatic representation of the divine names in the form of a sunflower (called "a Kabbalistic tree") that provides a striking visual parallel to Agrippa's summary. The corolla of the flower in the diagram has precisely the structure of the solar crown of 72 quinaries, its outer fringe of 72 petals clearly on display and meticulously numbered for visual emphasis. No less to the point, the diagram highlights the numerical correspondence between the 72 rays, the 72 names of Yahweh, and the 72 nations by correlating one divine and one ethnic name (all listed within the diagram) with each of the sunflower's petals.[68] Most important, here as in Agrippa and in its Slavonic parallels, the core message is the working of a universal law of numerical correspondences whose key is the mysterious divine name of 72 names.

One of the best studied—and most controversial—aspects of these cosmological ideas in the early Kabbalah is their relation to Gnosticism, especially to certain passages in *On the Origin of the World* and *The Apocalypse of James* that appear to be most explicitly dependent on the number 72.[69] The most significant, perhaps, is a well-known passage from *On the Origin of the World* that describes in detail the dwelling place that Yahweh has created for himself:

> It is a large place which is very excellent, sevenfold [greater] than all those which exist [in the] seven heavens. Then in front of his dwelling place, he created a great throne of a four-faced chariot called "cherubin." And the cherubin has eight forms for each of the four corners—lion forms, and bull forms and human forms and eagle forms—so that all the forms total sixty-four forms. And seven archangels stood before him. He is the eighth, having authority. *All of the forms total seventy-two. For from this chariot the seventy-two gods receive a pattern; and they receive a pattern so that they may rule over the seventy-two languages of the nations* [emphasis added].[70]

We can observe here the direct link between the 72 celestial powers (called "gods" in this passage, but apparently akin to the 72 angels who appear in Agrippa) and the division of the world into 72 languages and nations.[71]

Fig. 5. Sunflower diagram from Athanasius Kircher, *Oedipus Aegyptiacus*, vol. 1,
class 4, chap. 6, 281 (Rome, 1652). Reproduced by kind permission of the
Department of Special Collections, The University of Chicago.

The parallel linkage of the two concepts is already familiar to us, I should add, from the Aramaic translation of Genesis in *Targum Pseudo-Jonathan*, though there it is keyed to the number 70 instead.

No less interesting as a possible intertext is a fragment from *The Apocalypse of James*. Having found himself surrounded by hostile heavenly powers, James inquires about their number:

> The Lord said: " . . . I shall reveal to you that which has come forth from him who is without number; I shall indicate their number. That which has come forth from him who is without measure, I shall indicate their measure." James said: "Rabbi, behold, have I then received their number? Are there 72 measures?" The Lord said: "These are the 72 heavens which are their inferiors."[72]

The figure of the 72 heavens is particularly significant, for it is an apparent synonym to what Agrippa calls the 72 quinaries. And again, as in Agrippa's summary, the 72 parts of the heavenly realm here are presented as subordinate to 72 celestial forces.

On the basis of the extant sources, it is not entirely possible to disentangle the precise origin of the figure and the exact historical lineage of its complex cosmological implications. Gnosticism developed during the time when both Rabbinic Judaism and early Christianity were being constituted, and the three traditions sought their more mature articulation while negotiating a web of complex relations and multiple exchanges with one another.

To try to determine for sure whether the cosmological imagination that interests us here was originally Gnostic, as the chronology of the extant sources suggests, or to conjecture that it was indeed Judaic, as some authors argue, is far beyond the point of this study.[73] What concerns us remains unaffected by the answer to this largely unsolvable mystery. The sources reveal that the early Kabbalah is partial to a vision of the universe based on the number 72, where the structures of the celestial and the human sphere are perfectly symmetrical. This vision is largely supported by several Gnostic texts, with one notable exception. None of the available Gnostic sources relates this symmetrical design specifically to the divine Name of 72. It appears, therefore that the number of God's names first becomes the key to this cosmological program as a Kabbalistic innovation. Since in the Slavonic codex *Jerusalem 22* the parallel link between classes of 72 elements and a broader cosmic vision apparently stems from the 72 names of the Lord, we can claim with sufficient certainty that it reflects a Kabbalistic context. Such a conjecture is supported by several texts in the codex that point either generally to a Jewish background or specifically to Kabbalistic sources. Taken together, all of these Kabbalistic indices present this peculiar codex as perhaps the earliest extant document of a Kabbalo-Christian exchange that took place in a Slavic context.

CHAPTER NINE

Christian Culture and the 72 Names

Kabbalah in Christian Garb

Any speculation about the specific channels by which the Jewish Kabbalah may have influenced Christian communities prior to the European Renaissance remains, given the scant documentation, conjectural. What we know for certain is that the *teachings* of the Kabbalah and, by extension, the *theory* of the Name of 72, became known to the Christian world no earlier than the end of the fifteenth century. That period coincided with the Kabbalah's internal transformation from an esoteric system into an exoteric teaching, when, in the words of Moshe Idel, it "became more a lore that promoted the production of secrets, than a custodian of secret lore."[1] Historians usually correlate this shift with the expulsion of the Jews from Spain in 1492 and the subsequent migratory reconfigurations of the Diaspora in Europe. The enthusiasm with which Europe embraced the opportunity to dabble in the Kabbalistic secrets, however, was conditioned by phenomena that had little to do with the Kabbalah itself.

Christian interest in the Kabbalah first developed around the Platonic Academy in Florence, which aimed to revive Plato and the Platonic tradition as a way of life. In 1462 Cosimo de Medici gave Marsilio Ficino (1433–99) a villa near Florence together with several scrolls of Plato's works in Greek. In a matter of months, as the story goes, the translation was complete, and Humanism was born.

Christian Europe owed its acquaintance with the Kabbalah to Giovanni Pico della Mirandola (1463–94), one of the prodigies of Renaissance Humanism and a close associate of Ficino. Born into wealth and power, Pico abandoned both at fourteen in order to dedicate himself completely to philosophy and theology. During his extensive education in Italy and France, he "discovered" the Kabbalah and began his study of Kabbalistic texts with the help of the learned Jewish convert Raymond Moncada (a.k.a. Flavius Mithridates). In 1486, when he was only twenty-three, Pico put together nine hundred theses for a public debate in Rome, of which seventy-two (no doubt the number was carefully chosen!) summarized Pico's own conclusions about the Kabbalah in rather enthusiastic terms.[2] The most notorious of these conclusions stated, "There is no science that assures us more of the divinity of Christ than magic and Cabala."[3] Such was the controversial debut of the Kabbalah in the theater of Christian knowledge. Until then, even the word itself was unknown: one of Pico's detractors claimed—and people believed him—that Kabbalah was the name of an impious writer against Jesus Christ.[4]

Pope Innocent VIII (1484–92) swiftly declared thirteen of Pico's theses heretical. The proposed disputation was prohibited, and the manuscript itself interdicted. Pico's "discovery" of the Kabbalah, however, caused nothing short of a sensation in Humanist circles and quickly established a vogue of its own. The Kabbalah was embraced as a true divine revelation and as a key to understanding the ancients from Pythagoras and the Orphists to Plato, the uncrowned king of European Humanism.[5]

Humanists' enthusiasm for the Kabbalah was often founded on misconceptions, and misunderstandings compounded as the difficult romance of the Christian world with mystical and esoteric Judaism went on. Two examples of Pico's own distortions—both of them bearing directly on our subject—suffice to illustrate this point. The first is his conviction that Dionysius the Areopagite—who, let us not forget, was "the quintessential Platonist" for the members of the Florentine Academy—was "the master of the true Christian *cabbala*."[6] The second, not unrelated to the first, is Pico's evaluation of the Catalan philosopher and mystic Ramon Lull (ca. 1235–1316) in similar terms, as a great practitioner of "kabbalism."[7]

Including Lull in the same genealogical line as Dionysius is not a complete stretch. Lull, after all, was profoundly influenced by the Neoplatonic system of Scotus Eriugena, himself a follower of the Pseudo-Areopagite.[8] More to the point, the divine names were the very core of his own idiosyncratic vision. Around 1272, he reportedly had a mystical experience during which he saw the whole of creation infused with the names of God. In the good old tradition of Neoplatonism, he conceived of these divine attributes (*Dignitates Dei* in his vocabulary) as primordial causes. Only a system based on them could be truly universal, he concluded. From that moment on, he dedicated his entire life to constructing and perfecting such a system, a continual effort out of which his *Ars Magna* (1305–8) was born.

Unlike Dionysius, however, Lull was a missionary at heart. For him, the fact that all three Abrahamic religions—Judaism, Christianity, and Islam—are equally preoccupied with the names of God was not only a proof of his epiphany's universal validity, but also a missionary opportunity. His *Ars Magna*, he hoped, would be the perfect tool for conversion. In a manner of speaking, he believed it would not be difficult to teach a Jew or a Muslim the language of Christian Neoplatonism (the language of Dionysius), since the languages of all three are based on the names of God.

This dream must have been particularly appealing in thirteenth-century Spain, where the three religions coexisted in an uneasy symbiosis—in five kingdoms and six languages—through the politically volatile times of the Reconquista. And the unique historical context of Lull's project not only shaped its goals, but also appears to have provided some of its means. The synthesis that Lull strove to achieve, however fantastic its overarching goals, comes across as well-informed by the onomatological theories of his neighbors, especially those of the Kabbalah and Sufi mysticism.[9] We can see that Dionysius and Lull had something else in common apart from their explicit emphasis on the names of God: both were driven by a strong converging force toward a synthesis of several traditions, though admittedly the goals and the results of these consolidating projects were nothing alike.

All this does not explain, however, their being lumped together under the unlikely umbrella of the Kabbalah, a move that illuminates more the idiosyncrasies of the time than either of the two thinkers. The internal reasons for this triple association—Dionysius, the Kabbalah, and Lull—are rather heterogeneous in each case. The *Ars* of Lull, Frances Yates suspects, had a Kabbalistic core from the start: when he designated each divine name with a particular letter and practiced combining those letters in various patterns, he was "adapting a Cabalist practice to Gentile use."[10] Incidentally, Pico associated Lull with the Kabbalists precisely on that basis: he openly conflated the Kabbalist *ars combinandi* with "that which is called amongst us the *ars Raymundi*."[11] What is only a tentative index of a possible synthesis became for Pico proof of identification, leaving the door wide open to treat Lull not merely as a Kabbalist, but as a more valuable Kabbalist than most (since he was Christian). Confusions proliferated further. A number of pseudo-Kabbalistic treatises were fallaciously attributed to Lull over the next centuries, and Lullism (often in unrecognizable garb) assumed a place of honor in the pantheon of the Christian Kabbalah as its first harbinger.[12] The association of Dionysius with the Kabbalah stemmed from a transfer of a different kind: it was based on the Humanists' mythic version of intellectual history.

According to this myth, the continuity of the Platonic tradition, of which the Florentine Academy considered itself the proud heir, was maintained uninterrupted throughout the Middle Ages by the Jewish Kabbalah. Such a historical fantasy placed Dionysius and the Kabbalists on an equal footing as key makers of the Platonic tradition, a functional identification that enabled a variety of parallel alignments between them.

However dissimilar the two cases of misplaced Kabbalistic identity, they certainly share one thing: they both unequivocally use the name of the Kabbalah as a badge of honor. We may conclude that, at the close of the fifteenth century, Christian Europe had very little idea of the real intellectual content and religious praxis behind the name of the Jewish Kabbalah, yet the name itself, clouded in mystery, had already become a locus of collective cathexis and a sui generis investment for what Bourdieu calls symbolic capital.[13]

This intellectual climate ultimately led to the Christian elite's closer acquaintance with the real Kabbalah, just as it contributed to a closer examination and a more critical approach to it within the Jewish tradition.[14] A number of Christian scholars began firsthand studies of the Hebrew source. The pioneer among them was the great German Hebraist Johannes Reuchlin (1455–1522), who closely studied early Kabbalistic texts and published two milestone books on the Kabbalah: *De verbo mirifico* (The miracle-working name, 1494), the first ever written by a non-Jew, and *De arte cabalistica* (*On the art of the Kabbalah*, 1517).[15] Both works are especially concerned with the names of God and attempt a synthesis between relevant Kabbalistic ideas and the precepts of Christian theology. Cornelius Agrippa von Nettesheim (1486–1533) was active in the same context. Following a rather different path from the one Reuchlin had taken, though influenced by Reuchlin's ideas, Agrippa produced a no less influential body of texts. His three-volume *De occulta philosophia* accords the Kabbalah, and particularly its practical ramifications, a place of honor.[16]

Reuchlin and Agrippa were instrumental in making the secret Name of 72 familiar to the Western European reading public. We can trace the results of their work along two major pathways, erudition and magic, which in the sixteenth century still coexisted as interdependent and equally prestigious epistemological fields.[17] The first way gave us the Franciscan Petrus Galatinus, with his *Opus de arcanis catholicæ veritatis* (1518), and the Jesuit Athanasius Kircher, whose master work, *Œdipus Ægyptiacus* (1652), was mentioned in chapter 8. A larger group of scholars emerged in subsequent centuries, following in Reuchlin's footsteps to develop Christian Hebraism as an autonomous and respectable field of knowledge.

SCHEMHAMPHORAS.

N⁰ 1.

Seu septuaginta duo Divina Nomina in Lingua Hebraica, denotant semper Nomen dei, sive le-gantur à principio, fine, vel à dextris aut si-nistris: suntque ingentis virtutis.

(*Vordere Seite.*)

Fig. 6–7. Two circular representations of *shem ha-mephorash* from Andreas Luppius, *Semiphoras und Schemhamphoras* (1680). Reprinted in Johann Scheible, *Das Kloster*, vol. 3 (Stuttgart: Verlag des Herausgebers, 1846), between 330 and 331.

SCHEMHAMPHORAS.
№ 2.

(*Rückseite.*)

Fig. 7

The second way was linked to the name of Agrippa instead. It brought about particularly fantastic cross-practices in occult science and ceremonial magic. The most notorious example of this tradition is the *Grimoire of Honorius* (1629), reportedly "the blackest" of all magic handbooks, which prescribes in detail the ritual recitation of the 72 names of God during the Black Mass, in the context of such bizarre rituals as the slaughter and mutilation of a virgin kid and a black hen.[18] Due to the *Grimoire*, the 72 names entered the standard arsenal of magic practitioners throughout Western Europe, and can be traced from amulets and charms all the way to manuals of the Faustian tradition.[19]

The Christian Amulet East and West

Although the theory of *shem ha-mephorash* did not become known in Christian circles before the end of the fifteenth century, the fame of the powerful Name of 72 must have leaked out of insulated Kabbalistic circles much earlier, since by the twelfth century it was already making its appearance in the Christian texts of the Latin West.

The grafting of the Judaic notion onto Christian practice, however, was accompanied by a significant shift: the one singular name that is also 72 names was rendered simply as "the 72 names of the Lord." We cannot claim for certain whether this change was prompted directly by Kabbalistic lists of 72 divine names (which existed in abundance) or whether it reflects a more complicated process of adaptation,[20] but the direction of the shift was perfectly predictable. While a cryptogrammic, unpronounceable name of 72 three-letter combinations is a decidedly non-Christian concept, the notion of numerous individual divine names fits right into the framework of Christian onomatology.

Characteristically, the topos of the 72 names was linked from the very beginning to amulet use, which by itself points to the practical Kabbalah as the most probable source of the Kabbalo-Christian exchange.[21] The place of the transaction, judging by the evidence, must have been the South of France. Such a locale confirms the pattern of transconfessional exchange that we have observed thus far. Around approximately the same time, *Sefer ha-Bahir* surfaced in Provence, offering the first mature articulation of the *shem ha-mephorash* theory, and the region was a thriving center of the Jewish Kabbalah. No less notably, it was controlled at the time by one of the most radical dualist Christian sects, Catharism, which no doubt contributed to the general climate of doctrinal laxity that often accompanies confessional diversification. Though distinct from the fifteenth-century Balkan context,

Fig. 8. Hebrew silver amulet from Persia, inscribed with the 72-letter name. The
amulet contains 195 of the name's 216 characters, and the name of the owner, Esther
the daughter of Zipporah. Plate 27 from *Hebrew Magic Amulets: Their Decipherment
and Interpretation* by Theodor Schrire (copyright 1966, Routledge and Kegan Paul).
Reproduced by kind permission of Taylor and Francis Books, UK.

the heterogeneous religious milieu in Provence three-and-a-half centuries
earlier similarly enabled, if not directly encouraged, cross-practices and interreligious exchange.[22]

The first text to document the new Christian transformation of *shem ha-
mephorash* was the Provençal *Roman de Flamenca*, dating from the thirteenth century.[23] This early source already testifies to the double practice of
reciting and carrying the talismanic 72 names for protection and good fortune. The beautiful Flamenca is kept prisoner by her jealous husband in the
Castle of Bourbon. The protagonist of the poem is the knight William of
Nevers, who has fallen in love with her through hearsay. Having arrived in
Bourbon in the hope of winning Flamenca's heart, William zealously prays in
church to the Lord, the Virgin, and all saints for a chance to meet his beloved.
His long entreaty culminates in several *Pater Nosters* and

> a little prayer
> that a holy hermit had taught [him],
> and it is of the 72 Names of God,
> as one says them in Hebrew
> and in Latin and in Greek;
> this prayer renews one's love of God,

and every day makes one more courageous.
Everyone who says and believes it
will find mercy in the Lord God,
and no one who trusts in it with a good heart
or who carries a written copy on his person
will ever come to a bad end.[24]

Before the morning is over, William's wish is granted: he gets his first glimpse of Flamenca. Even if we do not read this prompt wish-fulfillment as a proof of the efficacy of the 72 names, the *Roman* clearly recommends them as a perfectly orthodox tool in the quest for happiness. Not only are they offered in church, in the context of canonical prayers from the Breviary, but their use in the poem is backed by spiritual authority: William has learned this potent prayer from none other than "a holy hermit." Curiously, the poem insists that the names are "in Hebrew, Latin, and Greek," suggesting that the reinterpretation of "the Name of 72" as "72 names" involved also a re-orientation of the topos toward the existing Christian practice of collecting divine names in the three sacred languages and storing them in expansive lists (a practice discussed briefly in chapter 4).

Sources from the end of the thirteenth and the beginning of the four-teenth century already provide the amulet itself. The earliest evidence comes in two languages, Slavonic and Provençal. In accordance with the *Roman de Flamenca*, both texts clearly relegate themselves to protective magic. The metapragmatic instructions are almost identical in the two texts. The Slavonic version is found in the *Berlin Codex*, a Bulgarian miscellany from the end of the thirteenth century, where it is lumped together with (three) names "when fearing death" and *The Ten Names of God*, and shares a common proviso with them: "These names, whoever carries them on his person purely, him the devil cannot touch, he will shed everything unclean, and will be neither slaughtered by knife, nor burnt by fire, nor drowned in water, and in the other world he will be saved from suffering."[25] The proviso of the Provençal text appears at the beginning of the amulet and shares with the Slavonic instructions not only their general model but also their specific idiom, often echoing phrases *verbatim*:

These are the 72 names of our Lord God Jesus Christ, found written for the salvation of all the Christian faithful, for every man or every woman who has them, in writing, on his person can neither be harmed by evil enemy, nor die in water or fire, nor be killed in battle by his enemies, nor can fire or storm harm him. And if a woman is suffering in childbirth and someone puts it [the text] on her, she will immediately be delivered by the will of God.[26]

The amulet itself represents an expansion of the new Christian topos "the 72 names of God" into an apotropaic numerical list where the missing names are supplied from the Bible or the sacred tradition. Interestingly, though both texts define themselves in their headings as lists of 72 names, in neither does the topos correspond to the actual number of the names. The Provençal text has 80, while the Slavonic version has only 70. This numerical incongruity clearly demonstrates that the topos and the list belong to two different traditions that are lumped together mechanically for the sake of producing a Christian equivalent to the Kabbalistic amulet. The names that substantiate the topos function mostly as a multitude, as a mass of respectable volume, rather than a specific quantity (which is hardly surprising, since the talismanic names are meant to be worn, not counted, and worn with faith, not critically analyzed).

The discrepancy between the numerical definition of a list and the actual number of the list's components is a recurrent "flaw" of medieval texts, a feature that—if only because of its persistence—is not easily explained by manuscript corruption, sloppiness, or the poor counting skills of the scribes. In reality it can be a veritable sign of sophistication, a game with the audience that revolves around quantity: a specific quantity pledged and then revoked, as Maria Tymoczko reminds us in her study of Joyce's *Ulysses*, where she provides several eloquent medieval examples of this kind.[27] In other cases, as in ours, the discrepancy has nothing to do with quantity at all: numerals here are used not descriptively but symbolically, designating quality instead of quantity.

Particularly important for this process of conflating the two traditions is the evident effort of both texts to furnish the list with a veneer of orthodoxy. The focus of this Christening project was the selection of names whose canonicity, I assume, was supposed to make the amulet legitimate in a Christian context, despite its overtly heterodox precept. Anyone familiar with magical texts, regardless of their time and place of origin, must be aware of their penchant for unintelligible, intentionally exotic, and obscure names. In fact, the magical efficacy of a name is usually thought of as a function of its abracadabric quality. The rule of thumb of name-magic, if there is one, may as well be "the more gibberish, the better" (for true wizards are those "who chirp and mutter," Isa. 8:19). Yet *The 72 Names*, despite the affiliation with protective magic so clearly declared in the proviso, displays no taste for strange-sounding, nonsensical names. Let us examine for proof the Slavonic list:

> Lord, Alpha, Leader,[28] the Word, Mountain, Bridegroom, Christ, Jesus, Love, Trinity, Shepherd, *Pantokrator* [Gr., "Omnipotent"], *Agios* [Gr., "Holy"], Wisdom, Might, the Firstborn, Effigy, Head, Shepherd, Jesus, Eternal, Unity, Messiah, Izios [*sic*], *Paraklit* [Gr., Intercessor"], the Beginning, Ram, Glory, the Light, Priest, the Father, the Creator, *Sabbaoth* [Heb., "(Lord) of Hosts"], *Kyrios* [Gr., "Lord"], I Am the One Who Is, Source, Lion, Sun, the Door, the Son of Man, *Emmanuel* [Heb., "the Lord is with us"], Eloil [*sic*], Earthly Way, Blossom, Stone, the Holy Ghost, Firstborn Son, *Adonai* [Heb., "My Lord"], the Man in Zion, Healer, Radiance, Rock,[29] Immortal, Omnipotent, the First [and] the Last, *Athanatos*, [Gr., "Immortal"], Saviour, Lamb, the True Mouth, Bread, Angel, Merciful, the Highest King, Good.

Only two names in this list can pass as unintelligible, or at least bewildering: Izios, and Eloil. The text contains several Cyrillic transliterations of commonly used Hebrew and Greek terms (I render them in italics above) that, even if not necessarily transparent to a Slavic speaker, are immediately recognizable as part of the canonical idiom and as distinct from the nonsensical names that are typical of magical texts. The fact that these transliterations are usually reduplicated by translation makes the effort to foreground the "meaningfulness" of the terms even more obvious.[30] We need only to compare this list with *The Ten Names of God* that follow it in the *Berlin Codex* (which I discuss in detail in chapter 8) to see how far removed it is from the magical standard. Against the backdrop of the ten names, which are all distorted Hebrew terms for Yahweh and barely recognizable under their Cyrillic camouflage, the semantic transparency and orthodox propriety of the 72 names provides an almost dramatic contrast. We may conclude that the Slavonic 72 *Names* are rather weird magic names precisely because they are not weird enough, or as Bronislaw Malinowsky would say, because their "coefficient of weirdness" is so weirdly low.[31]

We can extend the same observation to the Provençal amulet. The principal language of the list is not the Provençal vernacular of the proviso: most of the names are standard Latin terms for the divinity, with only a handful of Greek and Hebrew names rendered in their Latin transliteration. At least half of the names have direct correspondences in the Slavonic list.[32] Characteristically, the Slavonic text renders the Latin names from the Provençal text in Slavonic, while some of the Greek and Hebrew names (*Paroclitus*, *Ydonai*), presumably those that were identified as pan-Christian terms, appear in both versions in transliteration.[33]

The Provençal and the Slavonic texts are thus remarkably close to one another: they follow the same structural pattern, offer a similar inventory of God-terms, and have virtually identical provisos that prescribe the same employment. It seems only logical to assume that they are versions of the same text, one of them being a translation of the other. First Iatsimirskii and, more recently, Miklas and Zagrebin have suggested that the Slavonic text in the *Berlin Codex* is a translation from Latin, though none of them points either to specific sources or to specific textological proofs.[34] I am prepared to substantiate their conjecture.

The third and the fourth terms in the Provençal copy (which meticulously separates the names with crosses) read "Homo" and "Usyon." The names represent an obvious corruption of the Greek term *homoousion*, a substantive from the key Christological term in the Nicene Creed *homoousius* ("of one essence"). Toward the end of the Slavonic copy,[35] we encounter the pair *cheloviak* and *u sione* (literally "man" and "in Zion"), which, I suppose, was construed as one rather unusual name for Christ, "the man in Zion." What does this example prove? Evidently the Slavonic copy echoes the error of the Provençal text by translating *homo* and reinterpreting the puzzling *usion* by popular etymology. This means that the Slavonic text had as a source a Latin list, older than both of the extant sources, a list that already featured the corruption of the Greek term as it is registered in the Provençal copy. The translation could not possibly have gone in the other direction, from a putative Slavonic source to the Latin list, because the confusion of the Greek *homo-* (same) with the unrelated Latin *homo* (man) reflects a typical Romance linguistic instinct. To confuse the Greek *homo* with the Slavonic *cheloviak* (man) only because it sounds the same as the Latin word for "man" defies any plausible logic of textological change.

This same Latin corruption of the Greek term *homoousion* proves to be the key to demystifying the origin of the list's version in *Jerusalem 22* as well. Iatsimirskii sounded certain when he claimed that, unlike the version in the *Berlin Codex*, the one in *Jerusalem 22* had a Greek origin,[36] and the general assumption that the Slavonic list of 72 divine names must be a translation from Greek has been echoed again and again by scholars, although the search for the Greek original has proceeded in vain for more than a century. A close comparison of the names in the *Berlin Codex* and in *Jerusalem 22*, however, conclusively reveals a family connection that points to a common source. The problematic name "the man in Zion" (*cheloviak u sione*) is followed in the Berlin copy by the name "healer" (*istsialitel'*). The Jerusalem copy features neither, though in their place it offers the curious composite "man-healer"(*cheloviakoistsialitel'*). What we witness here is the domino effect of the initial error. At stage two, the prepositional phrase "in Zion" was dropped as nonsensical, and the remnant "man" was redefined as part of a compound word. Whatever the exact provenance of *Jerusalem 22*, its version of *The 72 Names of the Lord* clearly reflects an older South Slavic tradition that goes back to a Western European (rather than a Greek) source: the Provençal Christian adaptation of a Kabbalistic amulet.

In the absence of indisputable protographs for either the Latin or the Slavonic list, we are left with no clear beginning of our story and a labyrinth of speculations. Provence is certainly the most logical birthplace for the Christian amulet, and all clues, however scant, lead back to that region. The talismanic list was probably already assembled in the twelfth century, as *Roman de Flamenca* gives us ground to believe. But we cannot be certain about the channels that transmitted this amulet from Provence to the Southern Slavs or about the exact date when the Slavonic translation was made. Miklas and Zagrebin have suggested that the version in the *Berlin Codex* is the product of a "loose semi-oral delivery" ("einer lockeren halbmündlichen Überlieferung"),[37] but I would assume that the Slavic reinterpretation of *homo-ousion* that we encounter there clearly points to written transmission. One potential mediator for the text could have been the Provençal Cathars who flocked to Bosnia in the thirteenth century in search of a dualist "Promised Land."[38] Another possible channel was opened by the Crusades, especially by the Fourth Crusade (1201–4), which imposed a Latin Empire (1204–61) on the map of the Balkans for the better part of the thirteenth century.[39]

The paths of our text in the West are not well charted either, since the tradition is virtually unstudied.[40] What we do know for certain is that by the fifteenth century there existed several documented vernacular versions of the amulet, notably both French and German.[41] If Provence was indeed the epicenter of a diffusion whose waves had already reached the Balkans by the end of the thirteenth century, we would expect that the vernacular versions in the West developed at least as early as their Slavonic equivalent, and possibly even earlier.[42]

The text's inclusion in the printed editions of the notorious *Enchiridion*, one of the most popular Western books of white magic, appears to have boosted its popularity.[43] Though falsely attributed to Pope Leo III (795–816), the *Enchiridion* is essentially a collection of charms including, apart from *The 72 Names of the Lord*, its twin text *The 72 Names of the Theotokos*, and a prayer to Jesus Christ that specifically mentions "the 72 names of God" and concludes with an alternative list of God-terms. According to the legend, the book was given as a gift by the pontiff to Charlemagne on the occasion of his coronation in the year 800. The gift was intended to bring good luck to the new emperor and grant him protection from all kinds of enemies and perils.[44] To achieve this, however, the book-owner was supposed to maintain proper comportment, as specified meticulously in the book's proviso: to keep the book clean in a small bag of new leather and vow to carry it on himself with honor to the Almighty, and to read (on his knees and always facing East) at least one page a day in utmost devotion.

We can see that the entire book was carefully designed as an amulet, and there is little doubt that it was used accordingly on a large scale. No trace of an early manuscript tradition of the book exists. The earliest record of it refers to an alleged printed publication in Rome in the Latin language in 1523 (only three years after the first printed edition of the Slavonic 72 *Names of the Lord* that came out in Venice). Thereafter the book was said to have appeared in a half-dozen French and German editions in the course of a century. Regrettably, however, only two seventeenth-century editions have reached us (Lyons, 1633, and Rome, 1660), which makes all narratives about earlier publications highly uncertain, especially given the thick layers of mystification surrounding this book.[45] All these uncertainties contribute to the difficulties of discerning within the Western tradition of *The 72 Names of God* a clearer chronology and a more definite geography of its diffusion. However, solving these puzzles is beyond my objective in this book. So I leave the tracing of the Western routes of the text for future studies, while I return to the Balkans to explore the career of the amulet among the Slavs.

Before I abandon the Western tradition, however, let me offer a final word on the origin of the text, to close the Kabbalistic circle, so to speak. More than a century ago, Johannes Bolte polemicized with Moses Gaster about the Kabbalistic origin of the Western 72 *Names of the Lord*, and the debate was left unfinished. Gaster had claimed earlier that the Christian amulet drew directly on Kabbalistic sources and identified *Sefer Raziel* as the most plausible source.[46] Bolte countered that the list's descent from the Jewish Kabbalah was in no way as certain as Gaster would have us believe, and he proposed that the Christian text only freely improvised on a Jewish model, offering as a parallel Ramon Lull's composition of a song of praise to God adorned with 99 epithets recalling the Muslim 99 names of Allah.[47]

My position, as this chapter has made clear, is somewhere in the middle. I believe with Gaster that the text has a distinct Kabbalistic background, though it is a case of Christian adaptation of a Kabbalistic amulet, rather than a direct "translation" of *shem ha-mephorash*. This creative reinterpretation of a Kabbalistic practice is admittedly much less removed from its non-Christian source than are the free improvisations of Lull. However, Bolte's analogy still has heuristic value, as a reminder of the creative energy that spurred perpetual cross-fertilization in both the theory and practice of naming God whenever Christian, Jewish, and Muslim communities came in close contact with one another.

CHAPTER TEN

Printing and the Career of
the Slavonic Text

The remarkably successful career of the Slavic amulet of 72 divine names hinges on one central event in its history: its initial printed publication. The text first appeared in 1520 as part of a pioneering work of Cyrillic typography. The book, known as the *Miscellany for Travelers*, came out of the Venetian printing house of the Montenegrin entrepreneur Božidar Vuković—a central figure in the earliest chapter of modern Cyrillic bookmaking.[1]

Cyrillic typography appeared on the cultural map of Europe relatively late, lagging behind printing ventures in Latin and Glagolitic, the other two alphabets in use among Slavs at the time.[2] It was inaugurated in 1491 by the publication of an *Oktoechos* (a hymnographic book that contains offices for the services between the second Sunday after Pentecost and the first week of Lent) that came out of the Cracow shop of the German printer Schweipoldt Fiol. More active bookmaking in Cetinja (Montenegro), the first typographic center already in the territory of Slavia Cyrillica, followed later in the same decade. Yet early in the next century, the production of Cyrillic books moved almost entirely to Venice, which had established itself as perhaps the most important typographic center in Europe at the time.[3]

The publishing house of Božidar Vuković had much to do with the success of Cyrillic printing in Venice. It opened in 1519 as a branch of Božidar's trading company. As a result of his ambition and savvy, both the Pope and the emperor soon granted him exclusive privileges, and his publishing house quickly emerged as the major center of Cyrillic typography in the whole Italo-Balkan region.[4] The *Miscellany for Travelers* was one of Vuković's earliest releases and, as we shall presently see, his most successful publication.[5]

The *Miscellany for Travelers* and the Remaking of the Text

The *Miscellany for Travelers* offers a new version of *The 72 Names of the Lord*, distinct from both earlier copies that have reached us in the *Berlin Codex* and in *Jerusalem 22*. In fact, the numerous changes introduced into the text, in the list of names as well as in its frame, give us enough ground to consider this version a new redaction of the text:[6]

And these are the names of the Lord, 72 in number. Whoever has them and carries them purely on their person will be saved from every evil. Power, Strength, the Word, Life, Grace, Love, Wisdom, *Sother* [Gr., "Savior"], *Pantokrator* [Gr., "Omnipotent"], *Paraklit* [Gr., "Intercessor"], the Light, Meal, Shepherd, Ram, Stone, the Way, House, Garment, Blossom, the Foundation, Head, the Pure, Bridegroom, Ruler, Truth, Son of Man, Immanuel, the Beginning, Firstborn, Messiah, the Highest King, Jesus, Bread, the Father, the Creator, *Sabaoth* [Heb., "(Lord) of Hosts"], *Kyrios* [Gr., "Lord"], the Holy Spirit, Mercy, the Intercessor, Leader, Sun, Christ, Healer, Of the good womb, Merciful, Primordial, *Athanatos* [Gr., "Immortal"], Maker, Lamb, Lion, Bull, Effigy, Glory, I Am the One Who Is, Justice, Source, the True Mouth, Joy, Senior, *Eleon* [possibly from Hebr., *Elion*, "the Most High," or Gr., *Eleos*, "Mercy"], Priest, Prophet, Door, the Eternal, Justification, God, Indivisible Trinity, the King of Kings.

Why did He call Himself the Word? Because he was begotten of the Father, and as a word is begotten of the soul so was the Son of the Father. Why is He called Life? Because He resurrected us, who were dead. Why did He call Himself the Light? Because he changed us from darkness [to light]. Why did He call Himself Meal? Because I eat Him when I accept the Mystery [during the Holy Communion]. Why did He call Himself Shepherd? Because He watches over us. Why did He call Himself Ram? Because He sacrificed Himself for us and became [our] purification. Why did He call Himself the Stone? That you would achieve a firm and steadfast faith. Why did He call Himself the Way? Because through Him we come to the Father. Why did He call Himself House? Because we live in Him. Why did He call Himself Garment? Because when I was baptized I was clothed in Him. Why did He call Himself Blossom? Because we flourish in Him. Why did He call Himself the Foundation? That you should learn that He supports everything. Why is He called Head? That I should be part of His body. Why did He call Himself the Pure? Because He made me a virgin and I am His temple. Why did He call Himself Bridegroom?

Because He adorned me as a bride. Why is He called Ruler? That you should learn that we are His servants.

One name is not enough to represent all. He is named with innumerable names, so that we learn a little about God. For the divine being is not of the flesh and you are a man attached to a body. His grandeur is endless, His wisdom is countless, His destinies are inscrutable and His ways are true. I will glorify those who glorify me, says the Lord (1 King. 2:30). And not only with words but also with deeds let us glorify Christ, for unto Him are the glory and the power, the honor and worship, with the Father and the Holy Spirit, now and forever, and unto ages of ages. Amen.

The list features an entirely new selection of names compared to the two pre-typographic copies we possess (the *Berlin Codex* and *Jerusalem* 22). All traces of corrupted terms or occasionalisms have been carefully weeded out to produce a perfectly canonical series of God-terms. Moreover, the list is paired (in perfect accord with Dionysius' prescriptions) with an exegetical part that justifies the names' canonical status by means of biblical and liturgical proof texts. It includes sixteen names, introduced anaphorically by the same rhetorical question, "Why did he call himself X?" (or "Why was he called X?") and followed by an answer drawn from Scripture or the liturgical tradition.

I have identified as the source of this passage a homily on Psalm 45 (Slav. 44):10, "And the king will desire your beauty. Since he is your lord, bow to him."[7] The homily, falsely attributed to St. John Chrysostom, is a highly reputable text of Byzantine rhetoric that was part of the Eastern Orthodox liturgical repertoire for centuries (in the Slavonic tradition it usually appears as a reading for the First Sunday after Pentecost, known as the Sunday of All Saints). This Pseudo-Chrysostomian text shares with the amulet all but one of the explicated names (Blossom), but they are listed there in a different order and are supplemented by three additional epithets (Root, Food, Caretaker). The canonical "justifications" in both texts are virtually the same.[8] The rhetorical closure that follows the exegetical part of the amulet also relies on the same sermon by clipping phrases from it and gluing them together with biblical quotations. It is evident that, compared to the two earlier manuscript copies of the text, Vuković's version of *The 72 Names of the Lord* stands out as a new, well-informed, and well-balanced compilation, carefully veneered to fit both the conceptual framework of Christian onomatology and the traditional patterns of Orthodox ecclesiastical rhetoric. I have not been able to connect this redaction of the text to any other Latin or vernacular version; however, in view of the fragmentary evidence that is available to us, it would seem prudent to abstain for the moment from declaring it an original Slavonic compilation.

The text is paired in the book with *The 72 Names of the Theotokos*, following a pattern already established in *Jerusalem 22*. In the manuscript source, however, the two symmetrical texts were linked only as an afterthought by the numerological summary keyed to 72. Here, by contrast, the lists are introduced as a pair by a common proviso that immediately foregrounds their shared protective capacity and promotes their use *en bloc* as an amulet corpus:

> When you see these signs and read these names, you will be invincible in battle and saved from every enemy, and from sudden death, and from fear at night, and from the actions of Satan, and from every malice you will be protected by the sign of the holy and life-giving Cross, and by all the names of the Lord, 72, and by all the wondrous and untraceable signs of the most glorious and honorable Mother of Our Lord Jesus Christ to Whom there is glory in all the ages. Amen.

The version of *The 72 Names of the Theotokos* is equally new and improved. Compared to the one previous copy of the text that we possess, the list is revised and purged of any terms that could be viewed as doctrinally unsound. And, as in *The 72 Names of the Lord*, the names of the Virgin are also legitimated by an exegetical sequence drawn from a most respectable ecclesiastical text, this time a passage from a *Panegyric for the Birth of the Theotokos* by St. Andrew of Crete.[9] Whoever the compiler of the volume was (most probably the priest-monk Pahomije, mentioned in the book as the "typesetter"[10]), and whatever the level of his improvements on the sources he was working from, one thing is beyond doubt: the book, in its final form, presents a particularly well-crafted pair of amulet texts that aspire to be fully "canonical," on a par with the best examples of the official ecclesiastical repertoire.

The Spectacular Aftermath

It is difficult to overestimate the effect of Vuković's edition on the history of the Slavonic 72 *Names of the Lord*. The status of the text in the old pre-typographic times was shaky and marginal. Our only records from those times are two fairly discordant copies of the text, separated from one another by over a century. Despite textological proofs that tie them both to a putative common Provençal source, we cannot readily lump them into a hypothetical common "redaction," since they represent a sporadic and irregular tradition that was flickering here and there on the fringes of popular religious culture. This tradition could easily have died out had it not found its way to print—and instant popularity.

At the most obvious, the new technology granted the text a distribution of previously unimaginable proportions. Printing made it possible to reproduce an abundance of identical copies, ensuring both the *durability* of a particular text-version and its simultaneous *accessibility* in numerous distant locations.[11] Typography arrested the still immature scribal tradition of *The 72 Names of the Lord* and its twin text, *The 72 Names of the Theotokos*, in the fixed form of a single version and imposed this version as the standard text by distributing it on a hitherto unprecedented scale.[12] The result was overwhelming. Judging by the extant copies (which certainly represent only a fraction of the actual circulation), the tradition of the two texts reached an all-time high in the seventeenth century, their manuscript production more than quadrupling over a span of fifty years, while the lists were also enjoying multiple reprints—both by letterpress and from xylographic plates.

The wide distribution and the visibly more prolific and uniform tradition of the text, however, only laid the foundation for its spectacular career. The *72 Names of the Lord* did not just become a mainstream text of custom and convention, one of the most popular amulets of the time. It also became a magical text of gravity and consequence.[13]

Most of the post-Vuković sources of the list present it as the vanguard of textual clusters. The clusters open, as a rule, with the pair of *The 72 Names of the Lord* and *The 72 Names of the Theotokos* in its new combined version (inaugurated in Vuković's *Miscellany*), and include different combinations of other sacronymic lists, often restricted numerically to 72 or its variants (e.g., *The 73 Old Testament Prophets*, or *The 70 Disciples of Christ*). Perhaps the most elaborate among these corpora of talismanic lists is an ornate Serbian amulet from the end of the sixteenth or the beginning of the seventeenth century, carved on both sides of two wooden blocks for the xylographic production of amulet stamps.[14] Another corpus (the only one featuring a unique non-numerical list of the names of John the Baptist[15]) is represented by three almost identical seventeenth-century copies of a small-format manuscript prayer book that was certainly used as a personal phylactery. The modeling of these corpora after the successful pairing of *The 72 Names of the Lord* and *The 72 Names of the Theotokos* is evident, and clearly the source is again the Venetian *Miscellany*.

This list corpus, with its expandable boundaries, is loosely based on the number 72 and thus approximates (without ever coinciding with) the vision

Љубљанске плоче, плоча прва, страна 1.

Fig. 9. Woodblock print from the Ljubljana amulet (ca. 1500–1600) containing *The 72 Names of the Lord* and *The 72 Names of the Theotokos*. From Nikola Radojčić "Srpski Abagar," *Etnolog* 4, no. 2 (1931): 187–211.

of a 72-fold universe articulated by *Jerusalem* 22 and the later erotapocritical texts. As in those conceptual articulations, the 72 names of God are also
the organizing concept here. In view of the Christian hierarchical vision of
order, in which God-terms are ontologically superior to all other sacronyms,
we can claim that the list of the 72 divine appellations is superscribed upon
the entire corpus not merely as its *first* component, but also as its *archetypal*
text. Thus, the version of *The 72 Names of the Lord* that was popularized and
made standard by the Vuković edition established a model for the proliferation of talismanic lists that, by the seventeenth century, came to dominate
the production of both scribal and printed talismanic lists among the Balkan
Slavs.

It is hard to tell whether merit or luck was to blame for the amulet's good
fortune, though, as with any successful career, both probably played some
role. Appearing in print so early in the typographic age was a stroke of good
luck. But there must have been something other than wide exposure that
propelled the two texts to such popularity. I believe that something about
their new, well-groomed version and their successful balancing act between
orthodox propriety and magical efficacy must have struck a chord with the
Balkan religious communities. No doubt the credit for this achievement
should go to the unknown editor, whose personal version of the amulet dip-
tych was thereafter dutifully—and enthusiastically—reproduced by virtually all the subsequent sources of the two texts.[16]

Building Textual Affinities

We should also credit the compiler of the volume for establishing intertextual links between the two talismanic lists and several other amulet texts
that became increasingly associated with them in the subsequent tradition.

The first in the group is the *Eulogy of the Holy Cross*, essentially a list of
the most traditional epithets for the cross that, much like the lists of divine
and theotokian names, was designed to be used as an amulet.[17] In the post-
Vuković tradition of the texts, the *Eulogy* usually appears at the beginning of
an amulet corpus that always includes the two 72-fold lists of sacred names
with a varied entourage of other sacronymic lists. Its initial position in the
corpus resonates not only with the salient apotropaic function of the sign of
the cross in Christian culture, both high and low, but also with the standard
monastic practice of writing a cross at the beginning of each text as a silent
prayer for blessing.[18]

The other component of the larger amulet corpus in the *Miscellany* is
the Abgar Cycle. This group of texts is a much older and more popular Chris-

tian apocryphon than the other three amulets.[19] The story behind it is well known: Abgar, the toparch of Edessa, who ruled during the ministry of Christ (4 BCE–50 CE), suffered for nine years from an incurable disease. Upon hearing of the curative miracles performed by one Jesus of Nazareth, Abgar wrote a letter to him with a request for help. Jesus wrote back that he was unable to come himself, but he would send instead the apostle Thaddeus, "one of the 72 [disciples]," as most versions point out. According to one version, Abgar was immediately cured by the letter itself. Another version contends that he was cured instead by a piece of cloth sent by Christ in the letter, onto which the Lord's features were miraculously imprinted. Both versions gave rise to equally strong traditions of using Christ's letter or the "Edessa image" as curative amulets.

The cycle is believed to be of Syrian origin, but its earliest documented version is Greek, found in the fourth-century *Historia ecclesiastica* by Eusebius, the Bishop of Caesaria (ca. 268–ca. 338).[20] It includes the epistles of both Abgar and Christ, as well as a narrative commentary about the circumstances of their exchange. Over the next century, a narrative about the Edessa image was appended to them. This story about the miracle-working image of the Lord "not made by the hands of man" was singled out as a compelling theological argument in support of icon worship during the eighth-century icon controversy in Byzantium, and the political victory of the icon supporters in 787 boosted its reputation beyond imaginable bounds.

In the aftermath of these events, the Byzantine army, led by General John Carcuas, forced the city of Edessa to surrender its now invaluable Christian possession, and on August 16, 944, the relic was transferred to Constantinople with the utmost ceremony. The day was included in the Christian calendar as an official holiday, and the Edessa image became part of a standard iconographic program for Eastern Orthodox church decoration, a situation that remains unchanged to this day. In that same century, the celebrated Metaphrast collection of saints' lives offered a new, revised and expanded version of *Epistula Abgari* containing the two letters and a narrative about the Edessa image as a reading for the new holiday of the Constantinople transfer. This particular version became the standard text of the tradition and as such was soon translated into both Latin and Slavonic. Incidentally, its earliest Slavonic copy is documented in the *Berlin Codex* (though unrelated contextually to *The 72 Names of the Lord*), and that is the version on which the cycle in Vukovic's *Miscellany* rests, complemented as it is by a lithographic print of the Edessa image.

Even though the reputation of the Abgar Cycle rests on purely orthodox grounds, it has been transmitted mostly as an amulet. Abgar amulets are known across the Christian world in great variety and numerous languages, including Armenian, Georgian, Coptic, and Arabic versions, and almost everywhere the preponderance of available evidence is in the form of amulet.[21] One amusing example, which gives an idea of the scope and the complexity of the religious scene in which this abundant tradition thrived during the late Middle Ages, is a fifteenth-century Abgar amulet composed, reportedly, by a Catholic priest for Bosnian Muslims, written in Latin but using Cyrillic script.[22] Already in the fourteenth century the practice of wearing the Abgar letter as an amulet had gained such momentum in the Slavic milieu that the very name *abagar* (i.e., "Abgar" in Church Slavonic) became a synonym for written amulets and was appropriated as a cover-term for any codex or scroll worn for cure and protection.[23] Direct evidence of the popularity of this practice is provided by the anathema against those who "wear the Abgar Epistle on the neck" mentioned in a sixteenth-century copy of Metropolitan Kiprian's index of Slavic forbidden books.[24]

We can conclude that the *Miscellany*'s extended amulet corpus, while deliberately including texts with an orthodox veneer, is particularly well crafted from the standpoint of apotropaic magic. The corpus maximizes the potential of its heterogeneous components by merging them into a structural, conceptual, and functional unity that comes as close as possible to the perfect amulet. First, the *Eulogy of the Holy Cross* offers both protection and a blessing. Second, the two sets of names serve as a shield from every evil that might potentially strike people and their kin. Third, the *Abgar Letter* and the Edessa image ensure a divine cure from every ailment in case the names fail to deliver as promised.[25] And last but not least, the *Legend of King Abgar*, which directly testifies to the Christian mythological precedent of using written texts for cure and protection, offers a justification of these practices together with a guarantee of their success.[26] There is hardly anything more that a person could possibly want from an amulet, and we should not be surprised to learn that over the next century it was in great demand.[27]

Commercial Success

The real reason for the subsequent popularity of Vuković's amulet corpus, and by extension of the entire book in which it first appeared (for I believe that the two are intertwined), was purely commercial. I would argue that it lay not so much in the creation of a "perfect amulet" as in the pairing of a well-crafted magical product with its ideal consumer group.

The shift from scribal to printed culture involved more than merely a change in the technology of recording and distributing information. It transformed the entire spectrum of cultural mechanisms, attitudes, and meanings that accompanied the old ways of making and using books, effecting nothing short of a revolution in knowledge and culture.[28] One of the fundamental results of this transformation was the emergence of bookmaking as an industry that, like any industry, was ruled by the laws of the market. Walter Ong defines the change by a catchy opposition:

> Manuscript culture is *producer-oriented*, since every individual copy of a work represents great expenditure of an individual copyist's time. Medieval manuscripts are turgid with abbreviations, which favor the copyist although they inconvenience the reader. Print is *consumer-oriented*, since the individual copies of a work represent a much smaller investment of time: a few hours spent in producing a more readable text will immediately improve thousands upon thousands of copies.[29]

The new printed books were easier to read, more accessible, less mysterious—and so was the information they revealed. The printing revolution thus put an end to medieval elitism in book culture, an end to the cultural monopoly of the clergy. If knowledge and information is indeed power, as Michel Foucault and his followers contend, that power now became more evenly distributed, more "democratic." We can therefore rephrase Ong's formula in the idiom of power, a political idiom that is implied, I believe, in his overtly economic articulations: if the old scribal culture was an oligarchy of the enlightened few, the compilers and copyists of books, then the culture of print shifted power to the majority, the consumers, and laid the ground for the future tyranny of book buyers. That is why, by the way, we can talk about "the success" of a particular book. Success belongs to the vocabulary of the new book industry. It externalizes the links of that industry to the emerging book market and its dependence on the needs and tastes of some statistical, "average" potential consumer, always highly abstracted in the bookmaker's calculations, though materializing in the end as a group of book buyers who are very real indeed.

Exactly what kind of a consumer did the *Miscellany* of 1520 target? The intended audience is clearly defined in the volume's afterword: the book was to be "a soul-saving selection that is convenient to be carried by those who are on the road."[30] Both the format and the content of Vuković's *Miscellany*, in other words, were designed for a particular target-audience: travelers, mostly secular itinerants, that is, mobile entrepreneurs and traveling merchants, people with whom Božidar traded continually and whose tastes and needs he knew well.

The result was a new type of book: a religious digest for mobile laymen who, by the sixteenth century, constituted the core of the emerging middle class in the Balkans. Both the format and the content of the book were deliberately chosen to facilitate use by such people. The *Miscellany* was designed as a portable pocketbook, only 4.5 by 3.5 inches, that offered a mélange of devotional texts (daily prayers, hymns, and hagiographic narratives) and practical secular tools, such as calendars and metrical conversion tables. These readings, aimed specifically toward practical goals, were clearly selected on the basis of what Eisenstein calls "new single-minded, narrowly focused piety" to suit the religious mentality of the lay Christian majority.[31] This book stands out among the other editions of Vuković's publishing house because of its complex ornamentation, superb graphic composition, and numerous masterfully accomplished illustrations, which means that it was meant to appeal to buyers as a valuable and desirable Christian commodity.[32] We may conclude that Vuković's *Miscellany for Travelers* was the first Slavonic printed book addressed not to religious institutions, as was still the prevailing practice of the time, but to an individual secular buyer. Furthermore, it was made to appeal to the tastes and needs of the most promising potential consumers of the emerging book-market: people with a flow of cash who possessed—as businessmen—some level of literacy and a strong sense of private ownership, on which the market relied.

Let us now think for a moment about the specific needs of these secular itinerants to whom Vuković addressed his book. These people were always on the road, exposed, vulnerable, dependent on the kindness of strangers. What would such people need most? What would be the most invaluable commodity for them, if not stability and security in a changing and hostile world? In similar circumstances, we now buy travel insurance. In the sixteenth century, amulets were the only available alternative.[33] We can then treat the inclusion of the amulet corpus in Vuković's package of religious readings as a clever, consumer-oriented gesture aimed to fit the specific requirements of his intended audience and thus to increase the market appeal of the entire book.

Vuković's business acumen proved impeccable, for his *Miscellany* was evidently a great success (unlike the institution-oriented ritual codices, such as Psalters and Prayer Books, which he produced, reportedly, at a commercial loss). In the next forty years, the *Miscellany* had as many as four new editions, including one deluxe edition with rich illuminations published in 1547 by Božidar's son Vincenczo, who took over the company after his father's death.[34] All these new books, despite the numerous editorial changes, prominently featured an identical version of our amulet corpus—indicating that its presence in the book was considered expedient to the publishers' market goals.

We find further proof for the success of Vuković's book in the career of the next prominent figure of Venetian Cyrillic typography, the Bulgarian Jakov Kraikov, who bought the printing equipment of the Vukovićes after their printing shop closed. The first book that Kraikov published in 1566, called *Chasoslovec* (Book of hours), copied the format of the *Miscellany* of 1520, following the same design and targeting a similar audience. The textual material was almost entirely a new selection. Kraikov lifted only one group of texts directly from the masterpiece of his predecessor: the amulet corpus.[35]

Thus, from among no more than sixteen Cyrillic editions that were printed in Venice in the sixteenth century, more than one-third were religious books in the new, individual-oriented format, all of which featured an identical amulet corpus. Even though these books were designed primarily for reading, the presence of the same cluster of talismanic texts, diligently reproduced from one edition to the next, suggests an ancillary function of these books as amulets, or at least as sources for the manufacture of individual phylacteries. This assumption is supported by the persistent Christian practice of carrying small-format manuscript codices as amulets, a practice that print must have facilitated, at least in the beginning, by making such books more readily available. The elaborate provisos of the printed editions of the Latin *Enchiridion*, all of them urging the talismanic employment of the book, suffice to prove this point.

The extant exemplars of the Venetian editions further confirm such speculations by offering specific information about the ways actual buyers treated the amulet corpus. In two of the three copies of these books that I could actually see, the pages containing the 72 names of the Lord and the Theotokos have been torn out.[36] Considering the horrific Christian anathemas against those who damage or steal from books (especially if the texts contain the name of God!), there is little doubt that those who vandalized the books, targeting specifically the divine names in them, did so in order to wear the lists as personal phylacteries. In this case, the logic of orthodoxy (calling for veneration of the sacred name) works at cross purposes with the logic of heteropraxis (aspiring to the power of the name).

We can also observe how heteropraxis ultimately takes the upper hand in the mind of Vuković's audience, precisely because its voracious pragmatism collapses the distinction between the two logics; that is, it fails to register and respond to their incompatibility. Those who tore out the pages with the sacred names did it out of respect for the power instilled in them. Thus they venerated the list in the most intimate way they knew how—by appropriating it, by making it an extension of their physical bodies. As José Ortega y Gasset notes in another context, the instinct to possess is a gesture of worship, primitive and misguided perhaps, but always completely sincere. In the mind of the fortunate owners of the Venetian books, the pair of sacronymic lists must have been deemed so potent an amulet—and because of that, so desirable to possess—that the advantages of wearing it trumped all the possible negative consequences that might result from desecrating a sacred text. Neither the *Eulogy of the Cross* nor the widely popular *Letter of King Abgar*, synonymous with the very idea of an amulet, seem to have enjoyed quite the same reputation and trust.

To sum up, the Venetian editions of *The 72 Names of the Lord*, all of them dependent on Vuković's *Miscellany* of 1520, present us with a paradox. Some of the first Slavic texts to enjoy the benefits of the new printed medium—the same medium that ensured in perspective the emergence of a broad reading public—were actually magical texts that were not intended for reading. Instead, they were meant to be worn as magical objects for cure and protection, and were addressed not so much to the potential reading audience of the *literati* as to the still overwhelming majority of the semiliterate and those who could not read at all. Such an appropriation of print seems to go against the grain of both the medium and of modernity itself. At the very least, it challenges our preconceptions about both.

The paradox, however, lies only on the surface, because, as we have seen, the first priority of printed culture has always been not so much to create a reading public as to sell books. The creation of a reading audience is essential only to the degree that it creates possibilities for expanding the book market. Books emerged from the Gutenberg cultural revolution as new commodities. And, even though they admittedly are commodities for reading, to ensure that they would be read, books had first to be made into *marketable* commodities; they needed to sell well, even if that meant being sold for reasons that had nothing to do with reading. Such are the laws of the market.

Amulets have always been religious commodities, even in the old, pretypographic days—inscribed objects to have and profit from, items of private property. As such, they were particularly well-suited to the new commercialization of Cyrillic book production, beginning in the early sixteenth-century with the Balkan printers in Venice. Vuković and his successors had the keen market sense to capitalize on the cachet that printed amulets had with the most promising group of potential book buyers: the traveling Balkan merchants who not only had the means and the motive to invest in personal protection, but who could further enhance the wide distribution of the Venetian Cyrillic books by serving as live advertisers during their travels between Western Europe and the Balkan lands. In short, amulets sold well in the emerging Slavic market for printed books and helped make printed books more popular; so bookmakers made amulets, and thus the wheel of the book market went round and round.

The *Abagar* of Philip Stanislavov

The historical narrative about the felicitous marriage between *The 72 Names of the Lord* and the Gutenberg technology of letterpress print would be incomplete without mention of the most peculiar printed edition of the text, in a book published in Rome in 1651 under the explicit title *Abagar*.[37] The book was the work of the Bulgarian Catholic Bishop of Nikopol, Filip Stanislavov (1608?–1674), and was printed with the equipment and the sponsorship of the Vatican Polyglot Printing Office, a branch of *Congregatio de Propaganda Fide* founded in 1626 under Pope Urban VIII (1623–44) to spread religious propaganda among infidels and non-Catholic Christians. Despite its impressive background, this book appears to be deliberately designed as an amulet. The texts were printed only on the facing pages of five big folia and arranged in four columns bordered on both sides by a uniform ornamental frame. Such a graphic design was meant to facilitate the reshaping of the book into a scroll by cutting the columns and gluing them together. One of the extant copies, held at the Library of Bologna, is preserved in such an amulet form, the bulky scroll extending for about 5.5 meters (more than eighteen feet).

On the face of it, the content of the book also supports such a talismanic mode of employment. The brief envoy spells out clearly the apotropaic function of the texts: Bishop Stanislavov collected this *abagar* and gave it to the Bulgarian people (i.e., to his flock of newly converted Bulgarian Catholics) "to wear it about themselves instead of powerful relics."[38] No less conspicuously, the book is headed by the familiar amulet corpus from Vuković's *Miscellany*, though significantly abridged here and presented in a different arrangement.[39] All these elements make the book a particularly unlikely publication to come out of the Vatican Congregation of the Propaganda, especially considering the strict censorship policy of that institution. What was the agenda behind this peculiar edition? Was it published by omission or by design, and, if the latter, what could possibly be its raison d'être?

The first step in addressing these questions is to examine more closely the amulet façade of the book. Not surprisingly, it proves to be a rather shaky construction that is easily removed, like a patina or a mask. In fact, the way the book reshapes its vanguard of amulet texts suggests that it is

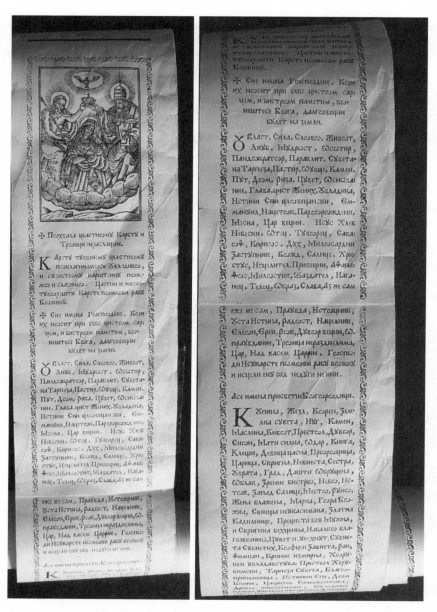

Fig. 10. Reprint of the *Abagar* of Filip Stanislavov (Rome, 1651) in the form of an amulet scroll. In the left panel can be seen the ornamental upper part of the scroll; in the right panel, a full view of *The 72 Names of the Lord* with a partial view of *The 72 Names of Theotokos*. Photographs courtesy of Krassimir Stantchev (Rome).

attempting to put a new spin on the practice. The lists are stripped of their magic provisos, and the *Letter of King Abgar* concludes with an impassioned and very personal sermon that condemns magical practices and religious superstitions. Local wizards, charmers, and cunning men are instructed by Satan to heal with herbs and false magic rituals, admonishes the preaching voice in a fervent tone, while Jesus, the True Healer, "heals only by word," as King Abgar testified himself, and that is how all Christians should heal and be healed. The remaining texts in the book are canonical prayers from the Catholic rite that form a kind of Catholic *rituale compendiosum*, as Jani Jerkov has proven convincingly in a series of articles.[40] This canonical part of the book opens with a prayer for a sick person immediately following the condemnation of magical healing and evidently functioning as its ideological counterpart, an example of true healing by the word. The heading of the text is no less emphatic in its attempt to distance itself from any kind of popular magical practices, as it specifies the three legitimate religious specialists who alone can perform the supplication: priests, monks, and school teachers (*daskali*).[41]

Thus, even though Stanislavov's book shares a corpus of amulet texts with the *Miscellany* of Vuković, its use of those texts has little to do with the commercial stratagem of its predecessor. The market-oriented *Miscellany* was designed as a reader for individual use, in which the editor strategically hid an amulet, like a kind of *Kindersurpise* in a chocolate egg, to increase the commercial appeal of the entire volume. By contrast, Stanislavov's *Abagar*, being in reality a ritual package of canonical Catholic texts, is cast overtly as an amulet, yielding superficially to popular religious practices with the hidden agenda of transforming them from within.[42] What it offers, in fact, is an alternative type of "amulet," meant to marginalize local magic specialists and the secret knowledge on which their repute rested, by imposing new values of religious enlightenment and literacy made available on a large scale by the new printed medium.

This unusual form of Catholic missionary propaganda was dictated by the specific circumstances of the small, new Catholic communities in seventeenth-century Bulgaria. The Catholic missions were successful only in limited areas of the Bulgarian territory, mostly among segments of the population that, until the late sixteenth century, adhered to an old, Christian dualist heresy known as Paulicianism (*pavlikianstvo*).[43] These former heretics embraced Catholicism only halfheartedly, while continuing to practice some of their old beliefs in a rather idiosyncratic version of Christianity.[44] The fact that this compendium of canonical texts was window-dressed as an amulet and that the particular texts chosen to camouflage it as a talismanic object were none other than the amulet texts from Vuković's *Miscellany* of 1520, speaks to the enormous appeal of these amulets for the former Paulicians and newly converted Catholics.

This last case reveals new aspects of the relation between print and magic that further illuminate the successful career of *The 72 Names of God*. I have already suggested that this text (together with its more or less traditional entourage of amulets) walks a thin line between Christian orthodoxy and heteropraxis, as it appeals simultaneously to the sense of orthodox propriety and to the deep longing for a safe and easy life on which heteropraxis relies. I suppose that it was precisely this liminal status of the text that made it an especially useful tool for courting both sides of the divide. Its fame as a powerful amulet could impart an instant magical allure to any collection of texts, while its apparent canonicity made it a much more widely acceptable amulet, one that could easily blend with an orthodox textual environment and become practically indistinguishable from it. As a result, it could be used with equal success to manipulate religious communities with rather opposite tastes and sensibilities. On the one hand, it could sell—solely on its appeal as an amulet—a whole packet of other texts in which the intended audiences had little or no interest: it could make traveling merchants buy a book (and fill the pockets of a bookmaker), or make yesterday's heretics interested in a book of Catholic ritual texts (and thus further the agenda of Catholic missionary propaganda). On the other hand, I imagine that this amulet had the ability to ease the conscience of people with Christian scruples who would yield to it (let us not forget how sensitive the middle class has always been to surface propriety), because the text's carefully crafted orthodox veneer reassured them that they had not crossed the line.

The text was thus particularly well-suited to the new relationship between bookseller and bookbuyer that complicated, in the new culture of printed communications, the old relationship between bookmakers and readers. Since publishers of printed books produce multiple copies, reaching out to a wide and anonymous readership over a large territory, they must cater to the tastes of a heterogeneous and highly unpredictable group of potential buyers in order to ensure their success in the market. The same edition must appeal simultaneously to people who might have little in common. The key to a book's success then becomes not so much the complete satisfaction of each customer's needs (something that is practically inconceivable), but the making of a product that offends as little as possible the sensibilities of a large portion of potential buyers.

We may conclude that much of the intricate history of early Slavic typography revolved around the talismanic list *The 72 Names of the Lord*.
And the dependence between the two worked, somewhat surprisingly, both
ways. If the successful career of the text was much indebted to the new
print medium, the medium itself benefited no less from its association with
the text, as did numerous actors who labored in the field of Slavic printed
books for private or institutional interests. Print produced the list as an ideal
amulet for the age of mechanical reproduction. It shaped a formerly awkward Christian calque of a Kabbalistic amulet into a respectable apotropaic
object that appealed to Christians of widely diverse background and tastes,
united only by a shared existential need to be in control and to be safe in a
world where uncertainty was the norm.

The 72 Names of the Lord thus emerges as the site of significant shifts
in Slavic cultural history. It was brought to maturity in the interim between
the reigns of the old scribal and the new printed Christian culture, or, more
generally, at the moment when the end of the Middle Ages met the birth
of modernity. On a less spectacular scale, but with even more relevance to
this study, it was the fruit of the transition from one type of religious (het-
ero)praxis to another: from magic, custom-made for face-to-face local communities, to commodified and commercialized magic, mass-produced for
the translocal, unstable, and highly unpredictable religious communities of
the modern age.

What remains?
—Jacques Derrida, *Glas*

The rose remains in the name alone,
we hold the naked names . . .
—Bernard of Morval, *De contemptu mundi*

The boundless cannot be bound!
—Kuzma Prutkov, *Aphorisms*

We began our journey with two texts and two conjectures. The texts were chosen to represent two alternative models for listing the names of God: an open-ended list and a closed series of 72 names. Both lists presume to be exhaustive. Their respective understandings of "all," however, are not identical. If they both comply with the axiom of monotheist onomatology that the single divinity has many names, each reflects a different position as to exactly how many they are. Theology vouches for an infinite number. Magic counters with 72, the numerical equivalent of finitude. The reasons behind such a radical split within the Christian practice of the name are not immediately obvious, and neither are its consequences. We can hypothesize, but we cannot assert anything before studying the two cases that manifest the split and getting to the bottom of how they emerged on the cultural scene, what they represented for whom, and how they were put to use.

Two simple conjectures guided our studies: that the names of God in Christianity are basic terms of sacred order, and that a list of such terms is itself an effective rhetorical tool for promoting visions of order. If that is indeed the case, the two alternative lists of divine names—the finite and the infinite—strive to impose upon social reality two alternative patterns of unity and coherence. In other words, they argue for two alternative models of Christian behavior.

The effort to test these assumptions took us much further in time and space than we originally intended. The initial questions kept increasing in number and difficulty the deeper we went into the messy collocation of texts, gaps, and contradictions that make up the available material. Our study of order, which repeatedly confronted the disturbing tendency of practice to transgress the limits it creates, embodied part of the same dynamic between order and disorderliness: it resorted to disjointed narratives and indecorous juxtapositions of subjects. Moreover, it came to acknowledge openly those breaks in the logic of practice that no theory can effectively erase.

Despite the uncertainties, a pattern—I will call it theological, for clarity—began to emerge by chapter 3, and it became more and more distinct as its alternative—the magical vision—appeared in full view in chapter 8. At that point it was tempting to conclude that the two visions of order are ideological rivals, that the second contests the first, especially since we already knew that it had its roots outside Christian thought, in Gnosticism and the Kabbalah. Yet the more we learned about the 72 *Names* in the Christian context, the less plausible such an easy explanation became. Before attempting a theoretical rearrangement of the historical narratives, however, let us first outline the two visions as they emerged from the narratives themselves.

Two Visions of Order

The central pronouncement of Christian theology on the naming of God—attributed to the authority of St. Dionysius the Areopagite—endorses the infinite list of names as the most adequate "name" for the unnamable divinity. This ideal list is envisioned as hierarchically ordered on an ascending scale of adequacy: from symbolic to conceptual names and to the collapse of naming in mystical silence. While symbolic names (such as "Lamb") index biblical narratives and thus represent specific scenarios for action, conceptual names (such as "Love") signify key Christian values. Despite their internal stratification, however, all names designate not a divine identity (God being beyond the reach of language), but a table of differentiations within the created world. Each name establishes a coordinate for evaluating human positions in the social sphere, and all of them in their unity chart our ascent to the divine, the route of human deification. The order implied in the names of the list, in other words, manifests the Creator directly within the confines of the created world in order to show a way out of these confines.

Such order resembles a ladder that, when properly used, negates itself, for it leads to its own beyond. We may conclude that the theological vision emerging from the text of Dionysius presents an asymmetrical system of order that posits its "beyond" as its condition of possibility—a transcendent divinity exempt from the order it generates.

The idea of order presented by the amulet *The 72 Names of the Lord* is based on an entirely different principle. The arrangement of the names in the list does not represent a particular vision of order. Instead, the list is circumscribed structurally as well as semantically by the number 72—a well-established Judeo-Christian symbol of limits and ideal totality. We observed, in abundant and rather heterogeneous Christian material, that *The 72 Names of the Lord* is the matrix for proliferating other lists of 72 members: the 72 names of the Theotokos, the 72 languages, disciples of Christ, prophets, and various personifications of evil (such as the 72 demons, the 72 hypostases of the child-stealing witch Gylou). We also recovered a much larger repertoire of 72-fold concepts where the potential list is represented by its "principle," as Stephen Barney calls it, which is to say, by the numerical topos alone.[1] In either form—as condensed to a topos, or extended into a list—these concepts tend to cluster in list-structures, as catalogues of all things that are 72 in number, or as corpora of 72-fold lists. The cumulative effect of this copious listmaking is a universal vision of perfect symmetry and finitude predicated on the number of the Creator's names. Its totalizing ploy is the exact opposite of Dionysius's strategy. While the theological vision of order is produced symbolically by a single, infinite list of divine names that approaches its unnamable referent only asymptotically, magic arrests our imagination within a self-enclosed and self-referential universe by rhetorically amassing an open set of finite, perfectly homologous lists that mirror, each in its 72-fold structure, the master list of the Master's names.

Two views of the world emerge from this comparison—two ways of making sense of human reality. The first world, as imagined by Dionysius, is open to a "yonder," to the possibility of becoming something that it is not. To live in such a world means living not with definitive answers but with provisional assumptions. Its order is only a temporary one. It prepares us to abandon our most cherished assumptions, as Dionysius abandons the names of God, yet abandon them respectfully, with utmost gratitude. For it also teaches us that without those crutches, without the support of that temporary order, we would never have made it this far. As Dionysius's order holds the promise of its own negation, it both humbles us about our limitations and inspires us to believe that we can overcome them. Thus the reality it represents is an endlessly demanding world that makes human perfectionism possible. For only the hope that, in some radically other life, we can be perfect could give us the courage to face our inadequacies here and now, and spend our lives trying to rise above them. Such a world does not sound very inviting. As in a Gothic cathedral, a person feels dizzy with awe, and a little lost—too small for an order of that magnitude.

By contrast, the alternative world—the world as imagined by magic—is built with human measure in mind, not only indulging, but even encouraging our human flaws. There is "no there there," no remainder, no beyond; all is here, and all is known. It is a world of complete interiority which, like a home—or a cave, if you prefer a Platonic trope—lulls us into the illusion that the world outside does not really exist. Since we are comfortable here, we must also be safe. It is minimally challenging because it implies no possibility for transformation. Its inhabitants know everything there is to know, which is the same thing each time. The promise is not ecstasy but stasis, maintaining the status quo, and the goal is not discovery or freedom (both problematic in their troublesome unpredictability), but safety and control, the healthy reinforcement of a few simple truths that allow us to ignore the rest.

Religion, Need, and Desire: A Reorientation

Those familiar with the ethical system of Emmanuel Levinas will hear in these descriptions echoes of his dual ethical model of "totality" and "infinity."[2] The correspondences are so thick, it is almost as if Levinas had our material in mind when building his model. Some of the categories he adopts to chart his distinctions are identical with those that emerge from our own analyses: finitude and infinity, interiority and exteriority. Others suggest instructive new implications: the "totalizers," in his idiom, are egocentrics who are downward-bound, preoccupied with material concerns, whereas the "infinitizers" are centered on the Other, their bodies "raised upward," "in the direction of heights," in an endless pursuit of the "spiritual." (At this point we are tempted to recall also Simone Weil's version of the same dichotomy: "gravity and grace," and the "wings" that she chooses for her controlling trope of grace.)[3]

Most instructive in the analysis of Levinas, however, is the correspondence that he posits between totality and need on the one hand, and infinity and desire on the other. The opposition between need and desire is a topos in postmodern thought that has been dealt with in a variety of ways in diverse theoretical systems, but the objectives of Levinas, with his intense ethical concern for order and the Other, are the closest to our own.[4] For Levinas, desire is always metaphysical: it is the yearning for "something else entirely," for the absolute Other. As such, it can never be satisfied but feeds instead on its own hunger.[5] "Desire," he proposes, is "a movement ceaselessly cast forth, an interminable movement toward a future never future enough."[6] Needs, conversely, are existential dependencies with regard to the world. "Material" needs, he calls them—for food and drink, for clothes, shelter, and contact—and, because they are material, "admitting of satisfaction."[7] From the viewpoint of behavior driven by needs, it is the "I" that matters: its philosophy is "I need, and I deserve." And, as in our magical model, the homogenization that the materially hungry human subject effects on his perception of reality produces a world of perfect interiority. In sharp contrast to the infinity-bound subject of metaphysical desire, an inhabitant of a need-driven world lives in "contentment with the finite without concern for the infinite."[8]

Behind the surface split that we observed in the field of Christian rhetoric, the split between infinite (or asymmetrical) and finite (symmetrical) listmaking, we may begin to discern now, with the help of Levinas, a deeper dichotomy that cuts through the core of Christianity as a way of life, a dichotomy that we may wish to reinterpret in terms of a need-desire polarity. Two ways of Christian life emerge, two kinds of human relationship with the divine.

The way of metaphysical desire implies an exclusive relationship with a personal divinity defined by the longing for absolute perfection. It requires perpetual labor in response to the uninterrupted presence of the divine, labor that is believed to empower the individual for a radical transformation. The alternative way, informed by existential needs, presupposes conversely a contractual—and rather "open"—relationship with the other world. It emphasizes not individual perfection but material well-being. Moreover, human gratification is understood in a very immediate sense, unlike the yonder-fixed, desire-based behavior that places all its hopes in the world to come.

The representative locus of a need-driven religious praxis is the existential crisis: we observe this model in its purest form when disaster strikes, when death, destruction, and chaos threaten to take the upper hand in immediate human reality. Such result-oriented religious behavior has little concern for ecclesiastical norms and doctrinal purity, just as a drowning person could not care less about proper bureaucratic procedures and hierarchies. In a moment of crisis, a religious subject desperately reaches to all available otherworldly forces for help, with no concern for their doctrinal status. What is important is that the crisis is overcome; the questions "how" and "by whom" are irrelevant. Hence, we may observe a peculiar, promiscuous behavior toward the other world, in sharp contrast with the unconditional loyalty demanded by the path of metaphysical desire. The loyalties and trusts of this down-to-earth religious pragmatism are all conditional: the most respected otherworldly force is the one that has recently proven to be the most helpful. Using a modern analogy, we may say that in this system the person is not, as the desire model would have it, an exclusive lover of God, but a client who is free to choose from an array of supernatural providers.

Put in another idiom, need-driven religious life is focused on miracles. The chief solace that it offers its practitioners is the sheer possibility of miraculous events. Unlike the desire-based model, which requires a radical denial of the self, with no material proof of any reward whatsoever, a miracle promises maximal gratification for only minimal effort. A miracle is not a reward for a job well done, it is not proportionally distributed to all according to some logical criterion; quite the contrary: it is completely extraordinary, an exemption from the habitual order of things. Doctrinally speaking, the Almighty can perform miracles because he himself is exempt from the order he generates. Miracles thus are supposed to depend entirely on the will— or the whim—of God. Yet the biblical precedents of miraculous help from above encourage humans to dream of producing miracles upon demand, be it by prayer or coercion. *Magic* is a cover term for various techniques of binding the divine to conform to human will against the established order or—which is the same thing—to make God make miracles that fit our specific need of the moment.

While these two hypothetical religious ways—of metaphysical desire and existential need—are indeed alternatives open to every believer, they clearly do not have the same cachet with everyone in the religious field. Of the two, the path of desire is far steeper, far more demanding and forbidding. While Dionysius's hunger for a "beyond" holds the irresistible promise of holistic and authentic experiences, it demands an intensity and ethical maximalism that few can sustain as a way of life. And luckily so, for otherwise humanity would be threatened by extinction, economically as well as biologically.[9] The option that, for most people most of the time, appears more practicable and accessible is the one defined by existential need. The need-driven religiosity of all those who wear the 72 *Names* "just in case" represents the silent majority in the field of religion. Its mass appeal is not hard to explain: it offers a workable model for coping with the anxieties of everyday life, here and now, something that the elegant system of Dionysius—

with its qualifications and dialectics and its focus on "a future never future enough"—fails to provide.

Levinas is instructive on this point as well. For him, desire requires distance from needs: "Having recognized its needs as material needs, as capable of being satisfied, the I can henceforth turn to what it does not lack. It distinguishes the material from the spiritual, opens to Desire."[10] A brief recourse to one of the major theoretical idioms of our discussion may add further points of reference. Pierre Bourdieu, reinterpreting the same relation in sociological terms (as a class distinction, as a matter of social distance), would replace the Levinasian desire with what he calls a "theoretical relation to the world." Such a relation requires distance from necessity, in contrast to the "practical" position of those who "do not have the freedom to distance the world."[11] Thus both thinkers, despite their distinct theoretical priorities, link the desire model to privilege: as a way of life, it belongs to the elite who can afford the leisure to desire.[12] Without those who lack the means to live with the metaphysical hunger of Dionysius, being forced instead to exist by the dictates of their needs, Dionysius—and his vision—could never have had a place in Christian life.

How are we to evaluate the dynamic of need and desire in the field of religion? We assumed early on in this book that whatever hypothetical visions the two different forms of listmaking propose, they must be ideological rivals, alternatives that mutually negate one another. Such a conjecture arose from the presumption that theology and magic occupy two opposing—even conflicting—positions in the Christian field. The presumption is too familiar, and reiterated in too many idioms, to require much attention here. I need only mention the ubiquitous magic/religion dichotomy that every scholar of religion with interests outside the orthodox norm seems compelled to use, while lamenting its multiple inadequacies.[13] Other dichotomies are even less satisfactory, but equally instructive. Each offers a contrasting pair of terms that reserves an unquestionably positive qualification for the orthodox center (religion as it should be) and opposes to it an inferior "other" that is plagued by a variety of deficiencies. It is "popular,"[14] "syncretic,"[15] "easy,"[16] that is, corrupted, contaminated, or profaned; or, in a word, removed from the respectable norm. This is religion as it should *not* be, but unfortunately is.[17]

To redefine the same split in terms of need and desire, understood as formative principles of religious practice, means to articulate it in less evaluative terms, to shift the discussion to more neutral ground. Yet the chief advantage of this approach, I believe, lies in its potential to unmask the fallacious representation of "magic" as a kind of parasite on the body of "religion." As we saw, the Levinasian pair of need and desire has exactly the opposite dynamic: desire presupposes needs and their fulfillment, not vice versa. Observing Christian practice through this theoretical screen allows us to acknowledge the dependence of elite or professional Christianity on the need-driven religious practice of the multitudes.[18] In the same breath I argue, extending further the model of Levinas, that desire is inscribed in the need model as its ideal horizon: it provides an impossible standard against which others can measure the seriousness of their religious commitments. Thus, the "need" and the "desire" models of Christian living are both indispensable parts of Christianity, as they are mutually dependent on one another. They sustain one another not as alternatives, but as a complementary pair of behavioral choices that, by balancing out the equally strong human longing for power *and* freedom (for "gravity *and* grace"), makes Christianity a viable religious system.

Such a hypothesis implies, contrary to popular assumption, that Christianity does not propose a single, unified vision of order.[19] Part of the historical struggle of Christianity to become a world religion can be seen as a struggle to make room for the two—apparently incompatible—visions of order that our material reveals: an asymmetrical order rooted in metaphysical desire, and a symmetrical order that revolves around material needs. A good way to observe their complementarity directly, and in distinctly historical terms, is to examine the Christian cult of saints. As it emerged in late antiquity, the cult of saints was a radical expression of metaphysical desire, promoting martyrs—including those who pursued the "slow" ascetic martyrdom of the flesh—as paradigms for a Christlike life on earth. In the sixth century, however, when Christianity began to dominate the religious life of the Roman Empire, and its membership exploded, the cult of saints gradually shifted its focus to existential needs, redefining saints predominantly as miracle workers.[20]

The Danger of Closures

A couple of weeks ago a student of mine who was particularly taken by my desire/need hypothesis asked me a question that took me by surprise. Is my project itself need- or desire-based? Much as I have been preoccupied with this dichotomy, I had never before applied it to my own intellectual practices. Pushed to the wall, I had to admit to myself that, even though this project is ostensibly need-driven (after all, this study is supposed to make me tenurable), it is a purebred product of desire. This may explain why it has always felt—as it still does, up to this final page—virtually unfinishable.

This realization suddenly empowered me to acknowledge that the only way I could end my book was to admit, facetiously, that it is indeed without an end. And what better way to do so than to recall one of the best texts written on the subject of divine names outside the realms of theology and magic: a short story by Arthur C. Clarke entitled "The Nine Billion Names of God."[21]

The story, a classic of science fiction written in the 1950s, envisions all of human history as teleologically organized by a single goal: the writing of a list that contains all the possible names of God. This monumental project was initiated, we are told, by a Buddhist lamasery in Tibet many centuries ago. Until recently, this colossal undertaking was deemed only vaguely commensurable with human limitations: the calculated time for its completion was about fifteen thousand years, which makes it, from the point of view of a human life—even of the life of a human institution, such as the Tibetan lamasery—a project open to infinity. Yet modern technology, represented in the story by an efficient New York computer company, boldly reduces infinity to a hundred days. Only when the computer is already programmed and set in motion, and the process of speedy listmaking becomes irreversible, is the real meaning of the project revealed. It is nothing less than a project for the End. For once the list is completed, mankind will have fulfilled its purpose and reached its final destination. And so, while the last names of God are coming out of the printer, the story about the end of the world comes to an abrupt close: "Overhead, without any fuss, the stars were going out."[22]

Some things may be better left unfinished . . .

NOTES

1. All references to the Bible follow the New Revised Standard Version (New York and Oxford: Oxford University Press, 1989).

2. Von Soden, "Leistung und Grenze"; cf. Jack Goody, *Domestication of the Savage Mind*, 74–111.

3. With regard to the formalists, see, for example, Black, *Models and Metaphors*; Ricoeur, *Rule of Metaphor*; Lakoff and Johnson, *Metaphors We Live By*; and Lakoff and Turner, *More Than Cool Reason*. With regard to the pragmatists, see, for example, Lévi-Strauss, *Savage Mind*; Tambiah, "Magical Power of Words"; Sapir and Crocker, *Social Use of Metaphor*; and particularly, the "an-trop-ology" of Fernandez in his *Persuasion and Performance*, *Beyond Metaphor*, and, with Huber, *Irony in Action*.

4. Burke, *Rhetoric of Religion*, vi.

5. Ibid., 25

6. See Foucault, *Order of Things*, 208. Note that any classificatory system is a complex mental construct that, although it depends on basic cognitive processes, is always socially embedded. Each society operates simultaneously with multiple systems of classification whose taxa may overlap, and whose differentiating boundaries may sometimes be rather fuzzy (see, e.g., Lévi-Strauss, *Savage Mind*, 139).

7. The phrase "exegetical totalization" comes from Jonathan Z. Smith, who offers one of the most engaging presentations of the religious ambition for total order. Significantly for us, his entire argument revolves around the role of lists in religious practice (see *Imagining Religion*, esp. 44–48).

8. Burke, Rhetoric of Religion, 25–26.

9. This prudent qualification comes from Northrop Frye's *Words with Power* (70). The connection between *vision* and *imagination* is a topos in Western culture. William Blake, for example, used the two terms interchangeably: "Vision or Imagination is a Representation of what eternally exists, Really and Unchangeably," he wrote in 1810 in "A Vision of the Last Judgment" (*Complete Poetry and Prose*, 555). In a similar vein, Shakespeare famously defined the three paradigmatic "visionaries"—the lunatic, the lover, and the poet—as being "of imagination all compact" (*A Midsummer Night's Dream*, act 5, scene 1.)

10. This is the opening sentence of James's lecture entitled "The Reality of the Unseen," the third of his Gifford Lectures on Natural Religion, which he delivered at the University of Edinburgh in 1901–02 and then published in his classic study *The Varieties of Religious Experience*. Most succinctly, he formulated religious belief as "a belief in an object which we cannot see" (61). Incidentally, Levinas, in *Totality and Infinity*, defines metaphysical desire—the desire for transcendence—in exactly the same idiom of the unseen, naming it "Desire for the Invisible" (33).

11. In a similar vein Clifford Geertz argues, in his essay "Religion as a Cultural System," that the vision of universal order is both an ontological and an ethical foundation of religious life. Having established that the main function of religious symbols is "to synthesize a people's ethos,...their most comprehensive ideas of order," he goes on to propose one of the most elegant and influential formulas in contemporary anthropological studies of religion: "Religious symbols formulate a basic congruence between a particular style of life and a specific (if, most often, implicit) metaphysics, and in so doing sustain each with the borrowed authority of the other" (*Interpretation of Cultures*, 90).

12. Cf. Rom. 10:17: "So faith comes from what is heard, and what is heard comes through the words of Christ." Note also that both the Greek term *enōtizein* and its Slavic calque *v"noushiti* (to instill, to convince) etymologically mean "to put something in one's ear," from Greek *en-*, Slavic *v"-* (in), and *ous-* / *ōtos-*, *oukh-*/*oush-* (ear).

13. The rhetorical form of the dictum is part of the message as well. Jesus uses the same beatitude formula—"Blessed are they"—that he uses in the Sermon on the Mount to link a particular type of Christian attitudes and actions to a direct promise of a reward in heaven (Matt. 5:3–11; cf. Luke 6:20–23). The formula's recurrence in the story of Thomas puts a clear soteriological spin on the ability to believe without seeing. The only other occasion in which Jesus uses this formula outside the Sermon on the Mount is a passage in Luke that describes the exorcising of demons. "Blessed is the womb that bore you and the breast that nursed you," says a woman who has witnessed Jesus's power over the evil spirits, to which the Christ responds, "Blessed rather are those who hear the word of God and obey it" (Luke 11:27–28). The formal parallelism between the corresponding passages in Luke and John points to a deeper semantic correspondence between "those who have not seen" and "those who have heard." Thus the very choice of rhetorical patterns in the Thomas episode amplifies further the triumph of the verbal over the visual.

14. A similar insight is proposed by Patti White, who calls listmaking directly "an imposition of order" and treats lists as "the very embodiment of order" (*Gatsby's Party*, 20–21). Significantly, this insight is brought about not by a study of religion but of postmodern British and American literature, a radically secular body of material that ostensibly resists the very idea of universal order.

15. The most compact presentation of Bourdieu's position appears in *Language and Symbolic Power*.

16. The Wittgensteinian term *game* is another name for *field* in Bourdieu's vocabulary (see Bourdieu, *Language and Symbolic Power*, 172–73).

17. One of Bourdieu's multiple definitions of symbolic capital is "credit founded in *credence*" (ibid., 192). In the same passage, Bourdieu quotes Benveniste to unpack further the etymological potential of the credit-credence pun, reminding us that *credo* means

literally "to place one's *kred*," that is "magic powers," in a person from whom one expects protection thanks to "believing" in him.

18. Bourdieu states clearly his focus on order and the legitimization of boundaries through ritual naming. In the opening argument of his essay "Rites of Institution," he claims that his revision of Arnold Van Gennep's rites of passage is based on the asking of questions "regarding the *social* function of ritual and the social significance of boundaries or limits which the ritual allows one to pass over or transgress in a lawful way" (*Language and Symbolic Power*, 116). Similarly, in "The Social Institution of Symbolic Power," he tersely remarks that "the act of naming helps to establish *the structure of this world*" (ibid., 105, emphasis added).

19. Ibid., 170.

20. Some of the views expressed here have been influenced by the lectures of Geoffrey Hartman at the 2003 Summer Faculty Seminar, "Religious Hermeneutics and Secular Interpretation," sponsored by the Erasmus Institute, an intellectual experience that has been particularly stimulating for my own thinking on what I call the production of outstanding texts.

21. For Bourdieu's concept of the "theory effect," see *Language and Symbolic Power*, 132–36.

22. I fancy it closest in intention (if not result) to Ginzburg's *Ecstasies*, to which I have often resorted for inspiration and counsel. One passage from this book's introduction in particular helped me through many a moment of queasiness: "When considering the long trail of research [this study] involved, I remember experiencing a sensation vaguely resembling vertigo. I naively asked myself whether I would one day have the necessary competence to tackle so vast and complex a theme. Today I know that I never will" (14).

23. The transliteration from Cyrillic follows the system of the Library of Congress without ligatures and diacritical marks. Front *jer* is rendered as ('), and back *jer* as ("). Church Slavonic etymological *u* is consistently transliterated as (ou), regardless of whether the source uses a digraph or not. The transliteration from Greek follows *The Chicago Manual of Style*.

CHAPTER ONE

1. The new critical edition of the Greek original is the two-volume *Corpus Dionysiacum*, edited by Beate Regina Suchla, Günter Heil, and Adolf Martin Ritter (1990–1991), and the standard English translation is *Pseudo-Dionysius: The Complete Works*, translated by Colm Luibheid and Paul Rorem (1987). All further references to the corpus will be to these two editions and cited in text and notes (often parenthetically) in the following format: abbreviated title of text, chapter and column number in the Greek edition, separated by a hyphen, and the corresponding page in the English translation, preceded by a slash (e.g., *DN* 1-596A/55). An excellent introduction to the Dionysian corpus with comprehensive, chapter-by-chapter commentaries on the individual texts is Paul Rorem's *Pseudo-Dionysius: A Commentary*.

2. The corpus first gained publicity in the context of the religious disputations in the East that followed the Council at Chalcedon (451). The earliest datable reference to it was

made by the Monophysite Severus, Patriarch of Antioch (512–18), in a treatise against Julian, Bishop of Halicarnassus. The treatise was certainly written before 528, when it was translated into Syriac, but it was made public in 532 at the Constantinople colloquy between the supporters of Chalcedon and their Monophysite (Antiochene) opponents. For details, see Rorem and Lamoreaux, *John of Scythopolis and the Dionysian Corpus*, 10–15.

3. The reputed historian of the Church Eusebius of Caesarea (263–ca. 340) himself identified the Areopagite with the first Bishop of Athens, basing his statement upon the testimony of another Dionysius, the Bishop of Corinth (Eusebius, *History of the Church*, 3.4). The Eastern Orthodox churches celebrate St. Dionysius's martyrdom on October 3. For the standard repertoire of Orthodox hagiographical texts in his honor, see Metropolitan Makarii's *Velikiia minei-chetii: Oktiabr' 1-3*.

4. The man responsible for this tradition is Hilduin, the Abbot of the monastery of Saint-Denis, north of Paris, and the first translator of Dionysius into Latin. About the year 838, when he completed his translation of the corpus, Hilduin wrote a hagiographical account of the *Passio sanctissimi Dionysii* (see Migne, *PL* 106: 23–50). In this text, he identified the Areopagite with the patron of his monastery and thus wove the Dionysian corpus into the tradition of that holy place which, according to the legend, was personally chosen by the martyred Saint-Denis as his resting place (see Louth, *Denys the Areopagite*, 121).

5. The best source on the scholia by John of Scythopolis and their context is the recent exhaustive and highly illuminating study by Paul Rorem and John Lamoreaux, *John of Scythopolis*, which includes an English translation of John's annotations and prologue.

6. The scholia by John and Maximus were intermixed in the tradition, and most surviving versions of the annotated Areopagite are in fact conflations of the two, attributed *en bloc* to Maximus (as in Migne's edition in *PG*, 4). Only recently Beate Regina Suchla identified an early recension of the scholia that contains only those comments authored by John. The results show John's considerable share in the extant commentaries: of the 1,675 individual scholia published by Migne, roughly 600 can be assigned to John. Since the scholia by John are as a rule longer, the total length of his commentaries makes up approximately 70 percent of the total text of the scholia (see details in Rorem and Lamoreaux, *John of Scythopolis*, 36–39).

7. Throughout the Middle Ages, voices of suspicion interrupted the continual panegyric of Dionysius only rarely, and without serious consequence. In the East, an isolated example of such inconsequential skepticism would be the fleeting doubts raised by Patriarch Photius of Constantinople (ca. 810–ca. 895), himself a rather problematic figure (see Rorem, *Pseudo-Dionysius: A Commentary*, 15).

8. McGinn's revealing comment deserves to be quoted here in full: "From the start [Dionysius's] writings were treated much like the Bible itself—as a divine message filled with inner life and mysterious meaning which could never be exhausted, but which needed to be reread in each generation and reinterpreted in the light of new issues. He himself, however, would probably not have been unhappy with this hermeneutical flexibility, since no one knew better than he the limits of words in the face of the true Mystery" (*Presence of God*, 1:182). Compare Rorem's metaphor of Dionysius's "wax nose" based on the medieval *bon mot* attributed to Alan of Lille, "Authority has a wax nose; it can be bent in diverse directions." Similarly, Rorem contends, the Dionysian writings have been

repeatedly stretched and bent every which way to serve the need of the interpreter (*Pseudo-Dionysius: A Commentary*, 238–40).

9. What Aquinas famously called Dionysius's "obscure style" (*In librum Beati Dionysii*, 1) is a topos in the responses of virtually everyone who ever attempted to translate the Areopagitical corpus, whether in medieval or modern time. Consider Eriugena's sober assessment, "In his usual way [Dionysius] expresses himself in an *involved and distorted language*, and therefore many find him *extremely obscure and difficult to understand*" (*Periphyseon* 1.50:106, emphasis added). One of the major stumbling blocks in Dionysius's style is his idiosyncratic lexicon. First, he delights in neologisms, some of which were picked up in later philosophical idiom (especially his original term *hierarchy*), but most of them remain to date outright perplexing. Furthermore, his pleonasms operate with an unusually broad range of near-synonyms; to quote Aquinas again, "he often multiplies words, which may seem superfluous, but nevertheless will be found to contain a great depth by those who consider them diligently" (Aquinas, *In librum Beati Dionysii*, 2). Finally, he has a penchant for "hyper-terms" (see McGinn, *Presence of God*, 1:76). These supereminent predications are usually elative adjectival forms (e.g., *hyperagathon*, "more-than-Good," or *hyperagnostos*, "more-than-unknowable") that strive to push language beyond affirmation and negation, and thus beyond its habitual boundaries.

10. See Louth, *Denys the Areopagite*, 111–13. The translation was made by Sergius of Reshaina in Mesopotamia (d. 536) and probably predated the Constantinople colloquy of 532, where the writings of Dionysius are first known to have been cited. Another translation was completed in 708 by Phocas bar Sergius of Edessa. Despite its early appearance in the Syrian context, however, the works of Dionysius never left serious traces there.

11. Having rejected the decisions of the Fourth Ecumenical Council of Chalcedon, the Church of Antioch, the Coptic Church of Egypt, the Armenian, and the Ethiopian Churches (collectively known as non-Chalcedonians) split off from the Pentarchy. The reasons manifested themselves as theological (controversies over the Christological articles of the Creed), but there were underlying political issues as well, mostly a growing resentment of the non-Greek and non-Byzantine Christians toward the idea that the conciliar dogmatic definitions should be imposed as imperial laws by Constantinople.

12. Antioch, the old Syrian capital, was destroyed first by the Persian army of Chosroes in 540, and then, in the famous battle of Jarmuk on August 20 of 636, it was conquered by the Arab army of the Caliph Omar. The new Arab Caliphate chose the Syrian city of Damascus for its capital, thus transforming the region into the cradle of the emerging world of Islam; for a complete historical background, see Cantor, *Civilization of the Middle Ages*, 131–37.

13. That exquisite manuscript, which was the Greek version most widely read by medieval Latin thinkers, is kept today in the Bibliothèque Nationale in Paris (Gr 437). An indispensable source for studying the Western tradition of the corpus is *Dionysiaca*, the line-by-line edition of the text in the major Latin translations prepared by Philippe Chevallier.

14. About the role of Eriugena, see McGinn, *Presence of God*, 2:80–118. Anastasius the Librarian (well known in medieval Slavic studies as one of the champions of the Slavic apostle St. Constantine-Cyril in Rome) brought out revisions of Eriugena's translation in 875 and added to it clarifying remarks.

15. The revival of interest in Dionysius among the Italian Humanists is related also to the efforts of the Florentine Academy to revive Plato and the Platonic tradition. For the members of the Academy, Dionysius was the quintessential Christian Platonist. Giovanni Pico della Mirandola praised him as the master of the true Christian Kabbalah, and Marsiglio Ficino, the head of the Academy, saw Paul, Plato, and Dionysius as the pillars of his own religious synthesis. Ficino even made new translations of *The Divine Names* and *The Mystical Theology* in 1492. For an excellent introduction to the significance of the corpus for the Italian Humanists, see Froehlich, "Pseudo-Dionysius," 33–46.

16. For a recent, comprehensive (though not always accurate) review of the Dionysian influence among the Slavs, see Denkova, Yaneva, and Ivanova, "Reception of Pseudo-Dionysius in Medieval Bulgaria," 87–103. See also Stanchev, "Kontseptsiiata na Psevdo-Dionisii Areopagit," and "Dionisii Areopagit"; cf. Ševčenko, "Byzantine Scientific and Pseudo-Scientific Literature," 328. Especially influential—or so it seems—was a passage from part 4 of *The Divine Names* that was read as a patristic endorsement of translation by sense over translation by form. Since at that early stage of Slavic culture translation was not only the predominant practice but also a critical theoretical issue, the passage, backed by the apostolic authority of Dionysius, soon became a commonplace.

17. For hesychast spirituality and its links to the mysticism of Dionysius, see Meyendorff, *St. Gregory Palamas and Orthodox Spirituality*, esp. 86–88 and 108. For specific aspects of Dionysius's influence in the fourteenth century, see Keipert, "Velikyj Dionisie sice napisa," 326–50 (cf. Denkova, Yaneva, and Ivanova, "Reception of Pseudo-Dionysius in Medieval Bulgaria," 100–102). For a useful comparative look at the impact of the Areopagitical corpus on Eastern and Western spirituality in the fourteenth century, see Louth, "Influence of Denys the Areopagite."

18. A complete edition of Isaiah's translation appears in Metropolitan Makarii, *Velikiia minei-chetii, Oktiabr' 1–3* (1870): 375–619. For a parallel Greek-Russian edition of *The Divine Names* and *The Mystical Theology*, see Prokhorov, *Dionisii Areopagit*.

19. According to latest count, more than eighty copies of Isaiah's translation have survived (see Denkova, Yaneva, and Ivanova, "Reception of Pseudo-Dionysius in Medieval Bulgaria," 97). The oldest among them belongs to a Serbian manuscript from 1579 that is held today in the State Public Library in Moscow, the collection of Gilferding, no. 46. Regarding the manuscript tradition, see Gelian Prokhorov, "Sochineniia Dionisiia Areopagita," and *Pamiatniki perevodnoi i russkoi literatury*, 42–59; see also the informative summary by Hermann Goltz, "Traditionsgeschichte des Corpus areopagiticum slavicum."

20. The first-century authorship of the corpus first came under attack when Desiderius Erasmus (ca. 1466–1536) circulated some brief but disturbing comments that Lorenzo Valla (ca. 1406–57) had made public in 1457. Valla had noticed that no Greek or Latin father before Gregory the Great ever quoted the Areopagite texts, and that parts of the corpus seemed blatantly fictional. Erasmus added to these doubts his own concerns about the much too elaborate liturgical rituals reflected in the corpus, which suggested a later (certainly post-Nicene) date. Martin Luther (1483–1546) adopted Erasmus's criticism together with his ironic way of referring to the Areopagite, "Dionysius ille quisquis fuerit" ("Dionysius whoever he may be"). Again, Froehlich's "Pseudo-Dionysius" offers a most succinct and reliable survey on this subject.

21. A large part of Proclus's treatise *On the Existence of Evils* was used in *DN*, and Dionysius drew from other works of his as well, even some written after 462. See Stiglmayr, "Der Neuplatoniker Proclus"; Koch, "Proklus"; and, more recently, Saffrey, "Pseudo-Dionysius and Proclus."

22. Rorem and Lamoreaux (*John of Scythopolis*, 9–11) summarize the arguments for pushing the *terminus a quo* of the corpus into the sixth century. As for the identification of the author, there have been, reportedly, about thirty-two attempts at this point, none of them conclusive. Hathaway provides a helpful summary of the leading hypotheses (*Hierarchy and the Definition of Order*, 31–35). The most recent attempt, proposed independently by Nutsubidze and Honigmann, identifies the anonymous author with the Georgian monk Peter the Iberian (ca. 411–ca. 491); for a more current development of that argument, see Khintibidze, "Novyi argument"; and van Esbroeck, "Peter the Iberian." So uncertain, in fact, is everything about this mysterious author that Paul Rorem semi-playfully questions even the confident gender reference to him (or her?); see his foreword to *Pseudo-Dionysius: A Commentary*, 1.

23. The Protestant Georg Calixt (1586–1656) is credited with having used the designation "Dionysius Pseudo-Areopagita" first in 1619. I generally avoid it because it appears to me not only clumsy but also slightly derogatory (cf. similar thoughts in Rorem, *Pseudo-Dionysius: A Commentary*, 3). About apophatic Christian thought and the place of Dionysius in it, see, for example, volume 2 of Raoul Mortley's panoramic study *From Word to Silence*.

24. See Rorem and Lamoreaux, *John of Scythopolis*, 4–5.

25. This last metaphor, a paraphrase of the biblical command of Yahweh to the Israelites to plunder the Egyptians in order to enrich themselves (Exod. 3:22; 12:35–36) was suggested to me by Jeauneau, "Neoplatonic Themes," 6. On the *spolatio* motif and Exod. 3:21–22, 11:2–3, and 12:35–37 as a paradigm for Christian appropriation of wisdom from the pagan world, see Frizzell, "'Spoils from Egypt.'"

26. Luther, "Babylonian Captivity," (1520), in *Martin Luthers Werke* 6:562.

27. Cf. Louth, *Denys the Areopagite*, 11.

28. The symbolic weight of Dionysius's gesture can be adequately evaluated only against a broader historical backdrop. As is well known, the sixth century marked the peak of the growing tension in the Byzantine Empire between the token site of the old pagan Greek culture and its new Christian counterpart, Athens and Constantinople. Many saw the Neoplatonic School in Athens, where Proclus had reigned for much of the fifth century as its last great figure (and which at the time of Dionysius was still a living center of classical education and thought), as the stronghold of the old tradition, a direct heir of Plato's Academy, and often referred to it by the same name. It is easy to imagine, then, how Proclean Neoplatonism emerged at the time as an ideological rival of Christianity, especially if we keep in mind that Platonism "was not only a school of philosophy, but a school of spirituality" (see Jeauneau, "Neoplatonic Themes," 4). The conflict culminated in 529 with the edict of Emperor Justinian to close the Academy, which—had Dionysius never written his works—might have been the death of Neoplatonism.

29. For a more inclusive approach to the question of synthesis in Dionysius, see, for example, David Tracy, "Divided Consciousness of Augustine," who presents

the Areopagitical corpus as the most successful Christian synthesis of Eros and Logos. One may even argue that the Areopagitical corpus externalizes, perhaps for the first time so dramatically, a tendency in Eastern Orthodoxy to favor synthesis over analysis, a tendency that is often seen (at least from an Eastern standpoint) as marking an important divide between the Christian East and West. To be sure, the capacity for synthesis is the one quality most frequently brought up by Eastern theologians to characterize both the Orthodox theological vision and Orthodox sacramental experience in opposition to their Western counterparts. Meyendorff, for example, claims that the Eastern Orthodox experience emphasizes *antinomies* and thus preserves "a sense of inadequacy between the formulae and the content of the faith" in opposition to the Western emphasis on "conceptual rationalism" and analytical formulae (*Byzantine Theology*, 124; cf. the more general scheme of synthesis/antithesis proposed by Fedotov in *Russian Religious Mind*, esp. 23–57).

30. When the so-called Monophysites brought up the Dionysian writings at the Constantinople colloquy of 532, the spokesman for their opponents, Hypatius, the Bishop of Ephesus, challenged the alleged apostolic authority of the author by pointing out that none of his works had ever been cited, or even mentioned, before. Thus the first reaction to the "discovery" of the corpus on the part of the Chalcedonians was reserved at best (see Rorem and Lamoreaux, *John of Scythopolis*, 15–18). I should note that the term "Monophysite" is not accepted by the Oriental Orthodox Churches to which it is applied.

31. An early Greek copy of the corpus (which Beate Regina Suchla dates from the first half of the sixth century and which she claims to be the antegraph for all later Greek manuscripts) already incorporated John of Scythopolis's *Scholia* and *Prologue* in the form of interlinear and marginal commentaries (see Suchla, "Eine Redaktion"). For further evidence of such Talmudic-style practice, consider the following: "In 875 Anastasius Bibliothecarius informed Charles the Bald that in Constantinople he had recently received a copy of the *Scholia* on the works of Dionysius. This is a text he translated and added *to the margins* of Eriugina's Latin version of the works of Dionysius" (Rorem and Lamoreaux, *John of Scythopolis*, 3 and 36, n. 56; emphasis added).

32. I have borrowed the phrase "limitrophic violence" from Derrida, though in the process—as is always the danger when quoting out of context—I may have reinvented it beyond recognition (see Derrida, *Margins of Philosophy*, xxv).

33. See Rorem and Lamoreaux, *John of Scythopolis*, 3.

CHAPTER TWO

1. On Judaism as a religion of the name, consult the fundamental works of Gershom Scholem, "The Name of God," and *On the Kabbalah*, especially 36–44; see also Peter Schäfer, *The Hidden and Manifest God*; and Joseph Dan, "The Name of God." David Burrell offers a noteworthy comparative analysis of Judaic, Muslim, and Christian onomatological views in "Naming the Names of God," and a good, comprehensive review of divine names across world religions appears in the entry "Names" in Jean Chevalier and Alain Gheerbrant's *A Dictionary of Symbols*, 693–95.

2. During the time of the Second Temple, the high priest alone was allowed to pronounce the ineffable name on Yom Kippur (the Day of Atonement), while reciting Lev. 16:30 during the confessional, and the people in the forecourt would prostrate themselves,

praying that he not be struck down for unworthiness (see Cohon, "The Name of God," 591).

3. The scriptural source of this Christian topos is the baptismal formula introduced in Matt. 28:19 ("baptizing. . .in the name of the Father and of the Son and of the Holy Spirit"). Friedrich Giesebrecht discusses the Hebrew origin and the initial ritual meaning of the formula "in the name of [God]" (*Die Alttestamentliche Schätzung des Gottesnamens*, 134–40). Walter Bauer, who mentions the rabbinical model of the accusative (directional) Greek construction *eis (to) onoma (theou)*, points out that it is used in New Testament Greek and in early patristic writings with the meaning of both "with regard to" and "while calling on the name of." He further asserts that the concept of dedication is crucial for the correct interpretation of the baptismal formula: "Through baptism *eis to onoma theou* the one who is baptized becomes the possession of and comes under the protection of the one whose name he bears" (*Greek-English Lexicon*, 572). The formula "in the name of" is present in all modern European languages, although today it is greatly trivialized, and the original meaning of "name" in it is largely lost. For further information on scriptural name-formulas, see Sergei Bulgakov, who provides an extensive list of biblical references to the name of God (*Filosofiia imeni*, 257–61).

4. The Jewish exegetes point out that the root for "wonderful" is the same one used to construct "name-for-the-name." Hence the rebuke is interpreted as a statement about the utmost secrecy and power of the name withheld (see Janowitz, "Theories of Divine Names," 366).

5. It is important to underline the relation of this passage to the most sacred name of God in the Jewish tradition, YHWH, which the Greeks called "the Tetragrammaton" (literally, "four letters"). The traditional pronunciation of this name is "Yahweh," the second syllable of which, "eh," is based on the assonance *ehyeh* ("I am"). The name was considered so immensely powerful and sacred that after the third century BCE it became practically a taboo, and the name *adonai* ("the Lord") was used instead. Christian exegesis relates the name YHWH to the statement "God is love" (John 4:8–16) by way of Exod. 34:6–7, the Lord's proclamation of his love and mercy which the rabbis call "the Thirteen Attributes" and which comes in response to Moses's request to see the glory of God (Exod. 33:18). See Martin Rose, *Jahwe*, for a comprehensive study on the subject.

6. Ricoeur, *Essays*, 94.

7. Note that this single, positive statement of God about his name documented in Scripture is given in the form of an I-identification ("I am X"). This circumstance opens the possibility of considering the abundance of other such identity statements of God from across the Old and the New Testaments as self-naming acts and their nominal predicates as the Lord's names: "I am the first and the last" (Isa. 44:6, 48:6; Rev. 1:17); "I am the bread of life" (John 6:35, 6:48); "I am the light of the world" (John 8:12); "I am the good shepherd" (John 10:11); "I am the Son of God" (John 10:36); "I am the resurrection and the life" (John 11:25), "I am the way, and the truth, and the life" (John 14:16); "I am the true vine" (John 15:1); "I am the Alpha and the Omega, the Beginning and the End" (Rev. 1:8).

8. Many scholars consider *ehyeh* to be the Hiphil form of the verb "to be" and thus construe a causative meaning, which would cohere with the phrase "Yahweh Sabbaoth," read as "the One who creates the heavenly Sabbaoth." Such an interpretation suggests an *a fortiori* argument: if Yahweh creates the Sabbaoth, the heavenly beings, how much

more is he to be regarded as creating the earthly world that we inhabit. The verb can also be construed as an imperfect form referring to the future: "I will be who I will be." The phrase, in turn, can be taken in the sense of reassuring presence—"I will be with you"— thus harmonizing with the context in Exodus, where God promises to be with Moses and the Hebrews on their journey to freedom.

9. Among the numerous contemporary studies on the subject, the most comprehensive are Taylor's *Names of Jesus*, Cullmann's *Christology*, Sabourin's *Names and Titles of Jesus*, and Hahn's *Titles of Jesus*.

10. Islam shares in the same dialectics. Based on the Koran (7:179), the Islamic tradition contends that Allah has ninety-nine Most Beautiful names (these legitimate appellations of the revealed God are discussed in detail by Al-Ghazzali (see Burrell and Daher, *Al-Ghazzali*). At the same time, it claims that Allah has only one Great Name (*al-ismu'l-a'zam*), the hundredth and most secret one, which alone represents his concealed essence.

11. See Bulgakov, *Filosofiia imeni*, 190 and 206. Gregory of Nyssa offers a similar proposition when discussing the baptismal formula: "What then does that unnamable name mean, about which the Lord said 'Baptizing them into the name' without adding the significant word which 'the name' indicates?...For how could a name be found for that which is above every name? But he gave the power that *whatever* name our intelligence by holy endeavor should discover, indicative of the transcendent nature, that that name should be equally applicable to the Father, Son, and Holy Ghost, whether the 'good' or the 'incorruptible,'...*whatever* name each may think worthy to be employed to indicate the undefiled nature" (Migne, *PG*, 45: 14–15, *Contra Eunomium*). I quote here the English translation of the passage provided in Mortley, *From Word to Silence*, 2:181 (emphasis added).

12. See Samuel Cohon's telling remarks about the indispensability of the notion of God's name for the establishment of the advanced Jewish monotheistic idea of God as a *personality*: "While personality is conceivable in nameless being, it is greatly crystallized by a name" ("The Name of God," 582).

13. A related issue, which would come to the fore with the transformation of Christianity into an imperial religion at the time of Justinian, is the question of the Bible. The Bible (both the source of Christian doctrine and a key element of Christian worship) was created in particular languages: Hebrew, Aramaic, and Greek. That circumstance proved to be at odds with the universalism of Christianity and its missionary character. It confronted Christian proselytizing with two equally imperfect alternatives: colonial bilingualism (a split between everyday and ritual language) or translation of the sacred texts (creation of multiple ritual languages across the Christian world). Each alternative implied a potential obstacle: the first of not being understood; the second of corrupting the Holy Writ.

14. Tracy, "Divided Consciousness of Augustine," 95.

15. See Hadot's compelling argument in *What Is Ancient Philosophy?* 237–52.

16. "Discourse" is the standard English translation today for the Greek term *logos*.

17. See Lossky, *In the Image*, 13. On the Neoplatonic negative method (*via negativa*) in its historical contexts, see Mortley, *From Word to Silence*, 1:125–58.

18. Concerning the Hebrew word *shem* (name) and its implications of a substantial relationship between the name and the name-bearer, see, for example, Giesebrecht, *Die Alttestamentliche Schätzung des Gottesnamens*, 7–21. See also Trachtenberg, who

presents insightful quotations from Hebrew texts on the matter such as "the man's name is his person," or "the man's name is his soul" (*Jewish Magic*, 78). It is interesting to note, however, that by the very act of the Septuagint translation (283–246 BCE), which consistently rendered the Hebrew *shem* by the Greek *onoma*, the entire spectrum of ambiguities of the Greek term, including those concerning the origin of names, was invested into the particular version of the Jewish Bible that later became the Christian Old Testament.

19. See Aristotle, *On Interpretation* 16a, 29, in *The Categories [and] On Interpretation*.

20. The works of Eunomius are extant only in fragments included in a series of polemical treatises against him (*Contra Eunomium*) written by Basil the Great (Migne, *PG*, 29–30) and Gregory of Nyssa (Migne, *PG*, 45).

21. Origen, *Contra Celsum*, bk. 5, sec. 45, p. 299.

22. See similar ideas in Janowitz's "Theories of Divine Names," where the author, at her own discretion, interprets Origen's theory of names in the terms of Peircian semiotics. Compare Bulgakov's idea that the divine name is a "verbal icon" (*slovesnaia ikona*; see his *Filosofiia imeni*, 186).

23. Regarding their translatability, Origen wrote, "If the names whose nature it is to be powerful in some particular language are translated into another language, they no longer have any effect as they did with their proper sounds" (*Contra Celsum*, bk. 5, sec. 45).

24. See Mortley, *From Word to Silence*, 2:223.

25. Despite the resistance it encountered, the cratylic idea continued to linger on the fringes of Christian intellectual life, never fully embraced as legitimate yet never really banished. The most recent proof of its vitality and potential to turn the tide in its own favor was the renewed controversy on Mount Athos that exploded early in the twentieth century when the Russian monk Hilarion proposed the provocative formula "The Name of God is as if God Himself" (*Imia Bozhe kak by sam Bog*). This startling pronouncement triggered waves of protest and resentment among the monks of Mount Athos, polarizing them into supporters of Hilarion, who called themselves *imiaslavtsy* (Russian: "those who glorify the Name" or "onomatolaters"), and his opponents, significantly named *imiabortsy* ("name-breakers" or "onomatoclasts"), with a clear reference to the Iconoclast controversy that had shaken the Eastern Orthodox world twelve centuries before. Though the name-breakers instigated the conflict and were initially much more vocal, Hilarion's camp eventually gained the support of broader religious circles both on Mount Athos and in Russia. In fact, their position became so strong that they might even have won the battle, repeating the triumph of the Iconodules (those who venerate icons) in 843, had not the October Revolution "resolved" the matter (among so many others) in its own radical way. For an informative account of this controversy and its influence on Russian religious thought, see N. K. Bonetskaia, "O filologicheskoi shkole P. A. Florenskogo." The best study of the controversy to date is the two-volume tour de force by Bishop Ilarion Alfeev, *Sviashchennaia taina Tserkv*.

26. See Gregory Nazianzen, *Hymn to God*, in Migne, *PG*, 37: 507.

27. Kolakowski, *Main Currents of Marxism*, 1:14.

28. See Mortley, *From Word to Silence*, 2:251.

CHAPTER THREE

1. See Lossky, *In the Image and Likeness*, 17.

2. Only two previous nonpolemical works discuss divine names, although neither focuses exclusively on this subject: Origen's *Peri Archon* (On the first principle) is a systematic statement of Christian faith, providing the basis for allegorical interpretation of the Bible; and Augustine's *De Trinitate* (On the Trinity), which discusses the proper naming of God in books 5–7 and seeks to clarify how ecclesiastical teaching can be understood in the light of previous Trinitarian controversies and their dogmatic resolution.

3. See Ep. 6–7, where Dionysius dismisses polemical theology as "superfluous" and, largely, a waste of energy. Note especially the following unqualified statement: "I have never wished to embark on controversies with Greeks or with any others. It is enough for me to know about the truth and then to speak appropriately of what I know. And may God grant me this!" (Ep.7-1080A/267).

4. Note that Dionysius characteristically articulates this common denominator of creation in the Johannine language of "yearning" and "love" (see esp. *DN* 4-709B–D/81). In the same line of thought, consider Andrew Louth's metaphoric definition of Dionysius's hierarchy as "not a ladder we struggle up by our own effort," but "the outreach of God's love" (*Denys the Areopagite*, 41).

5. I use the term "quality space" to refer to the topographic model of social relations that Fernandez proposes in *Persuasion and Performance*.

6. It is important to emphasize here the rich Christian implications of "gift" (*dōrea*). It is used in New Testament Greek exclusively as designating the gifts of God in opposition to the term for human gift, *dōron*, with its distinct connotations of contingency and deprivation. Furthermore, this Christian term encompasses a vast semantic field that includes not only that which is given, but also the act of sharing a particular perfection (attribute), the gratuitous stance involved in the bounteous act, and even the particular capacity bestowed upon the receiver, a peculiar "partaking" in the gift so benevolently shared by God with the creation. See, for example, the usage of "the gift (*dōrea*) of righteousness" by St. Paul: "If, because of the one man's trespass, death exercised dominion through that one, much more surely will those who receive the abundance of grace and the free gift of righteousness exercise dominion in life through the one man, Jesus Christ" (Rom. 5:17). About the anthropological concept of "gift circle" as a community sustained by a perpetual circulation of gifts, see Hyde, *The Gift*, 56–92. Needless to say, the classic study by Mauss, *The Gift*, is still indispensable for any social theory of gifts.

7. Dionysius first introduces the term *kenosis* in a reference to its original apostolic context (Phil. 2:7) and in accordance with its traditional Christological application. Yet in a crucial passage that follows almost immediately and recapitulates the entire differentiation/unity argument, Dionysius applies the same term to the entire Godhead, which "remains. . .full amid the emptying act of differentiation" (*DN* 2-649B/66). This expansion of the term is consistent with the general premise of the treatise that whatever term is applied to one of the divine hypostases refers to the entire divinity.

8. Dionysius compares the divine gifts to a seal that gives itself completely to each impression yet leaves differing impressions, because the substances receiving a share of the archetype differ in their receptivity (*DN* 2-644A–B/62–63).

9. McGinn, *Presence of God*, 1:174.

10. "In the divine realm unities hold a higher place than differentiation" (*DN* 2-652A/67).

11. Note that both "beyond" and "supra" (as preposition or as prefix) translate the Greek *hyper*; hence the standard reference to such words as "hyper-terms" (see McGinn, *Presence of God*, 1:176).

12. Lossky, *In the Image and Likeness*, 29. In a related passage that explicates the understanding of the Trinitarian relationship in Dionysius, Lossky elaborates, "Denied in their opposition, the two terms [Unity and Trinity] must be understood together, in a sort of synopsis or simultaneous vision which identifies by distinguishing" (27).

13. Ibid., 29.

14. Ibid., 13.

15. Dionysius is often seen as too heavily order-bound, an inhabitant of a rigid hierarchical universe of his own making. Andrew Louth's defense of Dionysius against such charges is by itself revealing of this prejudice: "For many the very notion of order and hierarchy seems constraining: people are allotted their role and are to be content within it. In favor of the notion of hierarchy it could be argued that the alternative to some order is no order, and that anarchy brings with it much greater evils, much greater constraints on freedom and fulfillment. But [Dionysius] himself has none of these doubts or questions. He is deeply committed to the notion of an ordered society" (*Denys the Areopagite*, 42). I believe that such a line of defense, however well-intended, does little justice to the remarkably holistic notion of order advanced in the Areopagitical corpus, mostly because it operates within the binary logic that the author of *The Mystical Theology* so elegantly transcends.

16. For revealing commentaries on the structure of the corpus, see Lossky, *In the Image and Likeness*, 25–26, and esp. Rorem, "The Place of *The Mystical Theology* in the Pseudo-Dionysian Corpus," 87–98, which discusses alternative opinions on the interrelation of the treatises.

17. The description of creation in terms of gradual "overflowing" is one of the most controversial points of this treatise and may be interpreted as verging on pantheism. Dionysius, however, is particularly careful in his attempts to protect himself from such charges. In the same chapter he includes an elaborate qualification about the discontinuity between God and the created things, emphasizing that "there is no exact likeness between caused and cause, for the caused carry within themselves only such images of their originating sources as are possible for them, whereas the causes themselves are located in a realm transcending the caused, according to the argument regarding their source" (*DN*2-645C/64). For more details, see Rorem, *Pseudo-Dionysius: A Commentary*, 168 and 176–77.

18. Rorem specifies that Pseudo-Dionysius consistently uses the word *theology* in its literal meaning as "the word of God" (i.e., "the Bible"), and the word *theologians*, used interchangeably with "God's wise men," designates unequivocally the Scripture writers ("Biblical Allusions," 63–64).

19. Rorem (ibid., 64) points out that this short passage includes 108 references to the Bible and, in the entire work of Pseudo-Dionysius, is the passage most densely saturated with scriptural quotations and allusions.

20. The main thesis of chapter 2 of *The Divine Names* is that all names attributed to one person of the Trinity—with the exception of the Trinitarian titles proper—must be taken to belong, without distinction, to the entire divinity (*DN* 2-637A/58, 637C/60, 640B/60, 652A/67). This thesis follows directly from the general principle of personal non-opposition within the Trinity, as discussed above.

21. On *theosis* (deification or divinization) and its strategic place in Eastern Orthodox thought, see Ware [Bishop Kallistos of Diokletia], *Orthodox Church*, 231–38. For an excellent introduction to the interrelatedness of deification and the knowledge of God (with a weighty share of attention to the works of Dionysius), see Lossky, *In the Image and Likeness*.

22. See Ep. 9-1104B–1109A/280–285; the other references to *The Symbolic Theology* include the following passages: *DN* 1-597B/57; *DN* 4-700C/75; *DN* 9-913B/117; *DN* 13-984A/131; *CH* 15-336A/187; and, most notably, *MT* 3-1033B–C/139.

23. The Bible explicitly testifies to the existence of the gifts prior to Creation. See, for example, Prov. 8:23–31, where Wisdom claims she was established from eternity before the Creation, or the opening pericope of the Gospel of St. John, where it is asserted that the Word was "in the beginning" "with God" and that "the Word was God" (John 1:1).

24. Fernandez, *Persuasion and Performance*, 13ff.

25. "Insofar that it is evil," Dionysius claims, "it neither is nor confers being" (*DN* 4-717C/86); "[it] cannot produce and cannot sustain anything, cannot make or preserve anything" (*DN* 4-729B/93), it "has no being nor does it inhere in the things that have being" (*DN* 4-733C/95). It does not have an ontological status and, in a manner of speaking, it does not exist, for it does not exist in and by itself but only as a function of Good. Evil is only "imperfect Goodness" (*DN* 4-721A/88), "a falling-short of goodness" (*DN* 4-725A/90), "a deficiency and a lack of the perfection of the inherent goodness" (*DN* 4-728A/92).

26. Dionysius specifically instructs his readers on this point: "Do not make a distinction between 'beautiful' and 'beauty' as applied to the Cause which gathers all into one. For we recognize the difference in intelligible beings between qualities that are shared and the objects which share them. We call 'beautiful' that which has a share in beauty, and we give the name of 'beauty' to that ingredient which is the cause of beauty in everything. But the 'beautiful' which is beyond individual being is called 'beauty' because of that beauty bestowed by it on all things, each in accordance with what it is" (*DN* 4-701C–704A/76–77).

27. This ontological dichotomy of names also has a grammatical consequence that, although left untouched by Dionysius, is still instructive for a philological systematization. Since the level of abstraction decreases with the "procession" from conceptual to physical reality, symbolic names, grounded in the realm of the senses, are related to the grammatical category of concreteness, contrary to the inherent abstractness of the conceptual names. Thus symbolic names are articulated mainly in concrete nouns or noun-groups, whereas conceptual names have the form of abstract nouns or qualifying adjectives.

28. Eric Perl provides the following revealing elaboration of Dionysius's concepts of hierarchy and participation: "When Dionysius says that the higher ranks of creation are 'closer' to God than the lower, therefore, this must not be taken to mean that they stand between God and the lower orders. It means rather that they participate in God in more and greater ways....The higher levels are not exempt from, but rather include in an

eminent way, the perfections of the lower in their own, and the lower do not lack but rather manifest in a lesser way the perfections of the higher" ("Hierarchy and Participation," 20–21).

29. Note that Dionysius makes a subtle differentiation between the perceptible symbolism of "Light-Sun" that is to be dealt with in *The Symbolic Theology* and the "conceptual content of the term 'light' as applied to the Good," namely, the concept of spiritual illumination (*DN* 4-700C–701A/75).

30. Dionysius discusses similar and dissimilar symbols at length in chapter 2 of *The Celestial Hierarchy*. Note, however, that, in his characteristic manner, he does not see the two groups as forming a binary opposition; instead, the corpus as a whole advances the idea that any image applied to God is simultaneously similar and dissimilar to him: "They are similar to him to the extent that they share what cannot be shared. They are dissimilar to him in that as effects they fall so very far short of their Cause and are infinitely and incomparably subordinate to him" (*DN* 9-916A/118; cf. René Roques, "Preface").

31. In the Hebrew *Aqedah* narrative, Isaac, the "sacrificial lamb" (Gen. 22:7–8) is miraculously and mercifully replaced by a ram at the moment of sacrifice. According to the traditional Christian reading of Gen. 22:1–19, which construes Isaac as prefiguring the Christ, the passage anticipates the New Testament title of Jesus "the Lamb of God" (John 1:29). Such a reading is reinforced by Isaiah's prophecy envisioning the suffering Messiah as "a lamb that is led to the slaughter" (Isa. 53:7).

32. For a definition of the term "grand narrative," see Lyotard, *Postmodern Condition*, xxiii.

33. Lossky, *In the Image and Likeness*, 14.

34. *DN* 1-592B. Here I prefer a more literal translation of the Dionysian paradoxical *paragmenon* to the one given by Luibheit and Rorem in the Paulist edition (*Pseudo-Dionysius*, 52—"with shape and form on things which have neither").

35. Lossky, *In the Image and Likeness*, 14–15.

CHAPTER FOUR

1. Foucault's claim that order exists in the tension between "the already 'encoded' eye and reflexive knowledge," that the experience of order is the middle ground where social practices and social theories of order could inform one another, is particularly important to my overarching concern with order (see Foucault, *Order of Things*, xx–xxi). No less enlightening is Bourdieu's insight that we can grasp the logic of practice only through theoretical constructs that expose its inner relative coherence by exaggerating it. This means that theoretical models have a heuristic value for discerning within "fuzzy" practices a logic that remains otherwise hidden (see Bourdieu, *Logic of Practice*, 11–15).

2. For Dionysius's emphasis on meaning, see a characteristic critique of formalist exegesis in his apology for using *eros* ("yearning") and *agape* ("love") interchangeably: "In my opinion, it would be unreasonable and silly to look at words rather than at the power of their meanings. Anyone seeking to understand the divine things should never do this, for this is the procedure followed by those who do not allow empty sounds to pass beyond their ears. . . . People like this are concerned with meaningless letters and lines, with syllables and phrases which they do not understand" (*DN* 4-708B–C/80).

3. For the Neoplatonic philosophy of numbers, see, for example, Schrenk, "God as Monad," 5. "Everything has been organized by the monad," reads the highly instructive anonymous text of *The Theology of Arithmetic* found in a corpus of works by the Neoplatonist Iamblichus (third or fourth century), "because it contains everything potentially: for even if they are not yet actual, nevertheless the monad holds seminally the principles which are all within numbers" (35). The anonymous author proceeds further to list various mathematical peculiarities of the number one, which "produces itself and is produced from itself"; it is both even and odd, linear and plane and solid, perfect and defective, proportional and harmonic, prime and secondary; diagonal and side (35–37). The discovery of these paradoxical qualities paves the way to a particular philosophy of mathematics centered on the monad, a mathematical monotheism of sorts. It opens up a transparent analogy between the cosmogonic potentials of the number one, the universal factor of all the integers, and the one and only God, who is "all in all" (1 Cor. 15:28), "all things through the transcendence of one unity," and "the cause of all without ever departing from that oneness" (*DN* 13-977C/128).

4. Note that *MT* follows *DN* in the structure of the corpus as presented in the extant manuscript tradition. In the "ideal" (or perhaps better said, "fictitious") structure of the corpus, *DN* was supposed to be followed by *The Symbolic Theology* (see Dionysius, *Pseudo-Dionysius*, 131, n. 269).

5. The Old Testament canon was closed by the second century AD with the deuterocanonical books of the Septuagint tradition. The New Testament canon was settled in local councils during the fourth century.

6. Foucault, *Order of Things*, 118.

7. Listmaking, broadly conceived, is not limited to the domain of the verbal. We can argue that serial representations of visual or plastic images (e.g., the medallions with portraits of all the popes inside the basilica San Paolo fuori la mura in Rome, or Peter Greenaway's pictorial "translations" of Sei Shonagon's lists in his film *The Pillow Book*) are indeed visual lists. In view of my general focus on rhetoric, however, I restrict my discussion of lists to the verbal variety.

8. The phrase belongs to Mark Morris's study of Sei's lists in *The Pillow Book*. The entire passage is particularly relevant to our discussion: "The metonymic serialization inevitably sets up a playful metaphorical bond between individual entries; *they become somehow alike in fitting to the [same] heading.* For the simple crime of contingency, they all receive (or rather, complete) the same sentence. Just as we enjoy moving through and second-guessing a collocation of things ridiculed by people or terribly incongruous things, so we appreciate the concocting of a world where scared dogs and singing girls, or Persians and sick doctors and dumb teachers turn out to be, temporarily at least, bedfellows" (Morris, "Poetic Catalogues," 43, emphasis added; cf. similar ideas in Spufford, *Cabbages and Kings*, 3).

9. The term that articulates that "thing in common" among the list members—their common denominator, if you will—is the subject of the list, or, as Stephen Barney calls it, its *principle*. "A list without a principle," he declares, "would seem bewildering if not pointless—we need to know what is being listed" ("Chaucer's Lists," 191). We may be aware of this principle only by implication, or the list may, as it often does, spell it out in an opening or concluding formula, but either way lists are always "lists of": a list *of* the

students in a class, *of* things to do, *of* books to read, *of* favored hates or hated lovers. I owe this observation to William Gass, *Habitations of the World*, 177.

10. Since lists do not explain or even externalize, let alone justify, the order they represent, they need a hermeneut to do it for them. I owe this insight to J. Z. Smith, who proposes two more terms that attest to the list's varying capacity for representing order: a catalogue is an ordered list; a canon, a closed catalogue. Smith argues that any canon needs a hermeneut to provide its fixity with the flexibility it needs in order to survive, an argument that fits perfectly the hermeneutical practice that Dionysius ascribes to Christian theologians of the Name. For the complete argument, see Smith, *Imagining Religion*, 36–52, esp. 44–49.

11. "The elements of a list are plural *(polla)* as they are 'happenings' *(gignomena)* and 'visibles' *(horatai)*," wrote Stephen Barney, one of the finest theorizers of lists ("Chaucer's Lists," 201).His study, though historically specific, is brimming with general insights about lists, and particularly about lists of "copious display."

12. Francis Spufford, to whom we owe the first anthology of literary lists—an illuminating and a highly entertaining list project—claims that "museums are frozen lists" (*Cabbages and Kings*, 3). More generally, on the coextensiveness of museums and catalogues (the "intellectually glorified lists"), see Robert Harbison, especially the chapter "Contracted World: Museums and Catalogues" (*Eccentric Spaces*, 140–62).

13. The Russian theologian Bishop Ilarion Alfeev offers a similar evaluation of Dionysius in his recent comprehensive study of the worship of divine names in Eastern Orthodoxy: the teachings of the Areopagite fit perfectly the liturgical practice of the Church, just as the liturgical practice is fully concordant with his teachings (*Sviashchennaia taina Tserkvi*, 166). Significantly, his prime illustration of this claim is the persistent enumeration of divine names across the liturgical genres.

14. See Foucault's more general hypothesis that classical Western *episteme* (which he stretches up to the sixteenth century) is by nature cumulative, monotonous addition being the only possible form of connecting its individual elements (see *Order of Things*, 30–32).

15. Von Soden's authorship of the *Listenwissenschaft* idea has been contested by Benno Landsberger, who claims that the idea was only "elaborated by W. von Soden" (quoted in Goody, *Savage Mind*, 165, n. 7). Jonathan Z. Smith attributes the term to Albert Alt, referring to Alt's "Die Weisheit Salamos," an article that was published fifteen years after von Soden's work (see Smith, *Imagining Religion*, 47).

16. Von Soden, "Leistung und Grenze," 113 (my translation).

17. The list-structure of the "scientific" project of Near Eastern Antiquity, however, survived intact in Jewish religious culture, yielding a rich tradition of listmaking practices. For analyses of biblical lists see, for example, Gerhard von Rad, "Job"; Hartmut Gese, "Idea of History,"; John G. Gammie, "Book of Daniel,"; and Peter W. Coxon, "The 'List' Genre." See also Wayne Towner's extensive analysis of rabbinic numerical lists in *Rabbinic "Enumeration of Scriptural Examples"*; and Jacob Neusner's insightful remarks on the use of lists in the classical rabbinic sources (*Transformation of Judaism*, 5, 113, and especially 173–91).

18. Antonomasia, the figure of repeated re-naming, derives its name from Greek *antonomazo*, "to name instead."

19. Cardinal Jean Batiste Pitra provides a handful of examples in volumes 2 and 3 of his monumental *Spicilegium* (2:137–38 and 143–45; 3:447–48). His selection includes a Greek list of 92 names (3:447–48), a bilingual Greco-Latin list of 144 appellations (2:143–45), and a Latin list of 100 names (2:145–47), among others.

20. The compiler has transcribed erroneously the *textus receptus* (Apoc. 1:[17–]18), which reads "I am the first and the last, I am the Living One; and I was dead." I owe the correction of the translation to Moshe Taube (Jerusalem).

21. The complete Greek text was published by Franz Diekamp in 1907 *(Doctrina Patrum)* and is almost identical to the text published by Jean Baptiste Pitra (*Spicilegium*, 2:137–38), who attributes it to Anastasius Monachus. An English translation of the catalogue alone was made available by Leopold Sabourin (*Names and Titles of Jesus*, 315–17).

22. The *Symeonic Florilegium* (whose earliest extant copy, the so-called *Sviatoslav Florilegium*, dates from 1073), is one rich source of such catalogues (see Pavlova, Raleva, and Doseva, eds., *Simeonov sbornik*). The codex contains "Names of the Prophets," fols. 254r–254v; "Names of the Apostles," fols. 262r–263v; a list of the (12) precious stones that appear on the high priest's breastplate (Exod. 28:17–21), fols. 152v–154r; the "Names of the (12) Great Mountains"; and the "Names of the (36) Great Rivers." The last two lists are included in the table of contents of the *Sviatoslav Florilegium*, but are missing in the body of the text and are extant only in much later copies (see Mikhaila, "Spiski Sbornika," 12).

23. Migne's edition of the treatise provides several versions of the list, including a trilingual Hebrew-Latin-Greek version (*PL*, 23:1329–40).

24. For a later, ninth-century extrapolation that provides the trilingual list alone under the title *The Names of Christ*, see Pitra, *Spicilegium*, 3:448.

25. See Boissande, *ANEKDOTA*, 460; cf. Pitra, *Spicilegium*, 3:447.

26. See Thorndike, *History of Magic*, 2:407.

27. It appears, for example, in the notorious seventeenth-century *Grimoire of Honorious* (see Waite, *Ceremonial Magic*, 281). This magic list of Hebrew terms bears a family resemblance to the Jewish mystical text of the same name, mostly known from Kabbalistic sources, where the names correspond to the ten *sefirot*, or emanations of the divinity (see Budge, *Amulets and Magic*, 370–73). For a good introduction into the Kabbalistic notion of the *sefirot*, see Idel, *Kabbalah*, 112–55.

28. The earliest Slavonic copy of the text is found in a miscellany from the end of the thirteenth century known as the *Berlin Codex*; see chapter 8 for details about the Slavonic tradition.

29. One of the most prominent thinkers of the Russian religious renaissance at the beginning of the twentieth century, Pavel Florenskii, has claimed that the entire format of Christian worship is a profession (*propoved'*) and a confession (*ispoved'*) of the Lord's Name (see Florenskii, "Imiaslavie kak filosofskaia predposylka," esp. 330).

30. Despite the efforts of the first four ecumenical councils, and especially the Council of Chalcedon (451), to complete the dogmatic foundation of the Christian Churches, some crucial issues remained unresolved in the East at least until the ninth century. We cannot posit a definitive conclusion of these debates before 787, when the Iconodules triumphed over the Iconoclasts at the seventh Ecumenical Council (Nicaea).

31. In his authoritative survey of Byzantine theology, Meyendorff singles out the sixth century as the time when the Orthodox liturgy was constituted in its elaborate form of ritual performance (*Byzantine Theology*, 29ff.). The first half of the sixth century also saw the inauguration of the most imposing Orthodox cathedral, Hagia Sophia, in Constantinople, which not only defined the liturgical practices of Eastern Orthodox Christianity for centuries, but was seen as incorporating the very idea of Orthodoxy. After five years of construction, the cathedral was inaugurated in 537 under Emperor Justinian.

32. *Akathistos* (lit. "not seated") designates that people should stand while the hymn is sung, and *Theotokos* (lit. "Mother of God," or "God-bearer") is the principal Orthodox title for Mary, which was attributed to her by the third Ecumenical Council (Ephesus, 431). The hymn was initially assigned for the Vigil of the Annunciation (March 25). In contemporary liturgical practice, its complete presentation has been shifted to the Vigil of the Fifth Saturday of Lent, called "the Sabbath of the Akathistos Hymn." The most popular hypothesis about its authorship is that it was written by Roman Melodos, probably early in the sixth century, although its origin has been associated also with the miraculous salvation of Constantinople from three consecutive foreign sieges in the seventh and eighth centuries. By the early ninth century, the hymn had already been translated into Latin. The earliest extant copy of a Slavonic translation dates from the twelfth century, but there is speculation that the translation was actually made in the Cyrilo-Methodian period (see Kozhukharov, "Akatist," 57–58). For a parallel edition of the Byzantine and Slavic texts, see Gove, *Akathistos Hymn*, and for an excellent study of the Byzantine tradition, see Wellesz, "Akathistos."

33. In Greek this salutation reads, *Chaire, nympha anymphaton*; the Slavonic translation, *Radui sia, neviasto neneviastnaia*, is literal, preserving the original paragmenon that is lost in the standard English rendition. All salutations in the Greek originals are marked by the anaphora *chaire* (rejoice), hence their generic name, *chairetismoi*.

34. On the Jesus prayer and its importance for the Orthodox worship of the Name of God, see Alfeev, *Sviashchennaia taina Tserkvi*, 166–287, and, specifically for the *Akathistos of the Most Sweet Jesus* and its background, 197–99; cf. Kozlov, "Akafist," 84–85.

35. As part of the Nicene Creed, this list belongs to the core of the liturgical repertoire.

36. See details in my article "Naming the Nameless," where I draw general conclusions about the preeminence of the catalogue pattern in Eastern Orthodox rhetorical practice.

37. From this point of the sequence, the speaking position ostensibly shifts from the community of Christians to the Church as a communal body.

38. This is my translation from the edition in Makarii, *Velikie minei-cheti: Noiabr'* *13–15*, 1132–61; for the Greek original, see Migne, *PG*, 52:395–414.

39. My source for the Slavonic text is a sixteenth-century copy of the encomium available on microfilm at the Hilandar Resource Center for Medieval Studies, The Ohio State University, Columbus, Ohio, catalogue description in Matejic and Thomas, *Catalog*, Hil. 440, fols. 116r–130r. For the Greek original, see Halkin, *Bibliotheca hagiographica graeca*, 2:59. The text was translated into Slavonic in Bulgaria in the late fourteenth century. In the Slavonic tradition, it is either erroneously attributed to Theodoros Daphnopatis (tenth century) or treated as anonymous.

40. The genre of figure poems, or *carmina figurata*, is treated comprehensively in Higgins, *Pattern Poetry*; Adler and Ernst, *Texts als Figur*; and Ernst, *Carmen Figuratum*.

41. For a photographic reproduction of the manuscript original of the poem, see Ernst, *Carmen Figuratum*, 184. The list poem is unpacked in the edition of the text by Ernst Dümmler, *Poetae Latini*, 156–57. Dümmler's edition includes a selection of other figurative list-poems by Josephus Scottus.

42. The beginning of a morning prayer to the Lord from *The Orthodox Prayer Book* (8). According to Florenskii, the names that follow the first unequivocal address function as "an ontological motivation" for the petition that follows ("Slovesnoe sluzhenie: Molitva," esp. 74–78). In accordance with this remark, we note that the appellations following the initial address are usually thematically related to the prayer's specific request. Thus, for example, if it is a prayer before a meal, the names will be semantically related to food and the Eucharist, such as "heavenly life-giving Bread, true Meal" (see Nachtigal, *Euchologium Sinaiticum*, 37), but if it asks for the fertility of a flock, the names will be fittingly pastoral, for example, "true Lamb" (33).

43. Sergieff, *My Life in Christ*, 431.

44. For the movement of the Ioannites, see Kizenko, *Prodigal Saint*, 197–232, esp. 200 for the special emphasis that Father John's followers placed on the saint's original prayers.

45. See Panteleimon, *Zhizn', podvigi, chudesa i prorochestva*, 205. I am grateful to Nadieszda Kizenko for referring me to this edition.

CHAPTER FIVE

1. The earliest extant version is known from seventh-century Latin sources, although it is presumably of Byzantine origin, and the earliest known Slavonic version is documented in a Russian fragment from the beginning of the twelfth century that is preserved in a single folio appended to a later manuscript in the Monastery of St. Catherine in Sinai (see Taube, "Kievan Fragment"). For a comprehensive review of the Slavonic erotapocritical tradition, see Santos Otero, *Handschriftliche Überlieferung*, 2, sec. 16, "Conversatio trium hierarcharum"; cf. Thomson, "Apocrypha Slavica," for numerous corrections and additions. Thomson's stipulations about the genre deserve to be quoted in full: "This title ["Conversatio trium hierarcharum"] is here used as a generic term to signify apocryphal erotapocritical literature in general, although strictly speaking its use should be restricted to collections of *erotapocriseis* in which the names of SS. Basil, Gregory, and John appear" (91). Hereafter, I use this title only in the latter, more restrictive sense.

2. Both texts were made available from eighteenth-century copies in Ivan Franko's *Apokrifi i legendy* (9, 16).

3. I quote the text from an apocryphal Prayer Book (seventeenth century), Serbian National Library, MS Slav 636, fols. 11v–13r. See Iatsimirskii, "K istorii," which includes the only existing study of the text and its history (no. 3 (1913): 1–22). The term *false prayer* (*orationes falsae, lozhnye molitvy*) is used in medieval studies to refer loosely to a vast and apparently amorphous area of texts that are overtly dedicated to magical ends, specifically healing and protection. They vary in structure from direct equivalents of orthodox prayers and exorcisms to instructions for magical rituals and inscriptions on magical objects. Such a distinction, however, is mostly academic, for they are equally credited with inherent

magical powers, and their modes of employment overlap accordingly. The term itself is laden with ambiguities. Originally an ecclesiastical label, it is designed to sanction a group of texts as unorthodox (i.e., not of the right doctrine) from the standpoint of official Church criteria for distinguishing between religion and magic. Therefore its taxonomic efficacy in secular scholarship is rather limited at best.

4. The exact provenance of this codex is unknown, but most scholars accept that it originated in the Western territories of Bulgaria. Though some scholars attribute the manuscript to the first decade of the fourteenth century, by content it is closer to the book production of the thirteenth century. The codex was clearly designed as a book for in-dividual reading and reflects a peculiar mixture of standard religious instructions with noncanonical and apocryphal texts. The abundance of examples from the latter group is particularly interesting: the codex includes, among other substandard readings, the earli-est Slavonic copy of the old apocryphal cycle about King Abgar and a copy of the Bogomil apocryphon, *Legend of the Cross*, attributed to the Bulgarian heresiarch Jeremiah. Slavists deem the codex especially valuable for its inclusion of the earliest extant copy of Monk Khrabr's *On the Letters*, a tenth-century eulogy of the Slavonic alphabet. For details, see the critical edition of the codex in Miklas and Zagrebin, *Berlinski sbornik*. A typeset edi-tion of the text itself is available in Iatsimirskii, "K istorii" (no. 3 (1913): 9–10).

5. I am familiar with twenty-six manuscript copies, which are available in the texto-logical appendix of Izmirlieva, *Christian Art of Listing* (192–211). The text was included in three early Cyrillic printed books (sixteenth/seventeenth century), one of which had as many as four separate editions. Even though we do not have precise information today about the actual number of printed copies for each of these editions, printing certainly ensured the text's circulation and continuity on a much larger scale.

6. By the end of th sixteenth century, the dissemination of the amulet extended to the Russian lands as well (Ryan, *Bathhouse at Midnight*, 294–95). This East Slavic tradition, which we still know only sporadically, appears to follow directly Vuković's printed edition of the text, retaining its South Slavic linguistic characteristics. That is why, I suppose, Iat-simirskii ("K istorii," 7–8) treats copies of both Balkan and East Slavic provenance as "South Slavic." Significantly, Ryan's single example, a sixteenth-century copy from the Iosifo-Volokolamsk Monastery published in Tikhonravov, *Pamiatniki*, 2: 339–44, is the only extant manuscript copy that completely reproduces Vuković's version, including the exegetical addendum (about this version and its routine truncation in manuscript copies, see chapter 10).

7. Some copies of the text feature an additional instruction for invoking the names daily as an exorcism. As such instructions are exceedingly rare in the extant sources, how-ever, we should assume that the text's principal use was as an amulet.

8. Most copies of the text instruct that the list should be "worn on one's person," and usually the formula is appended by the adverb "purely." This requirement for ritual cleanliness seems to refer to the state of the manuscript and to the documented practice of keeping the text-amulet in a leather bag close to the body to avoid staining or corruption.

9. Robert Mathiesen includes this text in his review article on Slavic magic, "Magic in Slavia Orthodoxa," under the rubric "Charms, Spells, Incantations, and Magical Prayers."

10. Note that Church Slavonic has no grammatical articles, so the proposition of the heading is ambiguous: it could be both "these are [some of the] names of God, 72 in number" or "these are *the* names of God, 72 in number."

11. For the symbolism of 72 in general, see Spiridakis, "Ο αριθμός εβδομήκοντα δύο"; [Kretzenbacher, "Die heilige Rundzahl 72"; and Izmirlieva, "72 i chisloviiat kod." Some reference books also provide useful overviews: see Schimmel, *Mystery of Numbers*, 264–68; and Meyer and Suntrup, *Lexikon*, 761–64; cf. Chevalier and Gheerbrant, *Dictionary of Symbols*, 866–87 and 989, for some pertinent details.

12. Some of the stubborn traces of the duodecimal system are visible even today: measurements in length and weight based on 12 are still current in the United Kingdom and the United States, and we still sell eggs, doughnuts, and oysters by the dozen everywhere in the Western world.

13. This item is missing in the second copy (see Franko, *Apokrifi i legendy*, 16). Otherwise, the two copies offer completely identical versions of the entry.

14. The text belongs to another version of the *Discourse*, published by Nikolai Tikhonravov from a seventeenth-century copy (*Pamiatniki*, 2:433). A shorter, seventeenth/eighteenth-century variation of the same entry is found in A. N. Pypin (*Lozhnyia i otrechennyia knigi*, 169). The answer in Tikhonravov's version concludes somewhat unexpectedly with a shift to another number: "And the different bones in men are 295, and just as many are the joints." This "deviation" supports my previous disclaimer about the dangers of generalizing an erotapocritical worldview without actually contradicting the validity of my more specific conclusions about the role of the number 72.

15. See Bychkov, *Katalog*, 188, MS #120, fol. 423. Note that the same manuscript has a particular focus on lists of names: it features, among other lists, the names of the days in Greek, the names of the letters in the Slavonic alphabet, the names of the great mountains and of the great rivers, and a list of biblical characters: the man who made the Holy Cross, the man who pierced the Savior's rib, the man who hit Christ on the cheek, the two thieves who were crucified with him, the woman with the flow of blood, and the paralytic.

16. *The 72 Names of the Theotokos* appears across the extant sources as a permanent text-satellite of *The 72 Names of the Lord*: only one of all the available copies is independent from the Lord's names, and only three copies of the Lord's names are not accompanied by it. Iatsimirskii pioneered the study of both texts, again in conjunction with one another (see Iatsimirskii, "K istorii," no. 3 (1913): 1–22).

17. Hereafter cited as *Jerusalem 22*. For this monument, see chapter 8.

18. *Jerusalem 22*, fol. 197r.

19. As I have already mentioned, one copy of the erotapocritical entry includes an additional class, the 72 members of the human body.

CHAPTER SIX

1. Faith medicine, also called somewhat misleadingly "medicinal magic," covers a large body of practices addressed to both curative and prophylactic ends. Most important for my purposes are the curative practice of exorcism and the prophylactic practice of wearing written amulets, or phylacteries. In his analysis of "magical healing," Keith Thomas emphasizes its advantage in a society with little or no science-based medical care: it is painless, it is psychotherapeutic in relying on the natural tendency of the human body to self-heal aided by the therapeutic power of imagination, and it can be positively

spectacular (see *Religion and the Decline of Magic*, 206–7). The prophylactic practices of faith medicine may be evaluated in a similar manner.

2. The most comprehensive study of these narratives in the Byzantino-Slavic context is Izmirlieva, "The Aetiology of the Seventy-Two Diseases." See also Pradel, *Griechische und süditalienische Gebete, Beschwörungen und Rezepte des Mittelalters* (36–37 and 73–75), and Spiridakis, "Ο αριθμός εβδομήκοντα δύο" (409–11), who offer useful references to the available Greek sources. The concept itself has been addressed only tangentially in broader studies of the number 72 and its cross-cultural symbolism, most notably in Marzell, "Die Zahl 72"; Kretzenbacher, "Die heilige Rundzahl 72"; and the still useful study by Steinschneider, "Die kanonische Zahl der muhammedanischen Secten."

3. The Greek version, which was consolidated in pre-Christian times, is considered to be the direct source of the other five, although, arguably, they all share a common Jewish origin. A synoptic edition, which includes the Greek and Latin texts in the original and translations of the Slavonic, Georgian, and Armenian versions, is available in Anderson and Stone, eds., *Books of Adam and Eve*. The standard edition of the Slavonic text in the original (with a parallel German translation) is Jagić, "Slavische Beiträge zu den biblischen Apocryphen." See Stone, *The Literature of Adam and Eve*, for a full treatment of the literature on this cycle, including a review of the hypotheses regarding its origin and time of consolidation (with comprehensive bibliography).

4. See Jagić, "Slavische Beiträge zu den biblischen Apocryphen," 21 and 86. The passage varies greatly across the Slavonic tradition (see, for example, I. Porfir'ev, *Apokrificheskiia skazaniia*, 213; cf. Tikhonravov, *Pamiatniki*, 1:302; and Sokolov, *Materialy i zametki*, 40–42). The Slavonic version is consistent in its use of 72, although the Greek evidence, despite the occasional registration of this number, favors its "rounded" variant 70, as do most of the other versions (see Anderson and Stone, *Books of Adam and Eve*, 28). For occasional occurrences of 72 in the Greek tradition of the text, see Wells, "Books of Adam and Eve," 142. For further details on the Byzantine and Slavic evidence, including the various terms for diseases used in this context, see Izmirlieva, "Aetiology," 184–85.

5. The pseudo-epigraphon is documented by two Greek recensions, one long and one short, both in Schmidt's *Le Testament grec d'Abraham*. Slavonic, Romanian, Coptic, and Ethiopian versions are also extant. For the manuscript tradition of the Slavonic and the Romanian versions (with a complete bibliography of the editions available), see Turdeanu, *Apocryphes slaves et roumains*, 201–38.

6. The English translation follows Box, *Testament of Abraham*, 35. The standard edition of the Greek text is in Schmidt, *Le Testament grec d'Abraham*, 164.20.1–2. The Slavonic version, which represents a truncation of the short Greek recension, does not register this passage.

7. As a possible source of—or at least a curious parallel to—this Semitic trope, we should recall the Egyptian myth of the cynocephalus who dies piecemeal over a period of 72 days, a belief that probably determined the identical length of the Pharaoh's funeral ceremonies in ancient Egypt (see Marzell, "Die Zahl 72," 71).

8. The standard Eastern Orthodox version of this verse, 89:10 according to the Slavonic numbering, reads, "As for the days of our years, in their span they be threescore years and ten."

9. Dante, *Banquet*, pt. 4, chap. 23, 181–82.

10. See Dante, *Inferno*, 344, note to canto 1:1–3.

11. The seventeenth-century text entitled *Discourse on How God Created Adam* is published in Pypin (*Lozhnyia i otrechennyia knigi*, 15). The text offers a curious numerological symmetry: God transforms the seven days that Adam spent in Paradise into the seventy years that number a man's life, and the week of creating the world into the seven thousand years that number the world's existence.

12. Novaković, "Apokrifske priče," 201.

13. See Pypin, *Lozhnyia i otrechennyia knigi*, 12–15.

14. See Kovachev, "Narodna astronomia i meteorologiia," 49–50. The number in that particular record is not 72 but 41: the devil makes 41 (71) holes, the Lord fills up 40 (70) of them. I suppose that the substitution could be explained by a confusion of 7 and 4 based on their graphic similarity (the published copy of the legend is from the nineteenth century and, as is to be expected, Arabic numbers are used throughout).

15. See Petrov, "Ugrorusskie zagovory," 55. The manuscript originated from the Carpathian homeland of the Slavic ethnic group usually referred to as Rusyns. Nowadays, the Rusyns populate the borderlands between Ukraine, the Slovak Republic, and Poland, have a diaspora in Vojvodina, and speak East Slavic dialects.

16. The amulet, reportedly made for a man named Dukas, was written on a paper scroll to be worn around the neck. The scroll was wrapped in a piece of linen cloth, sewn to a leather bag and then placed in a silver case for maximal protection (see Abbott, *Macedonian Folklore*, 238 and 365–66). The earliest available evidence of the text is found in a Greek fifteenth-century codex of false prayers and is published in Vassiliev, *Anecdota*, 323–27. The oldest extant Slavonic copy of the text is still unpublished. It is part of the seventeenth-century addendum to a fifteenth-century Psalter in the Slavonic manuscript collection of the National Library SS Cyril and Methodius, Sofia, Bulgaria, Manuscript and Rare Book Collection, MS Slav, 458, fols. 112v–115r (for details about the text and this particular copy, see "Appendix 1: A Slavic Exorcism of the 72 Diseases" in Izmirlieva, *Christian Art of Listing*, 183–91; cf. Izmirlieva, "Aetiology," 181–95).

17. Vassiliev, *Anecdota*, 324; cf. National Library SS Cyril and Methodius, MS Slav 458, fol. 114v.

18. Compare the following telling passage in the Slavonic version: "All you, evil powers. . .return to the head of the one who created you" (National Library SS Cyril and Methodius, MS Slav 458, fol. 115r).

19. For a variety of Greek texts with such topoi, see Spiridakis, "Ο αριθμός εβδομήκοντα δύο," which provides an extensive bibliography of primary sources. From the Slavic material see, for example, the formula "I chased you away from the 77 members and sent you to the 70 unholy nations" from a sixteenth-century prayer for shooting pain (Kačanovskij, "Apokrifne molitve," 156); or the mention of "70 joints in the arm and the leg and the elbow" in a prayer from a nineteenth-century codex (Vinogradov, *Zagovory*, 15). Savushkina provides rich East Slavic folk material in *Russkie zagovory*—see # 47 (73 joints); #145 (70 bones, 70 joints, and 70 tendons); #197 (73 herbs for 73 joints); #199 (77 joints with 77 tendons); and #223 (72 joints and 72 tendons). See similar examples in Ryan, *Bathhouse at Midnight*, 181 (77 veins/sinews); 183 (73 members).

20. See a reference to 70 seals used as protection from diseases in a fourteenth-century Missal in Kovačević, "Nekoliko priloga." Oikonomidis reports that one of the Greek

versions of the well-studied "legend" of St. Sissinios lists the 72 names of the disease-causing female demon Gylou ("Εξορκισμοί," 22). According to Ryan, "shaking fevers" (*triasavitsy*) are personified in Russian texts as 77 evil women or, conversely, the 77 fevers are identified with Herod's daughters, who were turned into 77 evil winds or 77 flies (*Bathhouse at Midnight*, 244–45).

CHAPTER SEVEN

1. I quote the passage from Weigand's article, "Two and Seventy Languages," 248. Weigand points out as his immediate source the edition by Alexander Turner Cory, *The Hieroglyphics of Horapollo Nilous* (London: William Pickering, 1840).

2. In some versions of the myth, the cynocephalus is said to have 72 limbs or joints, which means it is also made up of 72 parts and thus identical in structure to the populated lands (see Reitzenstein, *Poimandres*, 265–66, n. 3).

3. Cited in Weigand, "Two and Seventy Languages," 242.

4. Besides the indispensable article by Weigand, see Séd, "Les douze hebdomades"; and Sauer, "Ein mittelalterlicher Topos," and his "Ergänzungen."

5. Gen. 11:7. Note that the name Babel comes from the Hebrew verb *balal*, "to confuse": "It was called Babel, because there the Lord confused the language of all the earth" (Gen. 11:9).

6. The metonymic transfer is supported by the double meaning of tongue as "language" and as "people" in both Greek *(glossa)* and Church Slavonic *(iazyk)*.

7. Bruce Metzger provides an excellent summary of the sources ("Seventy or Seventy-Two," 303). See also Baumgarten ("Duodecimal Courts," 76, n. 66) and Burrows ("Number Seventy in Semitic," 391).

8. See Metzger, "Seventy or Seventy-Two," 303; cf. Scholem, *On the Kabbalah,* 62.

9. *Targum Pseudo-Jonathan, Genesis,* 50. In another version of the same Targum, "at that time he [the Lord] established the boundaries of the nations according to the total of seventy souls of Israel who went down to Egypt" (quoted in Baumgarten, "Duodecimal Courts," 68, n. 29). This version connects the triple homology of 70 angels, 70 nations, and 70 languages/writing systems with the number of the descendants of Israel who went to Egypt, thus reorienting the source of the 70 nations from Noah to Jacob, the progenitor of the 12 tribes. Compare the midrashic legend that angel Gabriel taught Joseph the 70 languages, as well as its offshoots found in Hebrew and Aramaic amulets (Schiffman and Swartz, *Hebrew and Aramaic Incantation Texts*, 23, 151, 156).

10. The number 72 is particularly visible in the late Jewish apocalyptic tradition; see details in Baumgarten, "Duodecimal Courts," 76, n. 66. There, note also his reference to the use of 72 for both the number of languages and the number of heavenly princes in 3 Enoch.

11. See Borst, *Der Turmbau von Babel*, 1:230; Migne, *PG*, 7:958; English translation in Roberts and Donaldson, *Ante-Nicean Fathers*, 1:455.

12. See Weigand, "Two and Seventy Languages," 249. Sauer offers a selection of relevant patristic passages in "Ein mittelalterlicher Topos," esp. 30 and 39–40; cf. his no less informative "Ergänzungen."

13. See St. Augustine, *De Civitate Dei* 16:3–12, in Migne, *PL*, 12: 343–44; cf. Weigand, "Two and Seventy Languages," 251–53.

14. For selected Greek sources, see Spiridakis, "Ο αριθμός εβδομήκοντα δύο," 412–18. Weigand provides a rich panorama of the dispersion of this idea in the Latin West. The same tradition also affected apocryphal revelations of the Eastern Church, such as the Syrian *Cave of Treasures* and the Ethiopian *Book of Adam* (see Weigand, "Two and Seventy Languages," 249). For the Ethiopian tradition, see Strelcyn "Une tradition éthiopienne"; and Cowley, *Ethiopian Biblical Interpretation*, 20–24.

15. Ostrowski, Birnbaum, and Lunt, eds., *The* Povest' vremennykh let, 18–19.

16. Miltenova, "Skazanie za Sivila," 63; there is also a Greek parallel. This otherwise unattested saying of Jesus is addressed to the 72 disciples and is evidently based on Luke 10:1. Paul Alexander, to whom we owe the most complete study of the Greek original, has argued that the passage was added to the fourth-century text of *Oracula Sibyllina* in the following form: "The word which you received from me, preach it to the people of the 72 languages." These peoples later reappear in the text as the population of Constantinople, thus making the city a true microcosm of the world (see details in Alexander, *Oracle of Baalbeck*, 136–37; cf. 56, 92–93, and 108).

17. The text belongs to another version of the *Discourse*, published from a seventeenth-century copy in Tikhonravov, *Pamiatniki*, 433.

18. Pypin, *Lozhnyia i otrechennyia knigi*, 169.

19. See Petkanova, *Stara b"lgarska literatura*, 1:341; cf. Miltenova, *Stara b"lgarska literatura*, 5:348, for a different compilation based on a copy from the end of the seventeenth century.

20. Miltenova, "Razumnik-ukáz," 34; the second redaction of the text features a similar passage (see 39). Cf. another version of the same text entitled *Questions: Of How Many Parts Was Adam Made?* published from two different copies in Tikhonravov, *Pamiatniki*, 446, and in Lavrov, *Apokrificheskie teksty*, 119. For Latin versions of the same *Interrogatio*, see Sauer, "Ein mittelalterlicher Topos," 40–41, #7.

21. The prayer is published in Almazov, "Vracheval'nyia molitvy," from a sixteenth-century Slavonic copy with a parallel edition of the Greek equivalent, also from a sixteenth-century copy (508–9). A similar Slavonic eighteenth-century version containing the same formula appears in Vinogradov, *Zagovory*, 79.

22. An edition of the Greek text with an English translation and excellent apparatus appears in Hadas, *Aristeas to Philocrates*. For a comprehensive account of the origin, transmission, significance, and study of the text, see Jellicoe, *Septuagint and Modern Study*, 29–58. For a Slavic version of the legend, see Taube, "Une Source inconnue."

23. On the 12 tribes of Israel, descended from the sons of Jacob, see 1 Kings 18:31. The lists of the 12 tribes do not always agree with one another, and the number varies from 11 to 13 with the exclusion of Joseph, the inclusion of his two sons, Ephraim and Manasseh, and the exclusion of Levy, the progenitor of the priestly tribe that was not assigned a special territory. For more details, see Whybray, "Tribes of Israel."

24. According to Aristeas, the translation of the *Septuaginta Duo* included only the five books of the Torah, but in the Christian tradition it was extended to include the entire Greek Old Testament. The first author to document this extension is Justin Martyr in the *First Apology* 31 (see Jellicoe, *Septuagint and Modern Study*, 42).

25. Although the oldest sources agree on the number 72, the number of the translators in the subsequent tradition varies predictably between 70 and 72 (see Metzger, "Seventy or Seventy-Two," 303), a discrepancy that is reflected also by the standard designation of the translation itself. It is generally accepted today that the number 70 is a natural syncope of 72, a shift that has been facilitated by the stable association of 70 with the Elders of Moses, whose commission as a representative body of the twelve tribes is directly related to the revelation of the Law at Sinai (Exod. 24).

26. The list is preserved in some of the later sources. Epiphanius of Salamis (ca. 315–406 CE) includes it in his own elaborated version in *De Mensuris et Ponderibus* (pt. 3ff.), extant in full only in Syriac (see an edition in Dean, *Epiphanius' Treatise on Weights and Measures*). Michael E. Stone reports on an Armenian excerpt from Epiphanius's treatise entitled *Concerning the Seventy-Two Translators Who Were on the Island of Pharos* (see Stone, "Concerning the Seventy-Two Translators," 334–35).

27. *Letter of Aristeas*, sec. 307 (emphasis added). I quote the source from the segments provided (in translation) in Peters, *Judaism, Christianity, Islam*, 2:15.

28. See Irenaeus, "Against Heresies," in Roberts and Donaldson, *The Ante-Nicean Fathers*, 1. Weigand ("Two and Seventy Languages," 250), erroneously identifies the source in question as Philo of Judea's *De Vita Mosis* (2.25–44), which does not mention separate cells, and, although it emphasizes that each version of the translation was identical to all others, "as though it had been dictated to each by an invisible prompter" (Peters, *Judaism, Christianity, Islam*, 2:16), it never explicitly points out their number. An explicit mention of 72 separate cells, however, is reportedly present in the Talmud (see Baumgarten, "Duodecimal Courts," 76, n. 65), which gave ground to Hadas to consider Ireneaus's embellishment as going back to the Tannaitic times (first or second century CE; see Hadas, *Aristeas to Philocrates*, 83).

Epiphanius offers a notable modification of the tradition in *On Weights and Measures*: the translators worked in pairs, isolated in 36 cells. Significantly, the Slavonic tradition follows the same pattern: "The 72 translators of the books were sent from Jerusalem, six from each tribe. Ptolemy built for them 36 huts on the island of Pharos and locked them in, two by two" (see Taube, "Une Source inconnue," 120). This peculiarity could have been introduced, as Sidney Jellicoe suggests, by the Gospel of Luke, where the 72 disciples are sent by the Lord "in pairs" (Luke 10:1; see Jellicoe, *Septuagint and Modern Study*, 45).

29. Peters, *Judaism, Christianity, Islam*, 2:14.

30. See Schimmel, *Mystery*, 122–23. Note that six is also a perfect number in the arithmetic sense—it equals both the sum of its factors and their product ($1 + 2 + 3 = 6$; $1 \times 2 \times 3 = 6$).

31. Schimmel calls the kind of "totality" represented by 72 "fullness composed of different elements" (*Mystery*, 266).

32. Bourdieu, *Language and Symbolic Power*, 203ff.

33. Ibid., 208.

34. In fact, the distribution of 70 and 72 is so balanced across both the early Greek and later versional evidence of these verses that the most fastidious among biblical scholars prefer to render the number by the clumsy hybrid "seventy(-two)." To repeat Metzger's competent summary of the manuscript data (see Metzger, "Seventy or Seventy-Two"), 72

is featured in Georgian and Persian sources, in the Vulgate, in most of the Syriac, and in the chief Alexandrian (Coptic) texts. Conversely, alternative Syriac and Coptic texts, and all the so-called Caesarean witnesses, along with the Ethiopian versions, Gothic texts, Luther's translation, and the Slavonic Bible, all favor 70 instead. Regrettably, however, Metzger leaves out of sight much of the conceptual scope of the number 72 that was cultivated in pre-Christian cultures.

35. See Jellicoe, "St. Luke and the 'Seventy (-Two).'"

36. If we accept the primacy of 72, as Jellicoe prompts us to do in "St. Luke and the 'Seventy (-Two),'" we can easily attribute the subsequent transformation of this number into 70 to the interplay of at least three independent factors. First, palaeographically, it is highly possible for a scribe to omit accidentally the second part of a number ("two"), especially since the word is repeated in the immediate context of Luke 10:1 (Luke 10:17). Second, the rounding of a precise number (i.e., of 72 to 70) is psychologically much more plausible than the opposite transformation. Third, the general synonymy of the two numbers in the Judeo-Christian culture and their interchangeability in shifting contexts (see above) largely facilitate the appearance of a variant of Luke's passage featuring 70 instead of 72 disciples, since the simplification of the number does not in fact alter the original symbolic implications of the numerical mention.

37. For patristic references, see Meyer and Suntrup, *Lexikon*, 762.

38. This interpretation is not exclusive. According to alternative patristic readings, the number of the disciples is prefigured by the bells on the robe of the high priest, which tradition holds to be 72 (Exod. 28:33). As the product of 8, a number associated with Christ's Resurrection on the "eighth" day after Sabbath, and 9, the number of the angelic orders, 72 is seen as a symbol for the triumphant celebration of the new messianic age on high. Last but not least, as the product of 24, the number of hours in each day, and 3, the number of the Holy Trinity, it is said to represent also continuous glorification of the Trinity, which is the essence of apostolic work (see Meyer, *Die Zahlenallegorese*, 168).

39. See Matt. 10:2–4 and Mark 3:16–19; cf. Acts 1:26 for the replacement of Judas by Matthias.

40. See Metzger, "Names for the Nameless," 547.

41. See editions in Schermann, *Prophetarum vitae fabulosae*, 107–70.

42. See Metzger, "Seventy or Seventy-Two," 304.

43. For further details about the Slavonic sources, see my article "From Babel to Christ and Beyond."

44. Baumgarten, "Duodecimal Courts."

45. "It [the Heavenly Jerusalem] has a great high wall with twelve gates, and at the gates twelve angels, and on the gates are inscribed the names of the twelve tribes of the Israelites. . . . And the wall of the city has twelve foundations, and on them are the twelve names of the twelve apostles of the Lamb" (Rev. 21:12–14). Note also that the function of the 12 apostles as a deliberative body of the Final Judgment is legitimated by Matt. 19:28 and Luke 22:30 as a central part of their legacy in the Christ.

46. "Whatever the Holy One, blessed be he, created above, he likewise created below" (*Exodus Rabbah* 33:4; cited in Baumgarten, "Duodecimal Courts," 78).

47. *Sanhedrin* is a Hebraized form of the Greek term *Synedrion*, "council" (lit. "sitting together"). The Greek term dates from antiquity, though in Christian language it is

associated with "the council of the Apostles" and its continuation in the Council of the
Presbyters, which inherits their esteem in the eyes of the Church. In the meaning of the
High Council (the Great Sanhedrin), it refers to the highest indigenous governing body
in Judea, which functioned under the presidency of the ruling high priest and included as
members adult male representatives of the most prominent priestly families, the elders
of the tribes, and scholars or scribes. It had the ultimate authority not only in religious
matters, but in legal and governmental affairs as well, as long as it did not encroach on the
authority of the Roman procurator. Its history goes back at least to Pompey the Great who,
in 66 BCE, reorganized Palestine as part of a bigger project of subjugating the Greek East
to the Roman Senate, dividing it into five councils. In the context of the New Testament,
the Sanhedrin is both the locus of opposition to Jesus and his movement, and the venue of
the trial of the Christ and his followers. In the Rabbinic period (ca. 200 CE), "Sanhedrin"
became a technical term for the rabbinic court, and the Mishnah devotes a special section
to its structure and function (see details in Overman, "Sanhedrin," in Metzger and Coogan,
eds., *Oxford Companion to the Bible*, 677–78).

48. For scriptural reference to the 70 elders, see Numbers 11:16, 24–25 and Exod. 24:1,
9; on the 70 descendants of Israel, see Exod. 1:5, "The total number of people born to Jacob
was seventy"; cf. Gen. 46:27: "All the persons of the house of Jacob who came into Egypt
were seventy."

49. Baumgarten, "Duodecimal Courts," 57.

50. The correspondence, in fact, is so exact that one is tempted to assume that
Ptolemy's request to get six translators from each tribe was modeled after the structure
of the Sanhedrin, though such an assumption is difficult to prove in historical terms. Both
the translation and, in all probability, the legend on which Aristeas based his account predate the rabbinic courts, although the *Letter* itself could have been composed around the
same time when the Sanhedrin was being constituted. The particular differentiation
within the number may be a later (first-century) addition, while the original number 72
in the original legend was undifferentiated, derived most probably from the older belief
that the number of peoples on earth were 72.

51. See Meyer and Suntrup, *Lexicon*, 732; cf. Schimmel, *Mystery*, 266, though her
biblical reference is erroneous.

52. Kaplan, *Bahir*, pt. 1, 94, 34.

53. The number 72 had a no less significant career in the making of the Islamic political imagination: from the 73 Muslim sects envisioned by the Prophet Mohammed, of
which 72 shall perish and 1 shall be saved, to the 72 martyrs in the battle at Karbala (680),
which was the constitutive Shi'ite event (see details in Steinschneider, "Die kanonische
Zahl"; cf. Schimmel, *Mystery*, 264–68). In that sense, the political significance of this numerical symbol is truly shared by all Abrahamic religions.

CHAPTER EIGHT

1. A microfilm of the codex is available in The Library of Congress in Washington,
D.C. (see *Checklist of the Manuscripts in the Libraries of the Greek and Armenian Patriarchates in Jerusalem*, Micro # 5017 Slav. 22). The most complete description of the
codex to date is Krasnosel'tsev, *Slavianskiia rukopisi*, 21–24. I am indebted to Klimentina

Ivanova for sharing with me her unpublished description of the codex, which is much more detailed than Krasnosel'tsev's. The codex is hereafter often cited parenthetically in the text: for example, (fol. 445v).

2. *The 72 Names of the Lord* is located on fols. 195r–196r, and *The 72 Names of the Theotokos* appears on fols. 196v–197r.

3. See Krasnosel'tsev, *Slavianskiia rukopisi*, 21–26; Rozov, "Srpski rukopisi," 120–21; Nedomački, *O srpskim rukopisima*, 94.

4. The colophon, in the handwriting of the (principal) scribe, reads as follows: "In the year 1498. Brethren, forgive that [we wrote] with a sinful hand or incorrectly from the source. You forgive us, and Christ the King [will forgive] you. Amen" (fol. 445v).

5. According to the written sources, the monastery (situated today near the Israel Museum in Jerusalem) was founded by the Georgian monk Prochor between 1039 and 1056 and remained for centuries the most important Georgian religious and spiritual center in the Holy Land (see Tsagareli, "Pamyatniki"). Since 1685, the monastery has been in the possession of the Greek Orthodox Patriarchate.

6. According to Klimentina Ivanova, the codex could have been written by two hands, the first one tentatively linked to fols. 78r–131v and the second one (which identifies the principal scribe—incidentally the one who also wrote our lists) with the rest of the codex. The handwriting, however, is fairly similar throughout, and the identification is uncertain.

7. The only existing article specifically dedicated to this feature is Ivanov, "Preglas na glasna U > O v b"lgarskite govori" (see also Mirchev, "Nevrokopskiiat govor," esp. 43).

8. Krasnosel'tsev, *Slavianskiia rukopisi*, 26; Rozov, "Srpski rukopisi," 121.

9. The larger part of the codex comprises hymnographic material for the calendar cycle.

10. Krasnosel'tsev's main example is a magic recipe "for love" that consists mostly of what appear to be names (see Krasnosel'tsev, *Slavianskiia rukopisi*, 23, 27). For later speculation on the possible Jewish connection, see Nedomački, "O srpskim rukopisima," 94).

11. Among the comprehensive studies of the Kabbalah available in English, see especially Scholem, *On the Kabbalah and Its Symbolism*; his invaluable "Kabbalah"; and Idel's more recent work, *Kabbalah: New Perspectives*.

12. For a succinct summary of the concept and the history of the practical Kabbalah, see Scholem, "Kabbalah," 632–38 (with bibliography).

13. Scholem, "Kabbalah," 634.

14. Scholem, *On the Kabbalah and Its Symbolism*, 99.

15. Gaster, *Sword of Moses*, 163.

16. For a definitive history of the Ottoman Empire from that period, see Inalcik, *Ottoman Empire*.

17. Ocak, "Religion," 187.

18. See details in Braude and Lewis, *Christians and Jews*.

19. The Eastern Orthodox Christians in the Balkan part of the Ottoman Empire were hardly a homogeneous group. Ethnically, they encompassed Greeks, Slavs, Albanians, and Walachians, among others. They also included a broad spectrum of Christian sects, most numerous of which were the Bogomils.

20. The relatively liberal religious policy of the Ottomans toward the other religions of the Book is a topos in Ottoman historiography. At the core of this inclusive attitude, scholars usually place the doctrinal emphasis of Islam on the unity of God. Historically, Muslims saw themselves as the true heirs to the faith of the biblical patriarchs and prophets, from Abraham and Moses all the way to Christ. Thus they openly acknowledged their links to both Jews and Christians, who, in contrast, had forged their respective identities through a painful process of separation that left a long-lasting legacy of hostility between them (see Peters, *Judaism, Christianity, Islam,* 1:xxiii–iv).

21. Mark Mazower repeatedly quotes an account by Ukrainian Catholics who visited Salonica in the eighteenth century and were struck by the perfunctory character of Orthodox observance (see his *Salonica,* 66). Though this source is from a later period, it reveals the end result of a process that began with the Ottoman annexation of the Balkan lands: one of the first decrees of Gennadios Scholarios, the first Greek patriarch after the fall of Constantinople (1454–60?), was to relax the official sacramental rules and the doctrinal norms within the new Christian *millet.*

22. For the history of the expulsion, see Yerushalmi, "Exile and Expulsion." For the Ottoman Empire as the preferred destination of the massive exodus, see, for example, Hava Tirosh-Samuelson, "Postexpulsion Philosophic Literature," 227; Ocak, "Religion"; and Mazower, *Salonica,* 46–52.

23. An excellent source on the role of Salonica in the exodus of the Sephardim is Mazower's *Salonica,* 49ff. On the lives and culture of the Ottoman Jews more generally, see Epstein, *Ottoman Jewish Communities,* and Shmuelevitz, *Jews of the Ottoman Empire.*

24. According to the old Babylonian calendar, the world was created 5508 years before the birth of Christ, which makes 1492 CE—the same year that marked the expulsion of the Jews from Spain—the end of the seventh millennium. The apocryphal belief that the world would come to an end at the end of the seventh millennium was based on the conflation of two biblical notions: first, that God created the world in seven days (Genesis 1) and, second, that in the eyes of God one day is like a thousand years (cf. Ps. 90:4 and 2 Peter 3:8; see Volz, *Die Eschatologie der jüdischen Gemeinde,* 135ff). The belief was shared by Jews and Christians alike, and the fear of the impending apocalypse exploded into a real epidemic during the second part of the fifteenth century, fueled no doubt by the fall of Constantinople.

25. Mazower, *Salonica,* 66.

26. Pierre Belon (Belon du Mans), quoted in Fernand Braudel, *Mediterranean World,* 809.

27. See Trachtenberg, *Jewish Magic,* 1.

28. See fols. 195r–196v. Even though the text does not include the number 72 in its heading, there is no doubt that it is a copy of our amulet text. Iatsimirskii, who included it in his study of the *The 72 Names of the Lord,* treated it without qualification as a copy of the same text; so did Krasnosel'tsev in his description of the codex. The fact that the text is followed here by the same names "for fear of dying" that follow it in the *Berlin Codex* (where the numerical designation in the heading is intact) also suggests that the two copies—the earliest ones we possess—stem from the same tradition. Given the evident unreliability of the scribes, who, it seems, often worked in a hurry and without understanding

or paying much attention to their sources, it is quite plausible to assume that the number was indeed present in the antegraph and was omitted by mistake.

29. The highly unusual reference to the desert, apparently in the literal sense of the word, could be an index to a possible Palestinian origin, or to an intended use of the text related to pilgrims or travelers to Palestine; the concern with dangers on the road also points to itinerants, who at the time would be pilgrims, missionaries, or traveling merchants.

30. See Fernandez, "The Dark at the Bottom of the Stairs," in his *Persuasion and Performance*, 214–38, where he suggestively defines the inchoate as the underlying and overlying sense of wholeness that we can never really grasp. Unlike the Freudian category of the unconscious, Fernandez's inchoate is a category at the interface of the psychophysiological and the sociocultural, and it is the sociocultural aspect—its dependence on predication and performance—that is most representative. That is how we are to take, I assume, Fernandez's claim that the inchoate for him is "above all a set of images" (215).

31. Rabbinic *mezuzot* were designed as a permanent reminder of Jewish monotheism and a pledge of personal commitment to Yahweh, as the initial verses of the corresponding Torah passage indicate: "The Lord is our God, the Lord alone. You shall love the Lord your God with all your heart, and with all your soul, and with all your might" (Deut. 6:4–5). The scriptural passage continues with instructions "to keep these words in your heart," "recite them to your children," and "write them on the doorpost of your house and on your gates," the latter demand corresponding directly to *mezuzah* pragmatics. The rabbinic practice was also oriented toward commemoration of the Jewish exodus from Egypt, at the eve of which the Lord instructed the Israelites to mark their doorposts with blood from the sacrificial lamb, so that he would pass over their houses and spare them when striking every Egyptian firstborn (Exod. 12:13). In the spirit of that event, and particularly in the context of religious and ethnic plurality that characterized the life of medieval European Jews, a *mezuzah* was meant to be a very public index of Jewishness. For details about the *mezuzah* tradition and its absorption into Jewish magic practices, see Trachtenberg, *Jewish Magic*, 146ff.

32. Ibid., 147.

33. The text is largely unstudied. Santos Otero, in his *Die handschriftliche Überlieferung der altslavischen Apocryphen*, limits his section on this text to a general description with no examples (241); Thomson, in his critical review of Santos Otero's book, gives only two bibliographic references ("Apocripha Slavica: II," 98). I am familiar with several different Slavonic texts that are designated in their headings as "Angelic names." The specific type to which the text in *Jerusalem 22* (fols. 194v–195r) belongs is known to me from fourteen copies, most of which appear in the context of other sacronymic lists and, more often than not, specifically of *The 72 Names of the Lord*. Almazov offers Greek parallels to the same text in his *Vracheval'nye molitvy* (315–16, #17–18).

34. Morton Smith, in "A Note on Some Jewish Assimilationists," sums up very nicely their successful assimilation in Christian context: "[There was] a minority group of Jewish immigrants who entered Europe from the Near East about the beginning of the present era, prospered mightily, after their (probably involuntary) conversion to Christianity, became an important part of the ruling class, and in many cases assimilated with, in others reportedly drove out, the earlier inhabitants of their own sort (this in spite of the fact that they also remained active in Jewish affairs). I refer to the angels" (207).

35. The most useful guide to Jewish angelology is the famous treatise *Sepher ha-Razim*, edited in an English translation by Michael Morgan. Trachtenberg's *Jewish Magic* offers a good introduction to the vast field; Davidson's *Dictionary of Angels* is a useful tool; Schwab's *Vocabulaire de l'Angélologie* should be taken with a grain of salt when it comes to his etymologies.

36. The list in transliteration (which preserves all its idiosyncrasies) reads: "Michail, Gavril, Uril, Raphail, Rugail, Pandaforannoil, Kaluil, Saresam, Melhisedol, Nefuil, Afarail, Sihail, Sinail, Ephig[?]pha[?]." The first four names, Michael, Gabriel, Uriel, and Raphael, which incidentally form the stable core of this list across its various copies and redactions, are all standard archangels' names. They are among the names of the Seven Archangels in almost all traditions. The other fairly common name on the list is Rugail, known from 1 Enoch (the Ethiopian version; see Knibb, *Ethiopic Book of Enoch*) and rendered variably as Raguel, Ruhiel, Ruagel, and Ruahel. This name also appears often in Slavonic amulets. All five, I should add, are among the names of the seven angels who, according to the Kabbalah, rule the earth (see Budge, *Amulets and Superstitions*, 375). The rest of the names are fairly cryptic, with the possible exception of the name Melhisedol, which recalls the biblical Melchizedek (Gen. 14:18–20; Ps. 110:4; Heb. 5:6 and 10, 6:20, and 7:1–17), who also appears in the Slavonic version of 2 Enoch. Because of the privileged place of this biblical king in the Gnostic tradition (and its later ramifications in dualistic heresies), the appearance of his name in the list could be an index to a Gnostic connection.

37. Their collective name itself reveals their mission: the Hebrew *mal'ak* means "envoy" or, by extension, "agent." The Greek term *angelos*, which has become standard in Christian use, is not quite an equivalent translation, meaning literally "messenger."

38. Trachtenberg, *Jewish Magic*, 77. "The name has swallowed up the Angel," aphoristically continues Trachtenberg, moving toward a summation of his argument. By the Middle Ages, an angel had become a dual category in Jewish popular religious life: "The one comprised the true angels as tradition painted them, the other, a vast multitude of mystical names, designated as angels and in theory accepted as such—an angelic host in suspension, so to speak, capable of being precipitated into its individual angelic components—but actually significant only for the mystical powers inherent in the name itself" (89).

39. Schäfer, *Hidden and Manifest God*, 106; cf. Lesses, "Speaking with Angels," 47.

40. See Trachtenberg, *Jewish Magic*, 148 and 150–51; see also the Kabbalistic *mezuzot* in Aptowitzer, "Les noms de Dieu."

41. See Miklas and Zagrebin, *Berlinski sbornik*, fol. 71v. I have come across another copy of the same list written on the back cover of a *Troparion* from the end of the fourteenth century, MS 343 of the Hilandar Monastery, a microform in the Hilandar Resource Center for Medieval Studies; see the description in Matejic and Thomas, *Catalog*, HM. SMS 343, where the list has the same proviso as in the *Berlin Codex* and reads: "Anekotnosh, Atanatosh, Shiu[...]ksha." The Greek origin of the second name is obvious (all three forms are a corruption of *athanatos*), and the first one suggests a Greek origin, clearly filtered through Latin in the case of the *Berlin Codex*.

42. This corpus comprises fols. 381r–383r.

43. Ibid., fols. 381v–382r.

44. For *The Ten Names of God* in the Christian tradition, see chapter 4 in this volume. The text in the *Berlin Codex* reads as follows: "The names are ten, as is given by the Jews, and by them the Lord is called: First name and second *elee*, third *eloi*, fourth *savaoth*, fifth *filoi*, sixth *asafai*, seventh *adonai*, eighth *gai*, ninth *tromini*, tenth *evanei*. In the beginning was the word. The Lord sent his angel in the days of Herod the King, in the names of the Father and the Son and the Holy Spirit."

45. Trachtenberg claims that it "assumed godlike proportions in the charms"; see *Jewish Magic*, 101.

46. Gaster, *Sword of Moses*; Naveh and Shaked, *Amulets and Magic Bowls*, 16, n. 11.

47. Trachtenberg, *Jewish Magic*, 202; cf. Schäfer, *Hidden and Manifest God*, 94–95, for similar techniques.

48. Between fols. 381r and 383r, there are five more such recipes.

49. Kabbalistic amulets often encode messages in a specific "angelic" script dubbed "eye writing," since its constitutive elements are lines and small circles resembling eyes (see Scholem, "Kabbalah," 635). For more specific detail about these Kabbalistic figures (with samples), see Trachtenberg, *Jewish Magic*, 141–42 and 150–51.

50. Note that the corresponding Torah verses to which the passage alludes (Ex. 23:20–21) make no mention of the name of God.

51. The English translation is borrowed from the verbatim quotation of the passage in Barrett, *Magus*, II.1.12:59. Cf. the original Latin text in the reprint edition of Compagni, *Cornelius Agrippa*, 473, v. 7–11: "Tunc singulae tres literae sibi subalternatae constituunt unum nomen, que sunt septuaginta duo nomina quæ Hebraei Schemhamphoras vocant; quibus, si in fine addatur nomen divinum El vel Iah producunt septuaginta duo angelorum nomina trisyllaba, quorum quilibet fert magnum nomen Dei sicut scriptum est: 'Angelus meus praecedet te; observes eum: est enim nomen meum in illo.' Et hi sunt qui praesident septuaginta duobus quinariis coelestibus totidemque nationibus et linguis et humani corporis artibus cooperanturque septuaginta duobus synagogae senioribus totidemque Christi discipulis." It is curious that, according to the appendix in Compagni's edition, chapter 25 of book 3 in which the passage occurs is a new addition to the Juvenile Draft of the treatise from 1509–10, one of the few chapters completely absent from the old version, which suggests that Agrippa based it on new or newly evaluated sources.

52. *Sefer Raziel*, 40b; quoted in Trachtenberg, *Jewish Magic*, 95–97.

53. Trachtenberg, *Jewish Magic*, 289, n. 22. Gaster discusses the early mystical thesis that the most sacred name of God consists of 72 parts (letters) in *Sword of Moses*, 8 (cf. Cohon, "Name of God," 596, and Scholem, "Name of God," 69).

54. Scholem, "Name of God," 69. For the creative power of the Name, see Scholem, *On the Kabbalah*, 41–44. The most eloquent source for the identification between the Name of God and the Torah is a passage by the thirteenth-century Spanish Kabbalist Gikatila, a passage strangely reminiscent of the prologue to the Fourth Gospel (John 1:1–4), which, however, features Word (the Greek *logos*) instead of Name (the Hebrew *shem*): "His Torah is in Him, [and] the Holy One, blessed be He, is in His Name, and His name is in Him, and...His Name is His Torah" (MS Jerusalem, 8/597, fol. 21v, cited in Scholem, *On the Kabbalah*, 43).

55. "The entire Torah consists of the names of God, and the words we read can be divided in a very different way, so as to form [esoteric] names," wrote Nahmanides (Moses

ben-Nahman of Gerona, ca. 1194–1270), the highest legal and religious authority of his time for the Jews in Spain and the person to whom the Catalonian Kabbalah owed much of its popularity (see Scholem, *On the Kabbalah*, 38).

56. *Bahir*'s place and time of origin are the focus of ardent debates among scholars. The Kabbalist legend attributes the book to Rabbi Nehuiah ben HaKana, a first-century Talmudic sage, and claims that it was transmitted orally within closed circles through the twelfth century. Some scholars accept that manuscripts may have existed, but claim that access to them was even more restricted. The first printed edition of the book appeared in Amsterdam in 1651. A bilingual Hebrew-English edition is available in Kaplan, ed., *Bahir*.

57. Kaplan, *Bahir*, pt. 110, 42. The complete reconstruction of the name is available in a number of sources in English; see, for example, the critical bilingual edition of Johannes Reuchlin's famous treatise *On the Art of the Kabbalah* (1517) in Reuchlin, *Art of the Kabbalah*, 263.

58. The key passage in *Bahir* opens with the statement, "There is *a name* that is derived from the three verses (*Exodus 14:19-21*)," and concludes, "These are *the 72 names*" (Kaplan, *Bahir*, pt. 110, 42, emphasis added). In a similar vein, another passage claims, "the Blessed Holy One has 72 names" (ibid., pt. 94, 34).

59. In the following century, the Spanish kabbalist Abraham Abulafia (1240–c. 1291) addressed this issue by proposing a complex system for vocalizing *Bahir*'s reconstruction of the name and reciting it as an instrument for mystical meditation; see Idel, *Mystical Experience*, 22–41.

60. Alternative reconstructions are registered in other Kabbalistic texts, none less peculiar in form. As many as twelve are reported by Petrus Galatinus in the section on the Kabbalah in his *Opus de arcanis catolicae veritatis* published in 1518 (lib. 2, cap. 17, pp. 97–98).

61. The term *quinary* belongs to the astrological idiom and refers to five degrees of the celestial sphere, which measure one 72nd part of it. The astrological imagination divides the heavenly sphere into 12 houses that harbor the 12 signs of the Zodiac and are said to correspond to the 12 principal rays of the sun. Each solar ray further splinters into three, and then into six smaller rays. The sun is thus surrounded by three radiant garlands, and the 72 rays of the outermost ($12 \times 6 = 72$) are the quinaries. In Agrippa's passage, evidently, the 72 quinaries refer to an imaginative 72-fold structure of the astral sphere, with each of the angels—the body of celestial creatures in charge—ruling over one of the 72 parts.

62. Thomas, *Religion and the Decline of Magic*, 273.

63. Compagni, *Cornelius Agrippa*, 41.

64. The notions of cosmic correspondences and universal harmony were borrowed by Agrippa from the Venetian humanist Zorzi (Francesco Giorgio Veneto); see especially Zorzi, *De Harmonia Mundi*. On the influence of Zorzi upon Agrippa at the last stage of his work on *De occulta philosophia*, see Compagni, *Cornelius Agrippa*, 35ff.

65. Kaplan, Bahir, pt. 1, 94, 34..

66. Kaplan, *Meditation and Kabbalah*, 141 and 168, n. 85.

67. Kircher, *Œdipus Ægyptiacus*, 281.

68. The diagram further explicates the connection between the 72 sunflower petals and the 72 leaves in the Tree of Life ("The Magic Tree") that grows in the center of Paradise, of which every leaf stands simultaneously for one of the names of God and one of the

nations, the nations continually saluting the names in eternity. The entire diagram is usually linked to a passage in the principal book of the Spanish Kabbalah, the *Zohar* (The book of enlightenment), saying that the "the crown of all legions rises in 72 lights," (see Schimmel, *Mystery*, 265). Another thirteenth-century Kabbalist text, written by Moses de Leon of Guadalajara, to whom Gershom Scholem attributes the greater part of the *Zohar*, links the figure of "72 roots" to the cosmic tree (see details in Idel, *Kabbalah*, 124). Scholem expounds more generally the homology between "the body" of the Torah and the Tree of Life based on the same source (*On the Kabbalah*, 46). Note also that in the late Jewish apocalyptic tradition, the number of the 72 nations is said to correspond to the 72 shining pearls in the heavenly Jerusalem that provide light for the nations (see Baumgarten, "Duodecimal Courts," 76, n. 66).

69. The texts are all part of the Nag Hammadi corpus discovered in 1945 in Upper Egypt; see Robinson and Smith, *Nag Hammadi Library*. The issue is discussed at some length, albeit from different points of view, in Schoedel, "Scripture and the Seventy-Two Heavens," and Idel, *Kabbalah*, 122–28. I rely on their competent summaries for my own cursory review of the Gnostic sources.

70. Quoted in Idel, *Kabbalah*, 123.

71. The Septuagint rendering of *b'nai elim/elim* ("sons of gods/gods") in the Bible is "angels." Deuteronomy 32:8, in both the Septuagint and the Qumran versions, postulates a guardian angel for each nation, whereas the Massoretic text reads "according to the number of the sons of Israel," to avoid a seeming allusion to henotheism. I am grateful to Fr. Lawrence Frizzell for this clarification. On guardian angels for nations, see also Dan. 19.

72. Quoted in Schoedel, "Scripture and the Seventy-Two Heavens," 121.

73. Moshe Idel contends that, even though the earliest extant sources are indeed Gnostic, they all show familiarity with Jewish texts. This allows him to conjecture that the cosmological views shared by Gnostic and Kabbalistic texts were Jewish in origin and that, while they infiltrated Gnostic circles, they were also passed down by the Jewish oral tradition until the emergence of the medieval Kabbalah (see Idel, *Kabbalah*, 116).

CHAPTER NINE

1. Idel, *Kabbalah*, 254.

2. A bilingual Latin-English edition of Pico's *Conclusions*, with extensive commentaries, is available in Farmer, *Syncretism in the West*.

3. "Nulla est scientia quae nos magis certificet de diuinitate Christi quam magia et cabala," ibid., 496–97.

4. See Lejay, "Giovanni Pico della Mirandola."

5. See Scholem, "Kabbalah," 643–44.

6. Froehlich, "Pseudo Dionysius and the Reformation," 36.

7. Yates, *Art of Memory*, 188–89.

8. See Yates, "Ramon Lull and John Scotus Erigena."

9. See Hames, *Art of Conversion*, and Yates, *Art of Memory*, 177. On the influence of the Sufi mystic Mohidin on Lull, see Palacios, *Mystical Philosophy*.

10. Yates, *Art of Memory*, 188.

11. Mirandola, *Opera omnia*, 180, cited in Yates, *Art of Memory*, 189.

12. For the alchemical treatises attributed to Lull under the rubric of the Christian Kabbalah, see Taylor, *Alchemists*, 110ff.

13. Note that Christian authors' admiration for the Kabbalah aroused angry responses in some Jewish quarters, particularly among the critics of the Kabbalah who opposed its diffusion in Christian circles and its potential use as a missionary tool (see Ruderman, *Renaissance Jew*, 52–56).

14. For the latter, see Idel, *Kabbalah*, 4.

15. The two books are published together in a modern reprint; see Reuchlin, *De verbo marifico*. For an English translation of *De arte cabbalistica*, see Reuchlin, *On the Art of the Kabbalah*. Another scholar of the Kabbalah who deserves honorary mention is the Frenchman Guillaume Postel (1510–81). He translated the *Zohar* into Latin even before it had been printed in Hebrew, and complemented it with his new theosophic commentaries.

16. For a review of Agrippa's contribution to the study of Kabbalah, see Müller-Jahncke, "Agrippa von Nettesheim et la Kabbale."

17. See Foucault, *Order of Things*, 32.

18. *The Grimoire of Honorius* is fallaciously attributed to Pope Honorius III (1216–27). Arthur Edward Waite's seminal study, originally published in London in 1898 as *The Book of Black Magic and of Pacts*, offers a detailed presentation of this remarkable monument (see Waite, *Book of Ceremonial Magic*, 96–194). As Waite himself notes, the book is exceedingly rare in the original and is better known in seventeenth- and eighteenth-century reprints. I am familiar with the text through a modern French edition of 1978.

19. See Butler, *Ritual Magic*, 157–58. Western magic manuals list 72 chief devils or demons and 72 seals that control them, "the number seventy-two [being] obviously inspired by the seventy-two divine names of the Shemhamphoras," as Butler observes (66).

20. Kabbalistic texts and practices use reconstructions of the name of 72 combinations as well as lists of 72 or 70 divine names. For the latter, see Dan, "Seventy Names of Metatron"; cf. Buchman-Naga, *Schlüssel zu der 72 Gottesnamen*. While none of these names are "attributes" of the divinity, the rabbinic tradition offers an alternative list of 70 divine names, which, much like the names promoted by Dionysius the Areopagite, are all meaningful terms identified through scriptural exegeses and supported by biblical proof-texts. Moreover, they are placed in the center of a corpus of several 70-fold lists, where all other classes (the 70 names of Israel, the 70 names of Jerusalem, the 70 names of the Torah) echo the number of the Lord's names as a gesture of deference; see *Midrash Zuta* on the *Song of Songs*. I have used the German translation available in Brasch, *Midrasch Schir Ha-Schirim*, 20–35. The parallels between this corpus and the Christian material that I discuss in this book are too striking to miss, although I still have found no evidence that proves—or even suggests—a direct influence.

21. Evidence of the amulet use of *shem ha-mephorash* in Kabbalistic context is provided by Theodore Schrire, who claims that, since the name was too large to be written on one amulet, it was divided into two groups that were to be worn on the two arms or by couples (*Hebrew Magic Amulets*, 99). Schrire also provides a photographic reproduction of one Hebrew amulet that features the entire name on a single plate (see plate 27 and its description on 154–55). The topos itself is apparently a common element in magical texts; see, for instance, a Hebrew healing amulet from the Cairo Genizah, which opens with an invocation of the Explicit Name and the 70 names of God (Schiffman and Swartz, *Hebrew*

and Aramaic Incantation Texts, 113; 115); compare a reference to the 70 names in another amulet from the same collection (ibid., 151).

22. Languedoc, the center of the Provençal Kabbalah at the time, was under the religious dominance of the Cathars, a dualist sect related to the Bulgarian Bogomils, whose own genealogy leads back to both Gnosticism and Manichaeism. Given the mutual affinities between Kabbalah and Catharism, their coexistence in Provence has prompted scholars to suspect direct transactions between them, and especially a Cathar influence upon the Kabbalists. No conclusive evidence, however, has been found to corroborate such conjectures. For a balanced view on the subject, see Stoyanov, *The Other God*, 192–93, esp. 282.

23. A masterpiece of thirteenth-century vernacular literature, the poem (approximately 8,100 verses) is preserved in a single thirteenth-century copy with missing beginning and ending. The most recent critical edition of the original text with an introduction, commentaries, and a glossary is Ulrich Gschwind, ed. *Le Roman de Flamenca*. For a bilingual Provençal-English edition, see Hubert and Poter, *Romance of Flamenca*.

24. Verses 2279–88 (cf. Hubert and Poter, *Romance of Flamenca*, 142). I am grateful to my colleague Michael Agnew for his help with this translation. A less literal translation is provided by H. F. M. Prescott: "He [William] also said…a short prayer that a holy hermit had taught him. This prayer was made up of the seventy-two Names of God as they are spoken in Hebrew and Latin and Greek. It renews and strengthens a man in the love of God, and makes him daily more worthy. Everyone who repeats it, and believes it, is rewarded of God, and no one who trusts in it heartily, or who carries a written copy of it about with him, comes to a violent death" (Prescott, *Flamenca*, 44–45).

25. Miklas and Zagrebin, *Berlinski sbornik*, fol. 71v.

26. For the edited text, see Meyer, "La prière des soixante-douze noms de Dieu"; it is reprinted in Bolte, "Über die 72 Namen" (446). I am grateful to my colleague Susan Boynton for consulting me on the translation of this passage. Note that the Provençal proviso differs from the familiar Slavonic model only in its inclusion of a clause on difficult delivery, a concern that does not seem to be characteristic of the Slavonic tradition of this text. See also Nelli, "La Prière," which unfortunately was unavailable to me while preparing this manuscript.

27. "And they entreated him by each of the seven universal things—sun and moon, dew and sea, heaven and earth, day and night" (see Tymoczko, *Irish* Ulysses, 148–49).

28. There is an inconsistent tendency in this copy to numerate the names, which is abandoned after the third name. In the Provençal text only the first name is numbered.

29. The original Slavonic term is *opoka*, glossed by Miklosich as *saxum*, that is, "rock" (see his *Lexicon*). "Rock" (Gr. *petra*) is part of the standard repertory of divine names; see, for example, the extensive Byzantine seventh-century list quoted in chapter 4. Moshe Taube, in personal communication, has suggested to me that the Slavonic noun could be etymologically related to the verb *opochati*, "rest" or "dwell." The name read as "rest" may point to Matt. 11:28, "Come to me, all that are weary and are carrying heavy burdens, and I will give you rest" (cf. Heb. 4:1). More broadly, such a reading may reflect the Hebrew term *Shekhina*, literally "indwelling," namely, of God in the world. I should mention that the Kabbalists, in a radical departure from Rabbinical theology, treat

Shekhina as a quasi-independent feminine element within God (see Scholem, "Kabbalah," 104–5).

30. *Athanatos* (Gr., "Immortal") and *Pantokrator* (Gr., "Omnipotent") are doubled by their Slavonic equivalents (*bes'mr'tnyi, vsedr'zhitel'*), just as the Slavonic term for "the Lord" (*gospod'*) is listed side by side with the transliterations of both the Hebrew *Adonai* and the Greek *Kyrios*. The only transliterated names that are not coupled by their translation are *Sabbaoth* (Hebr., "Of the Hosts") and *Paraklit* (Gr., "Intercessor"), both fairly common titles that are often used without translation in the liturgical idiom.

31. For Malinowsky's "coefficient of weirdness" and "coefficient of intelligibility," by which we may distinguish between religious (magical) and profane language, see Tambiah, "Magical Power of Words," 185ff.

32. One interesting exception is the name Utis, which, if it is not a complete distortion of another name, is an accurate Latin transliteration of the Greek *outis*, "Nobody," which is the name that Odysseus gave himself to fool the Cyclops Polyphemos (Homer, *Odyssey* 9:366–67). It is also notable that the Slavonic version renders the descriptive name "Tetragrammaton" (which replaces the tabooed YHWH) with the name revealed to Moses at the burning bush (Exodus 3:15): "I am who I am" (*az' esm' ezhe es'm'*). This awkward name later causes a lot of problems for the scribes who wrestle with it, to rather peculiar effect; see, for example, the double negative "I am not who I am not" (*az" ne sam izhe ne sam*; see Raikov, ed., *Abagar na Filip Stanislavov*, n.p.), or the deliciously elliptic "I am the one who" (*az" es'm" ezhe*; National Library SS Cyril and Methodius, Sofia, Bulgaria, Manuscript and Rare Book Collection, MS. Slav. 646 [44] from 1787, fol. 8v).

33. The Slavonic text, however, seems to have more taste for foreign terms: it includes a number of transliterations that, in the Latin list, are either translated or absent altogether.

34. Iatsimirskii, "K istorii," 9; Miklas and Zagrebin, *Berlinski sbornik*, 39.

35. The names are numbers 51 and 52 by my count.

36. "The original, no doubt, was Greek" (see Iatsimirskii, "K istorii," 10).

37. Miklas and Zagrebin, *Berlinski sbornik*, 39.

38. See Stoyanov, *The Other God*, 225.

39. The practice of wearing *The 72 Names of the Lord* as an amulet is documented also among the Romanians. Hasdeu quotes an eighteenth-century Romanian *Rojdanicul* (Zodiac), which instructs that a sickly girl, born under the sign of Scorpio, should "carry on herself the 72 names of Jesus Christ, so that no unclean spirit can come close to her," and provides a parallel Serbian version (Hasdeu, *Cărțile poporane*, 23); cf. Gaster, *Literatura populară romănă*, 401–2, and Cartojan, *Cărțile populare*, 135, who report earlier copies of the same text.

40. Apart from the short article by Johannes Bolte published at the beginning of the twentieth century, we have only separate publications by Nyrop, "Navnets magt" (see esp. 185–92), and Gaster, "Zur Quellenkunde Deutscher Sagen und Märchen." See also a seventeenth-century German text preserved in the form of an amulet roll in Hampp, "Sigilla Solomonis."

41. Bolte mentions a French version dated from 1454 and a German one from the fifteenth century; see "Über die 72 Namen," 447–49.

42. The Dominican friar Agostino Giustiniani (1470–1536), a well-known Christian Kabbalist, is credited with the authorship of a book entitled *Praecatio pietatis plena ad Deum omnipotentem composita ex duobus et septuaginta nominibus divinis, hebraicis, et latinis* (Prayer full of piety to the Almighty God, composed of 72 divine names in Latin and Hebrew). The book's first edition (Paris) has no date of publication, but the second edition came out in Venice in 1513; see details in Salone, "La fortuna editoriale," 137, and 142, n. 10; cf. Cevolotto, *Agostino Giustiniani*, 37–38). It is tempting to assume that this text may have informed the first printed edition of the Slavonic 72 *Names of the Lord* (1520), which was also published in Venice, but more information is needed before drawing such conclusions. Regrettably, I found the reference to Giustiniani's edition too late to be able to consult it and compare his prayer to the Provençal and the Slavonic lists.

43. About the book, see Waite, *Book of Ceremonial Magic*, 39–57. This study still remains the most thorough and illuminating presentation of the *Enchiridion* in its context.

44. Waite, *Book of Ceremonial Magic*, 40.

45. Waite, who appears to be somewhat skeptical about the authenticity of the 1523 edition, reports that it was mentioned as authentic by Pierre Christian in his *Historie de la Magie* (*Book of Ceremonial Magic*, 41). It is also mentioned by Nisard in his *Historie des Livres Populaires* (149), though he quotes the date of publication as 1525. Since I could find no traces of this edition in contemporary archives and libraries, I am not prepared at this point to make any statements about its authenticity.

46. The article, first published in the journal *Germania*, 1881, is reprinted in Gaster, "Zur Quellenkunde Deutscher Sagen und Märchen" (1071–85).

47. Bolte, "Über die 72 Namen," 447–48.

CHAPTER TEN

1. Vuković, ed. *Zbornik za putnike*. Stojan Novaković's, "Božidara Vukovića zbornici za putnike," is still the best study of this book and the tradition that stemmed from it. In another article, "Apokrifi iz štampanih zbornika Božidara Vukovića," Novaković edited the group of texts that I will be discussing here, including the amulet itself.

2. Slavic books using Latin script (mostly Bibles and liturgical books in Latin) began to appear almost simultaneously in Cracow and Pilsen in the early 1470s, only a decade and a half after the landmark publication of the Gutenberg Bible in 1456. The first Glagolitic book (a Missal that is claimed today by both Croats and Slovenes as their own) was published in 1483. For the history of Slavic typography, see Pantić, ed., *Pet vekova srpskog štamparstva 1494–1994* (cf. the papers from the 1991 conference in Cracow dedicated to the study of the oldest Slavonic printed books, edited by Rusek, Witkowski, and Naumow, *Rękopis a druk*.

3. See Schmitz's *Südslavischer Buchdruck in Venedig*, which offers invaluable information about all Slavic Venetian editions with corresponding bibliographic data on their extant copies. Cf. Pesenti, "Stampatori e litterati," esp. 105, for Cyrillic printing and the role of Božidar Vuković.

4. For the activities of Vuković in Venice, see Milović, ed., *Štamparska i književna djelatnost*.

5. Work on the book was completed on March 6, 1520. The only two books that the publishing house had issued before the *Miscellany* were a Psalter and a Typikon, both published in 1519 (see Vujošević, "O nekim biografskim podacima," 43).

6. One of the extant sources of the texts in the Vuković redaction, *Prayer Book of Niketa*, from 1787, held at the National Library SS Cyril and Methodius, Sofia, Bulgaria, Manuscript and Rare Book Collection, MS 646 (44), fols. 3v–6v, also features a different version of *The 72 Names of the Lord* that is closer to the versions in both the *Berlin Codex* and *Jerusalem 22* (fols. 8v–9r). The fact that the two versions appear together in a single codex is itself evidence that they were thought of as distinct textual items, complementary rather than equivalent to one another.

7. The Greek original is published in Migne, *PG*, 52:395–414. The standard Slavonic translation is Makarii, *Velikiia minei-chetii, Noiabr' 13–15*, 1132–61.

8. I have quoted this passage for another purpose in chapter 4.

9. The Greek original is published in Migne, *PG*, 97:861–81. For the Slavonic translation, see Makarii, *Velikiia minei-chetii: Sentiabr' 1–13*, 386–96.

10. It is hard to estimate exactly how much Vuković was involved in the making of the book, but the evidence suggests that he was mostly the man with the vision and the money. Apparently he knew little about bookmaking and possibly even less about the making of texts.

11. The classic study of the shift from manuscript to print culture and its aftermath is Eisenstein, *Printing Revolution*. *Durability* and *accessibility* are both her terms.

12. It appears that the career of the two Latin lists was similarly boosted by their first printed publication in the *Enchiridion* of Pope Leo III, which allegedly dates from 1523 (though the earliest editions of the book that we possess are from the seventeenth century). Only a comprehensive study of these amulets in their Western context, however, can substantiate such a superficial impression.

13. As a rule, the manuscript copies that follow Vuković's version omit the exegetical part. The only exception known to me is the sixteenth-century copy published in Tikhonravov, *Pamiatniki*, 2: 339–44. Note that this copy documents the dissemination of Vuković's version in Russia; see Ryan, *Bathhouse at Midnight*, 294–95.

14. The amulet is part of the collection of the State Library of Ljubljana, Slovenia. For a comprehensive study of the amulet, with a reproduction of the plates, see Radojčić, "Srpski Abagar." Apart from *The 72 Names of the Lord* and *The 72 Names of the Theotokos*, the amulet includes *The Names of the Angels*, *The Names of the 17 Prophets*, and *The Names of the 40 Martyrs*, together with an array of troparia, kontakia, and prayers addressed to numerous saints. See an edition of the corpus in Izmirlieva, *Christian Art of Listing*, 213–15.

15. To the best of my knowledge, there is no other extant Slavonic source of this text. My attempts to find possible rhetorical sources of the nominal series in the Slavonic hagiographic and hymnographic repertoire have proven fruitless. A Greek list of twenty-two names for the saint, edited in Pitra, *Spicilegium solesmense complectens sanctorum patrum*, 3:448, offers a clue to the possible source of this tradition, though the epithets listed there do not coincide with the Slavonic "names." The other sacronymic lists in the corpus encompass *The Names of the 17 Angels*, *The Names of the 70 Disciples*, and *The Names of the 40 Martyrs*. See an edition of the corpus in Izmirlieva, *Christian Art of Listing*, 215–18.

16. The only major editorial change introduced in the later tradition of the texts was the truncation of their exegetical parts, evidently considered redundant (they survived in only two of the total thirty-two available copies).

17. The text and its status as a written amulet have been studied by Iatsimirskii in conjunction with *The 72 Names of the Lord* and *The 72 Names of the Theotokos* (see Iatsimirskii, "K istorii," 22–50). In some cases, the list of epithets is replaced by a bona fide canonical text, the *Troparion for the Cross*.

18. The sign of the cross is still routinely made by Eastern Orthodox Christians whenever they fear a threat of any kind. The monks on Mt. Athos reportedly used to make it for protection against evil forces even over their open mouths each time they yawned, since demons were believed to be able to sneak in unnoticed through any open aperture of the body.

19. Geerard's *Clavis Apocryphorum Novi Testamenti* is an excellent bibliographical source for the Abgar tradition across the Christian world (65–89). For the most complete monograph on the cycle in the field of Slavic medieval studies, see Meshcherskaia, *Legenda ob Avgare*. On the Slavonic tradition, see Minchev and Skovronek, "Tsikulut za Tsar Avgar."

20. Eusebius, *History of the Church*, 1:13.

21. Minchev and Skovronek have proposed, on the basis of late seventeenth-century texts, that the epistles were also used liturgically in folk milieu, in a paraliturgical ritual for curing a sick person, where the reading of the Abgar Cycle over the head of the patient replaced the reading from the Gospels (see their article "Tsik"l"t za Tsar Avgar," 337–39). This use, while not amuletic, is certainly no less apotropaic in nature; in fact placing the sacred text of the Gospels over the head of a sick person (always with the written text facing downward!) is, as the authors point out, one of the most telling examples of an apotropaic use of the Word in official Eastern Orthodox practice.

22. [Č]. T[ruhelka], "Jedan zanimliv zapis"

23. See Raikov, *Abagar na Filip Stanislavov*, 26. Raikov notes that a similar use of the name with the meaning of "amulet" occurs also among Romanians (37, n. 62).

24. See Gorskii and Novostruev, *Opisanie slavianskix rukopisei*, 600–601.

25. A sixteenth-century manuscript copy of the *Letter's* Slavonic version, published by Tikhonravov, claims explicitly that "everything is possible for those who have with themselves the names of Christ." The claim is followed by a familiar proviso about keeping the names clean and a short list of divine names that is apparently a contracted version of *The 72 Names of the Lord* (*Pamiatniki* 2:16). This evidence suggests that the two talismanic texts are closely associated with one another, possibly to the point of being fused together.

26. Note also that the letter-amulet was delivered in the legend by "one of the 72 disciples." Therefore, in the context of a 72-fold universe (where to every evil God counterpoises one of his omnipotent names), the epistle itself can be construed as a metonymic symbol of the protective shield that God had extended over the 72 nations through the Apostolic Church.

27. The *Enchiridion* of Pope Leo III (at least in the 1740 edition that was available to me) includes all the texts from this corpus, showing particularly strong intertextual links between the two lists and the texts from the Abgar Cycle that follow them. This

clustering is further enhanced by a prayer to Jesus Christ that appears at the end of the Abgar Cycle and concludes with an invocation of "the 72 names of God," followed by another long series of divine appellations. The similarity between the amulet texts in the *Enchiridion* and in Vuković's *Miscellany* may prompt us to suggest that Vuković's *Miscellany* was based on earlier Latin models. We cannot seriously entertain such a conjecture, however, until the sources and the history of the *Enchiridion* are sufficiently studied.

28. The "printing revolution" first received a full-scale treatment in Eisenstein's monumental, two-volume work *The Printing Press as an Agent of Change;* see also her abridged and illustrated version of the same study, *The Printing Revolution in Early Modern Europe.*

29. Ong, *Orality and Literacy,* 122–23 (emphasis added). Cf. Eisenstein's similar observation that the printing revolution involved a shift "away from fidelity to scribal conventions and toward serving the convenience of the reader" (*Printing Revolution,* 22).

30. Novaković, "Božidara Vukovića zbornici za putnike," 138.

31. Eisenstein, *Printing Revolution,* 48.

32. Cf. similar observations in Vujošević, "O nekim biografskim podacima," 44.

33. Incidentally, Keith Thomas links the decline of protective magical devices to the growth of insurance in seventeenth-century England (see *Religion and the Decline of Magic,* 651).

34. For the most detailed information about the printing activities of Božidar and Vincenczo Vuković, see the contribution by Pašikan in Pantić, *Pet vekova srpskog štamparstva,* 76–92.

35. For details about this book, see Atanasov, "Iakoviiat chasoslovets."

36. The missing pages belong to the copy of the 1547 edition of Vuković's *Miscellany* held at the Museum of the Serbian Orthodox Church in Belgrade, pr. bk. no. 96, which I have seen on microfilm at the Serbian National Library, Belgrade, Yugoslavia, Manuscript and Rare Book Collection (microfilm # 3737–82), and to one of the two copies of Yakov Kraikov's *Book of Hours* held at the Public Library in Plovdiv, Bulgaria, Manuscript and Rare Book Collection, Slavonic Division, RTs 19.

37. For an offset edition of this rare book with an excellent study of its history, see Raikov, *Abagar na Filip Stanislavov.*

38. Raikov, *Abagar na Filip Stanislavov* (the edition of the text has no pagination).

39. While in the *Miscellany* the *Eulogy of the Holy Cross* is followed by a complete Abgar corpus and the two talismanic lists, here the lists (minus their exegetical parts) appear directly after the *Eulogy,* and the corpus concludes with a *Letter of King Abgar* (without any mention of the Edessa image).

40. See Jerkova, "Latinski izvori na Stanislavoviia 'Abagar'"; cf. Jerkov and Capaldo, "Razlicnie potrebii di Jakov di Sofia."

41. The surprising inclusion of teachers among the religious specialists indicates that the publication of the book also had an educational purpose. In support of that assumption, seventeenth-century documents attest to the use of the *Abagar* in Bulgarian Catholic communities as a primer from which young Catholics learned the ABCs of Catholicism (together with useful information about Calvinists and Lutherans, in tune to the agenda of the Counter-Reformation). It is also significant that the book was written mostly in the

vernacular and was thus more intelligible to its audience, which must have facilitated its educational function (see Raikov, *Abagar na Filip Stanislavov*, 29).

42. It is important to note that this book was not produced for the market as was Vuković's reader, but for distribution free of charge by a network of missionaries exclusively for propaganda purposes. (The Congregation had specifically banned several years earlier any commercial deals involving its own editions.)

43. About the heresy in the context of Christian dualism, see Stoyanov, *The Other God*, esp. 127–30 and 258. For details about the Bulgarian Paulicians, see Miletich, "Nashite pavlikiani"; and Iovkov, *Pavlikiani i pavlikianski selishta*. For the Catholic missions among the Bulgarian Paulicians, see the documents published in Primov, Sariiski, and Iovkov, *Dokumenti za katolicheskata deinost*.

44. Raikov offers some direct evidence that written amulets were especially popular among the Bulgarian Paulicians, who used to refer to them as *abgari* (see Raikov, *Abagar na Filip Stanislavov*, 37, n. 62).

EPILOGUE

1. Barney argues that a principle represents a list the way a title represents a book, which means it can *stand for* the list itself ("Chaucer's Lists," 191).

2. Levinas, *Totality and Infinity*. Significantly, this study has a profound concern with order: its ultimate thrust is toward a third way between anarchy and tyranny, a way to which the Dionysius who emerges from my reading is no stranger.

3. Weil, *Gravity and Grace*.

4. Among the other postmodern takes on the subject, Lacan's is perhaps the most recognizable. For his treatment of need and desire, see, for example, Vincent Crapanzano, *Hermes' Dilemma and Hamlet's Desire*, 89. Lacan, however, plays out the two categories mostly in the field of psychological motivation. The ethical reprisal by Levinas is much closer to my own approach, and more illuminating of my own problematic.

5. Levinas, *Totality and Infinity*, 33–34.

6. Ibid., 254.

7. Ibid., 116.

8. Ibid., 191.

9. To be sure, the prospect of a perfect apocalyptic moment brought about by human desire is most desirable for religious "infinitizers." One recent example is the apocalyptic "erotic utopia" of Vladimir Solovev (1853–1900), one of Russia's most influential modern religious thinkers, and the radical attempts to put it into practice in Russian symbolist circles (see Matich, *Erotic Utopia*).

10. Levinas, *Totality and Infinity*, 117.

11. Bourdieu, *Logic of Practice*, 14–15.

12. Stanley Cavell offers a similar argument in his exploration of the pursuit of happiness in early Hollywood comedies of remarriage. His entire argument implies a certain vision of order that emerges from these films. The lesson of the cinematic genre that interests him, as he notes in the introduction, is that "the achievement of human happiness requires not the perennial and fuller satisfaction of our needs as they stand, but the examination and transformation of those needs." Cavell goes on to directly qualify desire-driven

life as removed from need: "Even if we whole-heartedly agreed with such a thought (as voiced, say, in Plato and in Rousseau and in Thoreau and in Freud), no one would say that it is applicable in all human contexts. It applies only in contexts in which there is satisfaction enough, in which something like luxury and leisure, something beyond the bare necessities, is an issue. This is why our films must on the whole take settings of unmistakable wealth; the people in them have the leisure to talk about human happiness" (*Pursuit of Happiness*, 4–5). In this case, the "distance from need" is provided directly by luxury, though wealth and indulgence are far from constituting the exclusive source of the "leisure to desire." In the Christian ascetic tradition, it is achieved by *akēdia* (Gr., "apathy"), the cultivated indifference to needs, which is to say, by a way directly opposite to that of material luxury.

13. The classic text is Malinowski, *Magic, Science and Religion*. Scholars as distant from one another as Thomas, Tambiah, and Kieckhefer all adopt this dichotomy while working diligently to clarify—from their respective methodological points of view—its highly problematic nature; see Thomas, *Religion and the Decline of Magic*; Tambiah, *Magic, Science, Religion*; and Kieckhefer, *Magic in the Middle Ages*.

14. A good survey of the polemics surrounding the term *popular religion* is O'Neil, "From 'Popular' to 'Local' Religion." Dinzelbacher provides a relatively recent bibliography of studies in popular religion (see "Zur Erforschung der Geschichte der Volksreligion"). In Slavic ethnological studies, the equivalent terms are numerous, "everyday" and "folk" religion being the more popular alternatives (see the review article by Mikhailova, "Za s"d"rzhanieto na termina *bitovo/folklorno khristiianstvo*).

15. The Russian term *dvoeverie*, "dual faith," established in the nineteenth and early twentieth centuries, is based on the assumption that the peculiar form of Christianity embraced by the Russian common folk is Christian in name only, being in reality a blend of pagan beliefs and practices under a thin Christian veneer (see, for example, Zhivov, "Dvoeverie"). The Western term "syncretic" is less radical: it implies only contamination, not an ideological duality.

16. The distinction between the "easy" and "difficult" ways in religion belongs to Eliade (see *Shamanism*, 401; and *Images and Symbols*, 54–55; cf. Staal, *Exploring Mysticism*, 100–101 and 155–56).

17. I have been using, without explicitly defining it, the term *heteropraxis* as a way of avoiding this discussion before all the cards are on the table. The term is more neutral only if we think of it in opposition not to *orthopraxis* but to what we may call *homopraxis*—the emphasis being not on what is right or wrong, but on homogeneity of belief as opposed to the salient omnivorousness of certain Christian practices that, eclectic and redundant as they are, have no distinct doctrinal (or theoretical) counterparts. The term is useful for descriptive purposes, but it has rather limited theoretical potential, for it perpetuates the understanding of Christian alternatives as forms of corruption and contamination.

18. David Tracy offers a similar position when he presents a defense of "the ordinary ways" along with the "extraordinary expressions" of religion. "[T]he religions are carried along at least as much by the vast undertow of ordinary people leading ordinary religious lives as by the classic prophets, mystics, and saints," he argues passionately, and concludes with the assertion that "no exponent of religious intensifications can ignore the classics of ordinary religious life" (*Plurality and Ambiguity*, 96–97).

19. One example of a powerful theoretical hypothesis based on the assumption of a single and unequivocal "medieval order" is Umberto Eco's opposition between the Western European medieval (Catholic) Cosmos, driven by the homogenous "logic of the inventory," and the modern (nihilist) "Chaosmos," exemplified by the heterogeneous lists of James Joyce (see Eco, *Aesthetics of Chaosmos*, esp. 6–11).

20. See Cunningham, *Meaning of Saints*, 16; cf. Peter Brown's influential study *Cult of Saints*, esp. the chapter entitled "Potentia" (106–27).

21. The story, considered one of Sir Arthur's masterpieces, has numerous editions—see, for example, the eponymous selection *Nine Billion Names of God* (3–11). In this edition, put together by Clarke himself, he quotes the British biochemist and geneticist John Burdon Sanderson Haldane (1892–1964), who remarked of this story and the story "Star," "You are the only person to say anything original about religion in the last two thousand years" (3). He goes on to undercut his own solemnity: "In fact, you have said several mutually incompatible things. If you had stuck to one hypothesis you might have been a serious public danger."

22. Clarke, *Nine Billion Names*, 11.

Abbott, G. F. *Macedonian Folklore*. Cambridge: Cambridge University Press, 1903.

Adler, Jeremy, and Ulrich Ernst. *Text als Figur: Visuelle Poesie von der Antike bis zur Moderne*. Ausstellungskataloge der Herzog August Bibliothek 56. Weinheim: VCH, Acta Humaniora, 1988.

Alexander, Paul Julius. *The Oracle of Baalbeck: The Tiburtine Sibyl in Greek Dress*. Dumbarton Oaks Studies, no. 10. Washington, DC: Dumbarton Oaks Center for Byzantine Studies, 1967.

Alfeev, Bishop Ilarion. *Sviashchennaia taina Tserkvi: Vvedenie v istoriiu i problematiku imiaslavskikh sporov*. Vol. 1. St. Petersburg: Aletejia, 2002.

Almazov, A. I. "Vracheval'nyia molitvy." In *Letopis' Istoriko-Filologicheskago Obshchestva pri Imperatorskom Novorossiiskom Universitete*, 8:367–514. Vizantino-Slavianskoe Otdelenie. Odessa: Ekonomicheskaia Tipografiia, 1900.

Alt, Albert. "Die Weisheit Salamos." *Theologische Literaturzeitung* 76 (1951): 139–44.

Anderson, Gary A., and Michael E. Stone, eds. *A Synopsis of the Books of Adam and Eve*. Atlanta, GA: Scholars Press, 1994.

Aptowitzer, V. "Les noms de Dieu et des anges dans la mezouza. Contributions a l'historie de la mystique et de la Cabbale." *Revue des Études Juives* 60 (1910): 39–52; 65 (1913): 54–60.

Aquinas, Thomas. *In librum Beati Dionysii* De divinis nominibus *expositio*. Ed. C. Pera. Turin: Marettis, 1950.

Aristotle. *The Categories [and] On Interpretation*. Ed. Harold P. Cooke. The Loeb Classical Library. Cambridge, MA: Harvard University Press, 1967.

Atanasov, Pet"r. "Iakoviiat chasoslovets (1566–1966)." *Istoricheski pregled* 22, no. 2 (1966): 96–104.

Barney, Stephen A. "Chaucer's Lists." In *The Wisdom of Poetry: Essays in Early English Literature in Honor of Morton W. Bloomfield*, ed. Larry D. Benson and Siegfried Wenzel, 189–223. Kalamazoo, MI: Medieval Institute Publications, 1982.

Barrett, Francis. *The Magus, or Celestial Intelligencer, Being a Complete System of Occult Philosophy*. London: Lackington, Allen, 1801.

Bauer, Walter. *A Greek-English Lexicon of the New Testament and Other Early Christian Literature*. Trans. William Arndt and F. W. Gingrich. Chicago: University of Chicago Press, 1979.

Baumgarten, Joseph. "The Duodecimal Courts of Qumran, Revelation, and the Sanhedrin." *Journal of Biblical Literature* 95 (1976): 59–78.

Black, Max. *Models and Metaphors*. Ithaca, NY: Cornell University Press, 1962.

Blake, William. "A Vision of the Last Judgment." In *The Complete Poetry and Prose of William Blake*, ed. David V. Erdman, 554–66. Berkeley and Los Angeles: University of California Press, 1982.

Boissande, Jean François. *ANEKDOTA: Anecdota graeca e codicibus regiis*. Vol. 4. 1832; repr., Hildesheim, Germany: Georg Olms, 1962.

Bolte, Johannes. "Über die 72 Namen Gottes." *Zeitschrift des Vereins für Volkskunde* 13, no. 4 (1903): 444–50.

Bonetskaia, N. K. "O filologicheskoi shkole P. A. Florenskogo: 'Filosofiia imeni' A. F. Loseva i 'Filosofiia imeni' S. N. Bulgakova." *Studia Slavica Hungarica* 37 (1991–92): 113–89.

Borst, Arno. *Der Turmbau von Babel: Geschichte der Meinungen über Ursprung und Vielfalt der Sprachen und Völker*. 4 vols. Stuttgart: A. Hiersemann, 1957–63.

Bourdieu, Pierre. *Language and Symbolic Power*. Ed. John B. Thompson. Trans. Gino Raymond and Matthew Adamson. Cambridge, MA: Harvard University Press, 1999.

———. *The Logic of Practice*. Trans. Richard Nice. Stanford, CA: Stanford University Press, 1990.

———. *The Rules of Art: Genesis and Structure of the Literary Field*. Trans. Susan Emanuel. Stanford, CA: Stanford University Press, 1995.

Box, G. H. *The Testament of Abraham*. London: Macmillan, 1927.

Braude, Benjamin, and Bernard Lewis, eds. *Christians and Jews in the Ottoman Empire: The Functioning of a Plural Society*. 2 vols. New York: Holmes and Meier, 1982.

Braudel, Fernand. *The Mediterranean and the Mediterranean World in the Age of Philip II*. Vol. 2. Trans. Siân Reynolds. Berkeley and Los Angeles: University of California Press, 1995.

Brasch, Rudolf, ed. *Der "Midrasch Schir Ha-Schirim Suta": Übersetzung, Kommentarierung und Vergleich mit dem Midrasch Rabba*. Leipzig: Albert Teicher, 1936.

Brown, Peter. *The Cult of Saints: Its Rise and Function in Latin Christianity*. Chicago: University of Chicago Press, 1982.

Buchmann-Naga, Franz. *Schlüssel zu den 72 Gottesnamen der Kabbala: Praxis der kabbalistischen Invokation: Talismanische Theomagie*. Schriftenreihe der Gilde, no. 8. Gaustadt: Osiris, 1955.

Budge, E. A. Wallis. *Amulets and Magic*. London: Kegan Paul, 2001. First published as *Amulets and Superstitions*. London: Oxford University Press, 1930.

Bulgakov, Sergei. *Filosofiia imeni*. Paris: YMCA Press, 1953.

Burke, Kenneth. *The Rhetoric of Religion: Studies in Logology*. Berkeley and Los Angeles: University of California Press, 1961.

———. *Terms for Order*. Bloomington: Indiana University Press, 1964.

Burrell, David. "Naming the Names of God: Muslims, Jews, Christians." *Theology Today* 47, no. 1 (1990): 22–59.

Burrell, David, and Nazih Daher, eds. *Al-Ghazzali: The Ninety-Nine Beautiful Names of God*. Cambridge: The Islamic Texts Society, 1992.

Burrows, Eric. "The Number Seventy in Semitic." *Orientalia*, n.s., 5 (1936): 389–92.

Butler, Eliza Marian. *Ritual Magic*. Cambridge: Cambridge University Press, 1949.

Bychkov, Ivan A. *Katalog sobraniia slaviano-russkix rukopisei P. D. Bogdanova*. Vol. 1. St. Petersburg: Tipografiia V.S. Balasheva, 1891–93.

Cantor, Norman. *The Civilization of the Middle Ages*. New York: Harper Collins, 1993.

Cartojan, Nicolae. *Cărţile populare în literatura românească*. Bucharest, Romania: Editura enciclopedică română, 1974.

Cavell, Stanley. *Pursuit of Happiness: The Hollywood Comedy of Remarriage*. Boston, MA: Harvard Film Studies, 1981.

Cevolotto, Aurelio. *Agostino Giustiniani: Un umanista tra Biblia e cabala*. Genoa: Edizioni culturali internazionali Genova, 1992.

Checklist of the Manuscripts in the Libraries of the Greek and Armenian Patriarchates in Jerusalem. Washington, DC: Library of Congress, 1949–50.

Chevalier, Jean, and Alain Gheerbrant. *A Dictionary of Symbols*. Trans. John Buchanan-Brown. London: Blackwell, 1994.

Chevallier, Philippe. *Dionysiaca: Recueil donnant l'ensemble des traductions latines des ouvrages attribués au Denys de l'Aréopage*. 2 vols. Paris: Desclée, 1937–50.

Clarke, Arthur C. *The Nine Billion Names of God: The Best Short Stories of Arthur C. Clarke*. New York: Harcourt, Brace & World, 1967.

Cohon, Samuel S. "The Name of God: A Study in Rabbinic Theology." *Hebrew Union College Annual* 23, no. 1 (1950–51): 579–604.

Compagni, Vittoria Perrone, ed. *Cornelius Agrippa: De occulta philosophia*. Vol. 3. Studies in the History of Christian Thought, no. 48. Leiden: E. J. Brill, 1992.

Cowley, Roger W. *Ethiopian Biblical Interpretation: A Study in Exegetical Tradition and Hermeneutics*. Cambridge: Cambridge University Press, 1988.

Coxon, Peter W. "The 'List' Genre and Narrative Style in the Court Tales of Daniel." *Journal for the Study of the Old Testament* 35 (1986): 95–121.

Crapanzano, Vincent. *Hermes' Dilemma and Hamlet's Desire: On the Epistemology of Interpretation*. Cambridge, MA: Harvard University Press, 1992.

Cullmann, Oscar. *The Christology of the New Testament*. Trans. Shirley C. Guthrie and Charles A. M. Hall. Philadelphia, PA: Westminster Press, 1959.

Cunningham, Lawrence S. *The Meaning of Saints*. San Francisco: Harper & Row, 1980.

Dan, Joseph. "The Name of God, the Name of the Rose, and the Concept of Language in Jewish Mysticism." *Medieval Encounters* 2, no. 3 (1996): 228–48.

———. "The Seventy Names of Metatron." In *Proceedings of the Eighth World Congress of Jewish Studies*, Jerusalem, August 16–21, 1981. Division 3: "Talmud and Midrash, Philosophy and Mysticism, Hebrew and Yiddish Literature," 19–23. Jerusalem: World Union of Jewish Studies, 1982.

Dante Alighieri, *The Banquet*. Tr. Christopher Ryan. Stanford French and Italian Studies, vol. 61. Saratoga, CA: Anma Libri, 1989.

Dante Alighieri. *The Divine Comedy of Dante Alighieri: Inferno*. A verse translation by Allen Mandelbaum. New York: Bantam Books, 1982.

Davidson, Gustav. *Dictionary of Angels, Including the Fallen Angels*. New York: Free Press, 1971.

Dean, James Elmer. *Epiphanius' Treatise on Weights and Measures: The Syriac Version*. Chicago: University of Chicago Press, 1935.

Denkova, L., P. Yaneva, and K. Ivanova. "The Reception of Pseudo-Dionysius in Medieval Bulgaria." In *Die Dionysius-Rezeption im Mittelalter. Internationales Kolloquium in Sofia vom 8. bis 11. April 1999 unter der Schirmherrschaft der Société Internationale pour l'Étude de la Philosophie Médiévale*, ed. Tzotcho Boiadjiev, Georgi Kapriev, and Andreas Speer, 87–103. Turnhout, Belgium: Brepols, 2000.

Derrida, Jacques. *Margins of Philosophy*. Tr. Alan Bass. Chicago: University of Chicago Press, 1982.

Diekamp, Franz, ed. *Doctrina Patrum de Incarnatione Verbi. Ein griechisches Florilegium aus der Wende des siebenten und achten Jahrhunderts*. Münster: Aschendorffsche Verlagsbuchhandlung, 1907.

Dinzelbacher, Peter. "Zur Erforschung der Geschichte der Volksreligion: Einführung und Bibliographie." In *Volksreligion im hohen und späten Mittelalter*, ed. P. Dinzelbacher and D. Bauer, 9–27. Paderborn: Ferdinand Schöningh, 1990.

[Dionysius the Areopagite.] *Corpus Dionysiacum. Pseudo-Dionysius Areopagita: De divinis nominibus*. 2 vols. Ed. Beate Regina Suchla, Günter Heil, and Adolf Martin Ritter. Patristische Texte und Studien, no. 33. Berlin: Walter de Gruyter, 1990–91.

———. *Pseudo-Dionysius: The Complete Works*. Trans. Colm Luibheid and Paul Rorem. New York: Paulist Press, 1987.

Dümmler, Ernst. *Poetae Latini aevi Carolini*. Vol. 1. Berlin: Weidmann, 1881.

Eco, Umberto. *The Aesthetics of Chaosmos: The Middle Ages of James Joyce*. Trans. Ellen Esrock. Cambridge, MA: Harvard University Press, 1989.

Eisenstein, Elizabeth. *The Printing Press as an Agent of Change: Communications and Cultural Transformations in Early-Modern Europe*. 2 vols. New York: Cambridge University Press, 1979.

———. *The Printing Revolution in Early Modern Europe*. Cambridge: Cambridge University Press, 1983.

Eliade, Mircea. *Images and Symbols: Studies in Religious Symbolism*. New York: Sheed and Ward, 1969.

———. *Shamanism: Archaic Teachings of Ecstasy*. Trans. Willard R. Trask. Bollingen Series, no. 76. New York, Bollingen Foundation; distributed by Pantheon Books, 1964.

Emerton, J. A. "Tetragrammaton." In Metzger and Coogan, *Oxford Companion to the Bible*, 738.

Epstein, Mark Alan. *The Ottoman Jewish Communities and Their Role in the Fifteenth and Sixteenth Centuries*. Freiburg: K. Schwarz, 1980.

Eriugena, Johnnes Scottus. *Periphyseon: Editionem nouam a suppositiciis quidem additamentis purgatam, ditatam uero appendice in qua uicissitudines operis synoptice exhibentur*. Ed. Edouard A. Jeauneau. Turnhout, Belgium: Brepols, 1996.

Ernst, Ulrich. *Carmen Figuratum: Geschichte des Figurengedichts von den antiken Ursprüngen bis zum Ausgang des Mittelalters*. Cologne: Böhlau Verlag, 1991.

Eusebius, Bishop of Caesarea. *The History of the Church from Christ to Constantine*. Trans. G.A. Williamson. New York: New York University Press, 1966.

Farmer, Stephen Alan. *Syncretism in the West: Pico's 900 Theses (1486): The Evolutions of Traditional Religious and Philosophical Systems.* Medieval and Renaissance Texts and Studies, no. 167. Tempe, AZ: Medieval and Renaissance Texts and Studies, 1998.

Fedotov, George. *The Russian Religious Mind.* Vol. 1. Belmont, MA: Nordland, 1975.

Fernandez, James W., ed. *Beyond Metaphor: The Theory of Tropes in Anthropology.* Stanford, CA: Stanford University Press, 1991.

———. *Persuasion and Performance: The Play of Tropes in Culture.* Bloomington: Indiana University Press 1986.

Fernandez, James W., and Mary Taylor Huber, eds. *Irony in Action: Anthropology, Practice, and the Moral Imagination.* Chicago: University of Chicago Press, 2001.

Florenskii, Pavel. "Imeslavie kak filosofskaia predposylka. Ob imenem Bozhiem." In *Pavel Florenskii: Sobranie sochinenii,* ed. P. V. Florenskii and M. S. Trubachev, 2:281–333. Moscow: Pravda, 1990.

———. "Slovesnoe sluzhenie: Molitva." *Bogoslovskie trudy* 17 (1977): 172–95.

Foucault, Michel. *The Order of Things: An Archaeology of the Human Knowledge.* New York: Vintage Books, 1970.

Franko, Ivan. *Apokrifi i legendy z Ukraïn'skich rukopisiv.* Vol. 4. Lvov, Ukraine: Shevchenko, 1906.

Frizzell, Lawrence E. "'Spoils from Egypt,' between Jews and Gnostics." In *Hellenization Revisited: Shaping a Christian Response Within the Greco-Roman World,* ed. Wendy E. Helleman, 383–94. Lanham: University Press of America, 1994.

Froehlich, Karlfried. "Pseudo-Dionysius and the Reformation of the Sixteenth Century." In [Dionysius the Areopagite] *Pseudo-Dionysius,* 33–46.

Frye, Northrop. *Words with Power: Being a Second Study of the Bible and Literature.* San Diego, CA: Harcourt Brace Jovanovich, 1990.

Galatinus, Petrus. *Opus de arcanis catholicae veritatis, contra Judaeorum nostrae tempestatis perfidiam, ex Talmud aliisque hebraicis libris nuper excerptum.* Orthonae Maris: Hier. Soncinus, 1518.

Gammie, John G. "The Classification, Stages of Growth, and Changing Intentions in the Book of Daniel." *Journal of Biblical Literature* 95, no. 2 (1976): 191–204.

Gardiner, A. H. *Ancient Egyptian Onomastica.* 2 vols. Oxford: Oxford University Press, 1947.

Gass, William H. *Habitations of the World: Essays.* New York: Simon and Schuster, 1985.

Gaster, Moses. *Literatura populară romănă.* Bucharest, Romania: Haimann, 1883.

———. *The Sword of Moses: An Ancient Book of Magic.* London: Nutt, 1896.

———. "Zur Quellenkunde Deutscher Sagen und Märchen." In *Studies and Texts in Folklore, Magic Medieval Romance, Hebrew Apocrypha, and Samaritan Archeology,* collected and reprinted by Moses Gaster, 1071–85. New York: Ktav, 1971.

Geerard, Mavritii. *Clavis Apocryphorum Novi Testamenti.* Turnhout, Belgium: Brepols, 1992.

Geertz, Clifford. *The Interpretation of Cultures.* New York: Basic Books, 1973.

Gese, Hartmut. "The Idea of History in the Ancient Near East and the Old Testament." *Journal for Theology and the Church* 1 (1965): 49–64.

Giesebrecht, Friedrich. *Die Alttestamentliche Schätzung des Gottesnamens und ihre religionsgeschichtliche Grundlage.* Königsberg: Thomas & Oppermann, 1901.

Ginzburg, Carlo. *Ecstasies: Deciphering the Witches' Sabbath.* Trans. Raymond Rosenthal. Chicago: University of Chicago Press, 1991.

Giustiniani, Agostino. *Praecatio pietatis plena ad Deum omnipotentem composita ex duobus et septuaginta nominibus divinis, hebraicis, et latinis, cum interprete commentariolo.* Venice: Alessando de Paganini, 1513.

Goltz, Hermann. "Notizen zur Traditionsgeschichte des Corpus areopagiticum slavicum." In *Byzanz in der europäischen Staatenwelt: Eine Aufsatzsammlung,* ed. Jürgen Dummer and Johannes Irmscher, 133–48. Berlin: Akademie, 1983.

Goody, Jack. *The Domestication of the Savage Mind.* Cambridge: Cambridge University Press, 1977.

Gorskii, A., and K. Novostruev. *Opisanie slavianskix rukopisei Moskovskoi sinodal'noi biblioteki.* Vol. 2. 1862; repr., Wiesbaden, Germany: Otto Harrassowitz, 1964.

Gove, Antonina Filonov. *The Slavic Akathistos Hymn: Poetic Elements of the Byzantine Text and Its Old Church Slavonic Translation.* Munich: Otto Sagner, 1988.

Gschwind, Ulrich, ed. *Le Roman de Flamenca: Nouvelle occitane du 13e siècle.* 2 vols. Bern: A. Francke, 1976.

Hadas, M. *Aristeas to Philocrates,* New York: Ktav, 1973.

Hadot, Pierre. *What Is Ancient Philosophy?* Cambridge, MA: Harvard University Press, 2002.

Hahn, Ferdinand. *The Titles of Jesus in Christology: Their History in Early Christianity.* New York: World, 1969.

Halkin, François, ed. *Bibliotheca hagiographica graeca.* 3 vols. Brussels: Société des Bollandistes, 1957.

Hames, Harvey J. *The Art of Conversion: Christianity and Kabbalah in the Thirteenth Century.* Boston, MA: E. J. Brill, 2000.

Hampp, Irmgard. "Sigilla Solomonis: Eine 'Zauberrolle' aus dem 17. Jahrhundert." In *Zauberei und Frömmigkeit,* ed. Hermann Bausinger, 101–16. Tübingen: Tübinger Vereinigung für Volkskunde, 1966.

Harbison, Robert. *Eccentric Spaces.* Cambridge, MA: MIT Press, 2000.

Hasdeu, B. Petriceicu. *Cărțile poporane ale Românilor în secolul XVI în legătură cu literatura poporană cea nescrisă studiu de filologie comparativă.* Vol. 2. 1879, repr., Bucharest, Romania: Editura Didactică și pedagogică, 1984.

Hathaway, Ronald F. *Hierarchy and the Definition of Order in the Letters of Pseudo-Dionysius.* The Hague: M. Nijhoff, 1969.

Higgins, Dick. *Pattern Poetry: A Guide to Unknown Literature.* New York: SUNY Press, 1988.

The Holy Bible, Containing the Old and New Testament with the Apocryphal/Deuterocanonical Books. New Revised Standard Version. New York and Oxford: Oxford University Press, 1989.

Honigmann, Ernst von. *Pierre l'Ibérien et les écrits de Pseudo-Denis l'Aréopagite.* Brussels: Institut de philologie et d'histoire orientales, 1952. (Translated into Russian as *Petr Iver i sochineniia Psevdo-Dionisiia Areopagita.* Translated from the French by Shalva Nutsubidze. Tbilisi: Tbiliskii Universitet, 1955.)

Hubert, Merton Jerome, and Marion E. Poter, eds. *Romance of Flamenca: A Provençal Poem of the Thirteenth Century.* Princeton, NJ: Princeton University Press, 1962.

Hyde, Lewis. *The Gift.* New York: Random House. 1983.

[Iamblichus]. *The Theology of Arithmetic: On the Mystical, Mathematical and Cosmological Symbolism of the First Ten Numbers.* Attributed to Iamblichus. Trans. Robin Waterfield. Grand Rapids, MI: Phanes Press, 1988.

Iatsimirskii, Aleksandr. "K istorii lozhnykh molitv v iuzhno-slavianskoi pis'mennosti." *Izvestiia Otdeleniia russkogo iazyka i slovesnosti Imperatorskoi akademii nauk* 18, no. 3 (1913): 1–102; 18, no. 4 (1913): 16–126.

Idel, Moshe. *Kabbalah: New Perspectives.* New Haven, CT: Yale University Press, 1988.

———. *The Mystical Experience of Abraham Abulafia.* Tr. Jonathan Chipman. New York: State University of New York Press, 1988.

Inalcik, Halil. *The Ottoman Empire: The Classical Age 1300–1600.* London: Weidenfeld and Nicolson, 1973.

Iovkov, I. *Pavlikiani i pavlikianski selishta v b"lgarskite zemi XV-XVIII v.* Sofia, Bulgaria: Universitetsko izdatelstvo Sv. Kliment Okhridski, 1991.

Ivanov, Iordan N. "Preglas na glasna U > O v b"lgarskite govori." In *V pamet na profesor Stoiko Stoikov (1912–1969): Ezikovedeski izsledvaniia,* ed. Stoiko Ivanov Stoikov and Liubomir Andreichin, 195–99. Sofia, Bulgaria: B"lgarska Akademiia na naukite, 1974.

Izmirlieva, Valentina. "The Aetiology of the Seventy-Two Diseases: Investigating a Byzantino-Slavic False Prayer." *Byzantinoslavica* 59 (1998): 181–96.

———. *The Christian Art of Listing: Naming God in* Slavia Orthodoxa, Ph.D. diss., University of Chicago, 1999.

———. "From Babel to Christ and Beyond: The Number 72 in Christian Political Symbolism." *Starob"lgarska literatura* 35–36 (2007): 3–21.

———. "Naming the Nameless: Included Name-Catalogues across Medieval Genres." *Starob"lgarska literatura* 32 (2001): 83–98.

———. "72 i chisloviiat kod na tvorenieto v predkhristiianskata traditsiia: Istoricheski ekskurs." In *Medievistika i kulturna antropologiia: Sbornik v chest na 60-godishnina tvorcheska deinost na Prof. Donka Petkanova,* ed. Anisava Miltenova, 121–29. Sofia, Bulgaria: B"lgarska Akademiia na naukite, 1998.

Jagić, Vatroslav. "Slavische Beiträge zu den biblischen Apocryphen. Vol. 1. Die altkirchenslavischen Texte des Adambuches." *Denkschriften der Kaiserlichen Akademie der Wissenschaften in Wien. Philosophisch-historische Klasse* 42 (1893): 1–104.

James, William. *The Varieties of Religious Experience: A Study in Human Nature. Being the Gifford Lectures on Natural Religion Delivered at Edinburgh in 1901–1902.* New York: Modern Library, 1999.

Janowitz, Naomi. "Theories of Divine Names in Origen and Pseudo-Dionysius." *History of Religion* 30 (1991): 359–72.

Jeauneau, Edouard. "The Neoplatonic Themes of *Processio* and *Reditus* in Eriugena." *Dionysius* 15 (1991): 3–29.

Jellicoe, Sidney. "St. Luke and the 'Seventy(-Two).'" *New Testament Studies* 6 (1960): 319–21.

———. *The Septuagint and Modern Study.* Oxford: Clarendon Press, 1968.

Jerkova, Jani. "Latinski izvori na Stanislavoviia 'Abagar.'" *Literaturna istoriia* 2 (1978): 60–68.

Jerkov, Jani, and Mario Capaldo. "Razlicnie potrebii di Jakov di Sofia alla luce di un esemplare completo." *Orientalia Christiana Periodica* 45, no. 2 (1979): 373–86.

Jerusalem 22. Library of the Greek Patriarchate in Jerusalem, Israel. Manuscript and Rare Book Collection, MS Slav. 22 (192).

Kačanovskij, Vladimir. "Apokrifne molitve, gatanja i priče." *Starine* (Jugoslavenska Akademija znanosti i umjetnosti) 13 (1881): 150–63.

Kaplan, Aryel, ed. *The Bahir.* Northvale, NJ: Jason Aronson, 1995.

———. *Meditation and Kabbalah.* Northvale, NJ: Jason Aronson, 1995.

Keipert, Helmut. "Velikyj Dionisie sice napisa: Die Übesetzung von Areopagita-Zitaten bei Euthymius von Turnovo." In *T"rnovska knizhovna shkola.* Vol. 2. *Uchenitsi i posledovateli na Evtimii Turnovski,* ed. Penio Rusev, 326–50. Sofia, Bulgaria: B"lgarska Akademiia na naukite, 1980.

Khintibidze, E. G. "Novyi argument ob identifikatsii Petra Ivera s Psevdo-Dionisiem Areopagitom." In *Vizantinovedcheskie etiudy,* ed. N. Lomouri, 139–47. Tbilisi: Metsniereba, 1991.

Kieckhefer, Richard. *Magic in the Middle Ages.* Cambridge: Cambridge University Press, 1989.

Kircher, Athanasius. *Œdipus Ægyptiacus.* Rome: Ex typographia Vitalis Mascardi, 1652.

Kizenko, Nadieszda. *A Prodigal Saint: Father John of Kronstadt and the Russian People.* University Park: Pennsylvania University Press, 2000.

Knibb, Michael A., and Edward Ullendorff. *The Ethiopic Book of Enoch: A New Edition in the Light of the Aramaic Dead Sea Fragments.* Oxford: Clarendon Press, 1978.

Knowles, David, O. S. B. "The Influence of Pseudo-Dionysius on Western Mysticism." *Christian Spirituality: Essays in Honor of Gordon Rupp.* Ed. Peter Brooks, 79–94. London: SCM Press, 1975.

Koch, H. "Proklus als Quelle des Pseudo-Dionysius Areopagita in der Lehre vom Bösen." *Philologus* 54 (1895): 438–54.

Kolakowski, Leszek. *Main Currents of Marxism: Its Origin, Growth and Dissolution.* Vol. 1. *The Founders.* Trans. P. S. Falla. New York: Oxford University Press, 1978.

Kovachev, Iordan. "Narodna astronomia i meteorologiia: Prinos k"m b"lgarskiia folklor." *Sbornik za narodni umotvoreniia, nauka i knizhnina* 30 (1914): 1–85.

Kovačević, Lj. "Nekoliko priloga staroj srpskoj književnosti. Pt 1. Molitve." *Starine* (Jugoslavenska Akademija znanosti i umjetnosti) 10 (1878): 274–93.

Kozhukharov, Stefan. "Akatist." In *Kirilo-Metodievska entsiklopediia,* vol. 1, ed. Pet"r Dinekov, 57–58. Sofia, Bulgaria: Izdatelstvo na B"lgarskata Akademiia na naukite, 1986.

Kozlov, Protoierei Maksim. "Akafist v istorii pravoslavnoi gimnografii." *Zhurnal Moskovskoi Patriarkhii* 6 (2000): 83–88.

Kraikov, Iakov, ed. *Chasoslovets.* Venice: privately printed by the author, 1566.

Krasnosel'tsev, Nikolai. "Slavianskiia rukopisi Patriarshei biblioteki v Ierusalime." *Pravoslavnyi sobesednik* 12 (1888): 1–32.

Kretzenbacher, Leopold. "Die heilige Rundzahl 72: Zur Zahlenmystik in Legende und Sakralbau, in Volksglaube und Redensart." *Blätter für Heimatkunde* 26, no. 1 (1952): 11–18.

Lakoff, George, and Mark Johnson. *Metaphors We Live By*. Chicago: University of Chicago Press, 1980.

Lakoff, George, and Mark Turner. *More Than Cool Reason: A Field Guide to Poetic Metaphor*. Chicago: University of Chicago Press, 1989.

Lavrov, P. A. *Apokrificheskie teksty*. St. Petersburg: Tipografiia Imperatorskoi akademii nauk, 1899.

Lejay, Paul. "Giovanni Pico della Mirandola." *Catholic Encyclopedia*. Vol. 10 (1911). Online Edition: http://www.newadvent.org/cathen/10352a.htm.

Lesses, Rebecca. "Speaking with Angels: Jewish and Greco-Egyptian Revelatory Adjurations." *Harvard Theological Review* 89, no. 1 (1996): 41–60.

Levinas, Emmanuel. *Totality and Infinity: An Essay on Exteriority*. Trans. Alphonso Lingis. Pittsburgh, PA: Duquesne University Press, 1969.

Lévi-Strauss, Claude. *The Savage Mind*. Chicago: University of Chicago Press, 1966.

Lyotard, Jean-François. *The Postmodern Condition: A Report on Knowledge*. Trans. Geoff Bennington and Brian Massumi. Theory and History of Literature, no. 10. Minneapolis: University of Minnesota, 1984.

Lossky, Vladimir. *In the Image and Likeness of God*. Ed. John H. Erickson and Thomas E. Bird. Crestwood, NY: St. Vladimir's Seminary Press, 2001.

Louth, Andrew. *Denys the Areopagite*. Wilton, CT: Morehouse-Barlow, 1989.

———. "The Influence of Denys the Areopagite on Eastern and Western Spirituality in the Fourteenth Century." *Sobornost* 4, no. 2 (1982): 185–200.

Luther, Martin. *D. Martin Luthers Werke: Weimarer Ausgabe*. 15 vols. Weimar: Böhlaus Nachfolger, 2001.

Maguire, Henry, ed. *Byzantine Magic*. Washington, DC: Dumbarton Oaks, 1995.

Makarii, [Metropolitan of all Russia], ed. *Velikiia minei-chetii: Sentiabr' 1–13*. St. Petersburg: Arkhiograficheskaia kommissiia Imperatorskoi akademii nauk, 1868.

———. *Velikiia minei-chetii: Oktiabr' 1–3*. St. Petersburg: Arkhiograficheskaia kommissiia Imperatorskoi akademii nauk, 1870.

———. *Velikiia minei-chetii: Noiabr' 13–15*. St. Petersburg: Arkhiograficheskaia kommissiia Imperatorskoi akademii nauk, 1899.

Malinowski, Bronislaw. *Magic, Science and Religion, and Other Essays*. Introduction by Robert Redfield. 1948; repr., Prospect Heights, IL: Waveland Press, 1992.

Marzell, Heinrich. "Die Zahl 72 in der sympathetischen Medizin." *Zeitschrift des Vereins für Volkskunde* 23, no. 1 (1913): 69–71.

Matejic, Predrag, and Hannah Thomas. *Catalog: Manuscripts on Microforms of the Hilandar Research Library (The Ohio State University)*. Columbus, OH: Slavica, 1995.

Mathiesen, Robert. "Magic in Slavia Orthodoxa: The Written Tradition." In *Byzantine Magic*, ed. Henry Maguire, 155–77. Washington, DC: Dumbarton Oaks Research Library and Collection, 1995.

Matich, Olga. *Erotic Utopia: The Decadent Imagination in Russia's Fin de Siècle*. Madison: University of Wisconsin Press, 2005.

Mauss, Marcel. *The Gift*. Trans. Ian Cunnison. New York: W. W. Norton, 1967.

Mazower, Mark. *Salonica, City of Ghosts: Christians, Muslims and Jews, 1430–1950*. New York: Alfred A. Knopf, 2005.

McGinn, Bernard. *The Presence of God: A History of Western Christian Mysticism.* 4 vols. New York: Crossroad, 1992.

Meshcherskaia, Elena. *Legenda ob Avgare: Rannesiriiskii literaturnyi pamiatnik (Istoricheskie korni v evoliutsii apokrificheskoi legendy).* Moscow: Nauka, 1984.

Metzger, Bruce M., "Names for the Nameless." In Metzger and Coogan, *Oxford Companion to the Bible,* 546–48.

———. "Seventy or Seventy-Two Disciples?" *New Testament Studies* 5 (1959): 299–306.

Metzger, Bruce M., and Michael D. Coogan, eds. *The Oxford Companion to the Bible.* New York: Oxford University Press, 1993.

Meyendorff, John. *Byzantine Theology: Historical Trends and Doctrinal Themes.* New York: Fordham University Press, 1974.

———. *St. Gregory Palamas and Orthodox Spirituality.* [n. p.]: St. Vladimir's Seminary Press, 1974.

Meyer, Heinz. *Die Zahlenallegorese im Mittelalter: Methode und Gebrauch.* Munich: Wilhelm Fink, 1975.

Meyer, Heinz, and Rudolf Suntrup. *Lexikon der mitteralterlichen Zahlenbedeutungen.* Munich: Wilhelm Fink, 1987.

Meyer, Marvin, Richard Smith, and Neal Kelsey, eds. *Ancient Christian Magic: Coptic Texts of Ritual Power.* San Francisco: Harper, 1994.

Meyer, Paul. "La prière des soixante-douze noms de Dieu." *Romania* 14 (1885): 528.

Migne, Jacques-Paul, ed. *[PG]. Patrologiae cursus completus. Series Graeca.* 161 vols. in 166 vols. Paris: Garnier et J.-P. Migne, 1857–87.

———. *[PL]. Patrologiae cursus completus. Series Latina.* 221 vols. Paris, 1844–64.

Mikhaila, G. "Spiski Sbornika tsaria Simeona v Biblioteke Rumynskoi Akademii." *Palaeobulgarica* 11, no. 3 (1987): 3–20.

Mikhailova, Katia. "Za s"d"rzhanieto na termina *bitovo/folklorno khristiianstvo* v slavianskata folkloristika." *B"lgarski folklor* 3 (2000): 3–15.

Miklas, Heinz, and Vjačeslav Zagrebin, eds. *Berlinski sbornik: Vollständige Studienausgabe im Originalformat von MS. (Slav.) WUK 48 aus dem Besitz der Staatsbibliothek preussischer Kulturbesitz, Berlin und von MS. O.p. I.15 der staatlichen öffentlichen Bibliothek "M. E. Saltykov-Sčedrin," Leningrad.* Graz, Austria: Akademische Druck-u. Verlagsanstalt, 1988.

Miklosich, Franz von, ed. *Lexicon linguae slovenicae veteris dialecti.* Vindobonae: Gulielmum Braunmüller, 1850.

Miletich, L. "Nashite pavlikiani." *Sbornik za narodni umotvoreniia, nauka i knizhnina* 19 (1903): 1–369; 21 (1905): 1–155.

Milović, Jevto M., ed. *Štamparska i književna djelatnost Božidara Vukovića Podgoričanina.* Titograd: Crnogorska Akademija Nauk i Umjetnoisti, 1986.

Miltenova, Anisava. "Razumnik-ukáz (Tekstologichesko prouchvane. Izdanie na starob"lgarskiia tekst)." *Palaeobulgarica* 10, no. 4 (1986): 22–44.

———. "Skazanie za Sivila (Arkheografski belezhki, tekstologichesko izsledvane, izdanie na teksta)." *Palaeobulgarica* 8, no. 4 (1984): 44–72.

———, ed. *Stara b"lgarska literatura.* Vol. 5. Sofia, Bulgaria: B"lgariski pisatel, 1992.

Minchev, Georgi, and Malgozhata Skovronek. "Tsik"l"t za Tsar Avgar v"v vizantino-slavianskata traditsiia." In *Srednovekovna khristiianska Evropa: Iztok i Zapad (tsennosti, traditsii, obshtuvane)*, ed. Vasil Giuzelev and Anisava Miltenova, 324–39. Sofia, Bulgaria: Gutenberg, 2002.

Mirandola, Giovanni Pico della. *Conclusiones sive theses DCCCC Romae anno 1486 publice disputandae, sed non admissae.* Ed. Bohdan Kieszkowski. Geneva: Droz, 1973.

Mirchev, Kiril. "Nevrokopskiiat govor." *Godishnik na Sofiiskiia Universitet, Istoriko-filologicheski fakultet* 32 (1936): 1–134.

Morgan, Michael A., ed. and trans. *Sepher ha-Razim: The Book of the Mysteries.* Chico, CA: Scholars Press, 1983.

Morris, Mark. "Sei Shonagon's Poetic Catalogues." *Harvard Journal of Asiatic Studies* 40, no. 1 (Spring 1980): 5–54.

Mortley, Raoul. *From Word to Silence.* Vol. 1. *The Rise and Fall of Logos.* Vol. 2. *The Way of Negation, Christian and Greek.* Theophanea: Beiträge zur Religious- und Kirchengeschichte des Altertums, nos. 30 and 31. Bonn: Hanstein, 1986.

Müller-Jahncke, Wolf- Dieter. "Agrippa von Nettesheim et la Kabbale." In *Kabbalistes chrétiens*, ed. Antoine Faivre and Frédérick Tristan, 195–209. Paris : Albin Michel, 1979.

Nachtigal, Rajko. *Euchologium Sinaiticum: Starocerkovnoslovanski glagolski spomenik.* 2 vols. Ljubljana: Akademija znanosti i umetnosti v Ljubljane, 1942.

Naveh, Joseph, and Shaul Shaked. *Amulets and Magic Bowls. Aramaic Incantations of Late Antiquity.* Jerusalem: Magnes Press, The Hebrew University; Leiden: E. J. Brill, 1985.

Nedomački, Vidosava. "O srpskim rukopisima u biblioteci Grčke pravoslavne patrijaršije u Jerusalimu." *Arheografski prilozi* (Beograd: Narodna biblioteka Srbije) 2 (1980): 71–118.

Nelli, René. "La Prière aux soixante-douze noms de Dieu," *Folklore* (Carcassonne, France), no. 8 (1950): 70–74.

Neusner, Jacob. *Sources of the Transformation of Judaism: From Philosophy to Religion in the Classics of Judaism.* Atlanta, GA: Scholars Press, 1992.

Nisard, Charles. *Historie des Livres Populaires.* Vol. 1. Paris: E. Dentu, 1864.

Novaković, Stojan. "Apokrifi iz štampanih zbornika Božidara Vukovića." *Starine* (Jugoslavenska Akademija znanosti i umjetnosti) 16 (1884): 57–66.

———. "Apokrifske priče o Bogorodičinoj smrti i još neke sitnice apokrifske o Bogorodici." *Starine* (Jugoslavenska Akademija znanosti i umjetnosti) 18 (1886): 188–202.

———. "Božidara Vukovića zbornici za putnike." *Glasnik Srpskog učenog društva* 45 (1877): 129–67.

Nutsubidze, Shalva. *Taina Psevdo-Dionisiia Areopagita.* Tbilisi: Akademiia nauk Gruzinskoi SSR, 1942.

Nyrop, Kristoffer. "Navnets magt: En folkepsykologisk sudie." In *Opuskula philologica: Mindre Afhandlinger*, Filologisk-historiske Samfund, 118–209. Copenhagen: Forlagt af Rudolph Klein, 1887.

Ocak, Ahmet Yasar. "Religion." In *History of the Ottoman State, Society and Civilization*, vol. 2, ed. Ekmeleddin Ihsanoglu, 2:177–238. Istanbul: Research Center for Islamic History, Art and Culture IRCICA, 2002.

Oikonomidēs, D. B. "Εξ ορκισμοί και ιατροσοφία εξ Ηπειρωτικού χειρογράφου." *Epeiris tou Laographikou Archeiou* 8 (1953–54): 14–40.

O'Neil, Mary R. "From 'Popular' to 'Local' Religion: Issues in Early Modern European History." *Religious Studies Review* 11 (1986): 222–26.

Ong, Walter J. *Orality and Literacy: The Technologizing of the Word.* London: Routledge, 1988.

Origen. *Contra Celsum.* Ed. and trans. Henry Chadwick. Cambridge: Cambridge University Press 1980.

The Orthodox Prayer Book. South Canaan, PA: St. Tikhon Press, 1959.

Ostrowski, Donald G., David J. Birnbaum, and Horas G. Lunt, eds. *The Povest'* vremennykh let: *Interlinear Collation and Paradosis.* Harvard Library of Early Ukrainian Literature. Texts. No. 10, pt. 1. Cambridge, MA: Harvard University Press, 2003.

Palacios, Maguel Asín. *The Mystical Philosophy of Ibn Masarra and His Followers.* Trans. Elmer H. Douglas and Howard W. Yoder. Leiden: E. J. Brill, 1978.

Panteleimon, Arkhimandrit, ed. *Zhizn', podvigi, chudesa i prorochestva sviatogo pravednogo ottsa nashego Ioanna, Kronshtadtskogo chudotvortsa.* [no place, no pub.], 1976.

Pantić, Miroslav, ed. *Pet vekova srpskog štamparstva 1494–1994: Razdoblje srpskoslovenske štampe 15–17 v.* Beograd: Srpska Akademija nauka i umetnosti, 1994.

Pavlova, Rumiana, Tsvetana Raleva, and Tsenka Doseva, eds. *Simeonov sbornik (po Svetoslavoviia prepis ot 1073 g.).* Vol. 1. Sofia, Bulgaria: B"lgarska Akademiia na naukite, 1991.

Perl, Eric. "Hierarchy and Participation in Dionysius the Areopagite and Greek Neoplatonism." *American Catholic Philosophical Quarterly* 68, no. 1 (1994): 15–30.

Pesenti, Tiziana. "Stampatori e litterati nell'industria editoriale a Venezia e iu terraferma." In *Storia della cultura Veneta. Il Seicento,* vol. 4, *Il Seicento,* pt. 1, ed. Gioralamo Arnaldi and Manlio Pastore Stocchi, 93–129. Venice: Neri Pozza, 1983.

Peters, F. E. *Judaism, Christianity, Islam: The Classical Texts and Their Interpretation.* 3 vols. Princeton, NJ: Princeton University Press, 1990.

Petkanova, Donka, ed. *Stara b"lgarska literatura.* Vol. 1. Sofia: B"lgariski pisatel, 1982.

Petrov, Aleksei. "Ugrorusskie zagovory i zaklinaniia nachala XVIII v." In his *Stat'i ob Ugorskoi Rusi,* 51–64. Zapiski istoriko-filologicheskago fakul'teta Imperatorskago Sankt-Peterburgskago universiteta, no. 81, supplement. St. Petersburg: Senatskaia tipografiia, 1906.

Pitra, Jean Baptiste. *Spicilegium solesmense complectens sanctorum patrum scriptorumque ecclesiasticorum anecdota hactenus opera, selecta e græcis orientalbusque et latinis codicibus.* 3 vols. Paris: Prostat apud Firmin Didot fraters, 1985.

Porfir'ev, Ivan. *Apokrificheskiia skazaniia o vetkhozavetnykh litsakh i sobytiiakh po rukopisiam Solovetskoi biblioteki.* Sbornik Otdeleniia russkogo iazyka i slovesnosti Imperatorskoi akademii nauk, no. 17, pt. 1. St. Petersburg: Tipografiia Imperatorskoi akademii nauk, 1877.

Pradel, Fritz. *Griechische und süditalienische Gebete, Beschwörungen und Rezepte des Mittelalters.* Religionsgeschichtliche Versuche und Vorarbeiten, no. 3, pt. 3. Giessen: Alfred Töpelmann, 1907.

Prescott, H. F. M., ed. *Flamenca. Translated from the Thirteenth-Century Provençal of Bernardet the Troubadour.* New York: Richard R. Smith, 1930.

Primov, Borislav, Pet"r Sariiski, and Milcho Iovkov, eds. *Dokumenti za katolicheskata deinost v B"lgaria prez XVII vek.* Sofia, Bulgaria: Universitetsko izdatelstvo Sv. Kliment Okhridski, 1993.

Prokhorov, Gelian Mikhailovich, ed. *Dionisii Areopagit. O bozhestvennykh imenakh. O Misticheskom bogoslovii.* [Greek and Russian edition]. St. Petersburg: Glagol, 1995.

———. *Pamiatniki perevodnoi i russkoi literatury XIV–XV vekov.* Leningrad: Nauka, 1987.

———. "Sochineniia Dionisiia Areopagita v slavianskoi rukopisnoi traditsii: Kodiko-logicheskie nabliudeniia." In *Russkaia i armianskaia srednevekovye literatury,* ed. K. V. Aivazian, and D. S. Likhachev, 80–94. Leningrad: Nauka, 1982.

Pypin, Aleksandr N., ed. *Lozhnyia i otrechennyia knigi russkoi stariny.* Pamiatniki starin-noi russkoi literatury, izdavaemye Grafom Grigoriem Kushelevym-Bezborodko, vol. 3. 1862; repr., The Hague: Mouton, 1970.

Radojčić, Nikola. "Srpski Abagar." *Etnolog* 4, no. 2 (1931): 187–211.

Raikov, Bozhidar, ed. *Abagar na Filip Stanislavov: Rim, 1651.* Phototype edition. Sofia, Bulgaria: Narodna prosveta, 1979.

Reitzenstein, R. *Poimandres: Studien zur griechisch-ägyptischen und frühchristlichen Literatur.* Leipzig: B. G. Teubner, 1904.

Reuchlin, Johann. *On the Art of the Kabbalah.* Trans. Martin and Sarah Goodman. Lincoln: University of Nebraska Press, 1983.

Reuchlin, Johannes. *De verbo marifico, 1494. De arte cabbalistica, 1517. Faksimile-Neudruck in einem Band.* Stuttgart-Bad Cannstatt: F. Frommann Verlag, 1964.

Ricoeur, Paul. *Essays on Biblical Interpretation.* Ed. Lewis S. Mudge. Philadelphia, PA: Fortress Press, 1980.

———. *The Rule of Metaphor: Multi-Disciplinary Studies of the Creation of Meaning in Language.* Trans. Robert Czerny, Kathleen McLaughlin, and John Costello. Toronto: University of Toronto Press, 1977.

Roberts, Alexander, and James Donaldson, eds. *The Ante-Nicean Fathers: Translation of the Fathers down to A.D. 325.* Vol. 1. *The Apostolic Fathers, Justin Martyr, Irenaeus.* Grand Rapids, MI: W. B. Eerdmans, 1981.

Robinson, James McConkey, and Richard Smith. *The Nag Hammadi Library in English.* Translated by members of the Coptic Gnostic Library Project of the Institute for Antiquity and Christianity, Claremont, CA. James M. Robinson, general editor. 4th ed. Leiden and New York: E. J. Brill, 1996.

Roques, René. "Preface." In [Dionysius the Areopagite], *Pseudo-Dionysius,* 5–7.

Rorem, Paul. "The Biblical Allusions and Overlooked Quotations in the Pseudo-Dionysian Corpus." *Studia Patristica* 23 (1989): 61–65.

———. "The Place of *The Mystical Theology* in the Pseudo-Dionysian Corpus." *Dionysius* 4 (1980): 87–98.

———. *Pseudo-Dionysius: A Commentary on the Texts and an Introduction to Their Influence.* New York: Oxford University Press, 1993.

Rorem, Paul, and John C. Lamoreaux. *John of Scythopolis and the Dionysian Corpus: Annotating the Areopagite.* Oxford: Clarendon Press, 1998.

Rose, Martin. *Jahwe: Zum Streit um den alttestamentlichen Gottesnamen*. Theologische Studien, 122. Zurich: Theologischer Verlag, 1978.

Rozov, Vladimir. "Srpski rukopisi Jerusalima i Sinaja." *Južnoslovenski filolog* (Belgrade) 5 (1925–26): 118–29.

Ruderman, David B. *The World of a Renaissance Jew: The Life and Thought of Abraham ben Mordecai Farissol*. Cincinnati, OH: Hebrew Union College Press, 1981.

Rusek, Jerzy, Wiesław Witkowski, and Aleksander Naumow. *Rękopis a druk: Najstarsze druki cerkiewnosłowiańskie i ich stosunek do tradycji rękopiśmiennej*. Materiały z sesji Kraków, 7–10 XI 1991 r. Cracow: Instytut Filologii Słowiańskiej, 1993.

Ryan, William Francis. *The Bathhouse at Midnight: An Historical Survey of Magic and Divination in Russia*. Stroud, UK: Sutton Publishing, 1999.

Sabourin, Leopold. *The Names and Titles of Jesus: Themes of Biblical Theology*. Trans. Maurice Carroll. New York: Macmillan, 1967.

Saffrey, H. D. "New Objective Links between the Pseudo-Dionysius and Proclus." In *Neoplatonism and Christian Thought*, ed. Dominic J. O'Meara, 64–74. Albany: SUNY Press, 1981.

Salone, Anna Maria. "La fortuna editoriale di Monsignor Agostino Giustiniani e della sua opera." In *Agostino Giustiniani annalista genovese ed i suoi tempi: Atti del Convegno di studi, Genova, 28–31 maggio 1982*, ed. Giorgio Costamagna, 119–34. Accademia di S. Chiara, Sezione studi storici. Genoa: Gompagnia dei Librai, 1984.

Santos Otero, Aurelio de. *Die Handschriftliche Überlieferung der altslavischen Apokryphen*. 2 vols. Patristische Texte und Studien, no. 23. Berlin: Walter De Gruyter, 1981.

Sapir, J. David, and J. Christopher Crocker, eds. *The Social Use of Metaphor: Essays on the Anthropology of Rhetoric*. Philadelphia: University of Pennsylvania Press, 1977.

Sauer, Hans. "Die 72 Völker und Sprachen der Welt: Ein mittelalterlicher Topos in der englischen Literatur." *Anglia* 101 (1983): 29–48.

———. "Die 72 Völker und Sprachen der Welt: Einige Ergänzungen." *Anglia* 107 (1989): 61–64.

Savushkina, Nina I., ed. *Russkie zagovory*. Moscow: Pressa, 1993.

Schäfer, Peter. *The Hidden and Manifest God: Some Major Themes in Early Jewish Mysticism*. Trans. Aubrey Pomerance. New York: SUNY Press, 1992.

Scheible, Johann. *Das Kloster: Weltlich und Geistlich. Meist aus der ältern deutschen volks-, wunder-, curiositäten-, und vorzugsweise komischen Literatur. Zur Kulter- und Sittengeschichte in Wort und Bild*. Vol. 3. Stuttgart: Verlag des Herausgebers, 1846.

Schermann, Theodor. *Prophetarum vitae fabulosae, Iudices apostolorum discipulorumque Domini, Dorotheo, Epiphanio, Hippolyto aliisque vindicat*. Leipzig, Germany: B. G. Teubneri, 1907.

Schiffman, Lawrence H., and Michael D. Swartz. *Hebrew and Aramaic Incantation Texts from the Cairo Genizah: Selected Texts from Tylor-Schechter Box K1*. Semitic Texts and Studies, no. 1. Sheffield, UK: JSOT Press, 1992.

Schimmel, Annemarie. *The Mystery of Numbers*. New York: Oxford University Press, 1993.

Schmidt, Francis. *Le Testament grec d'Abraham*. Tübingen: J. C. B. Mohr, 1986.

Schmitz, Werner. *Südslavischer Buchdruck in Venedig (16.–18. Jahrhundert): Untersuchungen und Bibliographie*. Giessen: Wilhelm Schmitz Verlag, 1977.

Schoedel, William R. "Scripture and the Seventy-Two Heavens of the First Apocalypse of James." *Novum Testamentum* 12, no. 2 (1970): 118–29.

Scholem, Gershom. "Kabbalah." *Encyclopedia Judaica*. Ed. Cecil Roth and Geoffrey Wigoder, 10:489–653. Jerusalem: Keter, 1971.

———. "The Name of God and the Linguistic Theory of the Kabbala." *Diogenes* 79 (1972): 59–80; 80 (1972): 164–94.

———. *On the Kabbalah and Its Symbolism*. Trans. Ralph Manheim. New York: Schocken Books, 1965.

Schrenk, Lawrence P. "God as Monad: The Philosophical Basis of Medieval Theological Numerology." In *Medieval Numerology: A Book of Essays*, ed. Robert L. Surles, 3–10. New York: Garland, 1993.

Schrire, Theodore. *Hebrew Magic Amulets: Their Decipherment and Interpretation*. New York: Behrman House, 1982.

Schwab, Moïse. *Vocabulaire de l'angélologie, d'aprés les manuscrits hébreux de la Bibliothèque nationale*. Paris: Klincksieck, 1897.

Séd, Nicolas. "Les douze hebdomades, le char de Sabaoth et les soixante-douze langues." *Novum Testamentum* 21, no. 2 (1979): 156–84.

Sergieff, John Iliytch [John of Kronstadt]. *My Life in Christ*. Trans. E. E. Goulaeff. London: Cassell, 1897.

Ševčenko, Ihor. "Remarks on the Diffusion of Byzantine Scientific and Pseudo-Scientific Literature among the Orthodox Slavs." *Slavonic and East European Review* 59, no. 3 (1981): 321–45.

Shmuelevitz, Aryeh. *The Jews of the Ottoman Empire in the Late Fifteenth and Sixteenth Centuries: Administrative, Economic, Legal, and Social Relations as Reflected in the Responsa*. Leiden: E. J. Brill, 1984.

Smith, Jonathan Z. *Imagining Religion: From Babylon to Jonestown*. Chicago: University of Chicago Press, 1982.

Smith, Morton. "A Note on Some Jewish Assimilationists: The Angels (P. Berlin 5025b, P. Louvre 2391)." *Journal of the Ancient Near Eastern Society* 16–17 (1984–85): 207–12.

Sokolov, Matvei. *Materialy i zametki po starinnoi slavianskoi literature*. Vol. 1. Moscow: Universitetskaia tipografiia, 1888.

Spiridakis, Geōrgios. "Ο αριθμός εβδομήκοντα δύο," In *Apheirōma eis K. I. Amanton*, 409–18. Athens: K. L. Kuriakoulē, 1940.

Spufford, Francis. *The Chatto Book of Cabbages and Kings: Lists in Literature*. London: Chatto and Windus, 1989.

Staal, Frits. *Exploring Mysticism*. Harmondsworth, UK: Penguin Books, 1975.

Stanchev, Krasimir. "Dionisii Areopagit." In *Kirilo-Metodievska entsiklopedia*, ed. Pet"r Dinekov, 1:587–89. Sofia, Bulgaria: B"lgarska akademiia na naukite, 1985.

———. "Kontseptsiiata na Psevdo-Dionisii Areopagit za obraznoto poznanie i neinoto razprostranenie v Srednovekovna B"lgariia." *Starob"lgarska literatura* 3 (1978): 62–76.

Steinschneider, M. "Die kanonische Zahl der muhammedanischen Secten und die Symbolik der Zahl 70–73, aus jüdischen und muhammedanisch-arabischen Quellen nachgewiesen." *Zeitschrift der Deutschen morgenländischen Gesellschaft* 4, no. 2 (1850): 145–70.

Stiglmayr, Joseph. "Der Neuplatoniker Proclus als Vorlage des sogen. Dionysius Areopagita in der Lehre vom Übel." *Historisches Jahrbuch* 16 (1895): 253–73, 721–48.

Stone, Michael E. "Concerning the Seventy-Two Translators: Armenian Fragments of Epiphanius, On Weights and Measures." *Harvard Theological Review* 73 (1980): 331–36.

———. *The Literature of Adam and Eve: The History of a Tradition.* Early Judaism and Its Literature, no. 3. Atlanta, GA: Scholars Press, 1992.

Stoyanov, Yuri. *The Other God: Dualist Religions from Antiquity to the Cathar Heresy.* New Haven, CT: Yale University Press, 2000.

Strelcyn, Stefan. "Une tradition éthiopienne d'origine juive yéménite concernant l'écriture." *Rocznik Orientalistyczny* 23, no. 1 (1959): 67–72.

Suchla, Beate Regina. "Eine Redaktion des griechischen Corpus Dionysiacum Areopagiticum im Umkreis des Johannes von Skythopolis, des Verfassers von Prolog und Scholien." *Nachrichten der Akademie der Wissenschaften in Göttingen* (Philologisch-historische Klasse), no. 4 (1985): 177–93.

Tambiah, Stanley Jeyaraja. *Magic, Science, Religion, and the Scope of Human Rationality.* Cambridge: Cambridge University Press, 1990.

———. "The Magical Power of Words." *Man*, n. s., 3, no. 2 (1968): 175–208.

Targum Pseudo-Jonathan, Genesis. Tr. Michael Maher. The Aramaic Bible, no. 1B. Collegeville, MN: Liturgical Press, 1992.

Taube, Moshe. "An Early Twelfth-Century Kievan Fragment of the *Beseda trekh sviatitelei.*" *Harvard Ukrainian Studies* 12–13 (1988–89): 346–59.

———. "Une Source inconnue de la Chronographie Russe: Le *Dialogue de Timothée et Aquila.*" *Revue des études slaves* 63, no. 1 (1991): 113–22.

Taylor, Frank Sherwood. *The Alchemists: Founders of Modern Chemistry.* New York: Schuman, 1949.

Taylor, Vincent. *The Names of Jesus.* London: Macmillan, 1953.

Thomas, Keith. *Religion and the Decline of Magic.* London: Weidenfeld & Nicolson, 1971.

Thomson, Francis J. "Apocrypha Slavica: II." *Slavonic and East European Review* 63, no. 1 (1985): 73–98.

———. "The Symeonic Florilegium: Problems of Its Origin, Content, Textology and Edition, Together with an English Translation of the Eulogy of Tzar Symeon." *Palaeobulgarica* 17, no. 1 (1993): 37–53.

Thorndike, Lynn. *A History of Magic and Experimental Science.* 8 vols. New York: Macmillan, 1923–58.

Tikhonravov, Nikolai. *Pamiatniki otrechennoi russkoi literatury.* 2 vols. Moscow: Universitetskaia tipografiia, 1863.

Tirosh-Samuelson, Hava. "The Ultimate End of Human Life in Postexpulsion Philosophic Literature." In *Crisis and Creativity in the Sephardic World 1391–1648*, ed. Benjamin R. Gampel, 223–54. New York: Columbia University Press, 1997.

Towner, Wayne Sibley. *The Rabbinic "Enumeration of Scriptural Examples": A Study of a Rabbinic Pattern of Discourse with Special Reference to Mekhilta d'R. Ishmael.* Leiden: E. J. Brill, 1973.

Trachtenberg, Joshua. *Jewish Magic and Superstition: A Study in Folk Religion.* New York: Behrman, 1939.

Tracy, David. "The Divided Consciousness of Augustine on Eros." In *Erotikon: Essays on Eros Ancient and Modern,* ed. Shadi Bartsch and Thomas Bartscherer, 91–106. Chicago: University of Chicago Press, 2005.

———. *Plurality and Ambiguity: Hermeneutics, Religion, Hope.* Chicago: University of Chicago Press, 1987.

T[ruhelka], [Č]. "Jedan zanimliv zapis, pisan bosančicom." *Glasnik Zemaljskog muzeja Bosni i Hercegovini* 18 (1906): 349–54.

Tsagareli, A. "Pamyatniki gruzinskoy starini v Svyatoy Zemle i na Sinae." *Palestinskiy pravoslavniy sbornik* 4, no. 1 (1888): 89–111.

Turdeanu, Émile. *Apocryphes slaves et roumains de L'Ancient Testament.* Leiden: E. J. Brill, 1981.

Tymoczko, Maria. *The Irish Ulysses.* Berkeley and Los Angeles: University of California Press, 1994.

van Esbroeck, Michel. "Peter the Iberian and Dionysius the Areopagite." *Orientalia christiana periodica* 59 (1993): 217–27.

Vassiliev, Afanasii. *Anecdota Graeco-Byzantina.* Sbornik pamiatnikov Vizantiiskoi literatury. Moscow: Universitas Caesarae, 1893.

Vinogradov, Nikolai. *Zagovory, oberegi, spasitel'nyia molitvy i proch.* St. Petersburg: Kushnerev, 1907.

Volz, Paul. *Die Eschatologie der jüdischen Gemeinde im neutestamentlichen Zeitalter, nach den Quellen der rabbinischen, apokalyptischen und apokryphen Literatur dargestellt.* Tübingen: Mohr, 1934.

von Soden, Wolfram. "Leistung und Grenze sumerischer und babylonischer Wissenschaft." In *Die Eigenbegrifflichkeit der babylonischen Welt. Leistung und Grenze sumerischer und babylonischer Wissenschaft,* by Benno Landsberger and Wolfram von Soden, 21–124. Darmstadt: Wissenschaftliche Buchgesellschaft, 1965. Orig. pub. 1936.

von Rad, Gerhard. "Job XXXVIII and Ancient Egyptian Wisdom." In his *The Problem of the Hexateuch and Other Essays,* 281–91. New York: McGraw-Hill, 1966.

Vuković, Božidar, ed. *Zbornik za putnike.* Venice: Privately printed by B. Vuković, 1520.

Vujošević, Rajka. "O nekim biografskim podacima o Božidaru Vukoviću Podgoričaninu i o Molitveniku—Zborniku za putnike iz Marcijane." In Milović, *Štamparska i književna djelatnost,* 43.

Waite, Arthur Edward. *The Book of Ceremonial Magic: The Secret Tradition of Goëtia, Including the Rites and Mysteries of Goëtic Theurgy, Sorcery and Infernal Necromancy.* New Hyde Park, NY: University Books, 1961.

Ware, Timothy [Bishop Kallistos of Diokletia]. *The Orthodox Church.* London: Penguin Books, 1991.

Weigand, Hermann. "The Two and Seventy Languages of the World." *German Review* 17, no. 4 (1942): 241–60.

Weil, Simone. *Gravity and Grace*. Trans. Emma Graufurd. 1952; repr., London: Routledge, 1992.

Wellesz, Egon. "The Akathistos: A Study in Byzantine Hymnography." *Dumbarton Oaks Papers* 9–10 (1956): 141–74.

Wells, L. S. A. "The Books of Adam and Eve." In *The Apocrypha and Pseudepigrapha of the Old Testament*, ed. R. H. Charles, 2:123–54. Oxford: Clarendon Press, 1913.

White, Patti. *Gatsby's Party: The System and the List in Contemporary Narrative*. West Lafayette, IN: Purdue University Press, 1992.

Whybray, R. N. "Tribes of Israel." In Metzger and Coogan, *Oxford Companion to the Bible*, 778–79.

Yates, Frances A. *The Art of Memory*. Chicago: University of Chicago Press, 1966.

———. "Ramon Lull and John Scotus Erigena." *Journal of the Warburg and Courtauld Institute* 23 (1960): 1–44.

Yerushalmi, Hayim. "Exile and Expulsion in Jewish History." In *Crisis and Creativity in the Sephardic World 1391–1648*, ed. Benjamin R. Gampel, 3–22. New York: Columbia University Press, 1997.

Zhivov, Viktor M. "Dvoeverie i osobyi kharakter russkoi kul'turnoi istorii." In *Filologia slavica: K 70-letiiu akademika N. I. Tolstogo*, ed. V. N. Toporov, 50–59. Moscow: Nauka, 1993.

Zorzi (Francesco Giorgio Veneto). *De harmonia mundi totius cantica trie*. Venice: In aedibus Bernardini de Vitalibus Calchographi, 1525.

Page numbers in italics refer to illustrations.